CHOSEN INSTRUMENT

CHOSEN INSTRUMENT

A History of the Canadian Wheat Board: The McIvor Years

by William E. Morriss

Canadian Cataloguing in Publication Data

Morriss, William E.
Chosen Instrument
Bibliography
ISBN 0-919091-34-2
1. Canadian Wheat Board—History 2. Wheat trade—Canada—History 3. Wheat trade—Government policy—Canada—History
I. Title
HD 9049.W5C25 1987 338.1'7311'0971 CB7-091357-3

Distributed by:
Reidmore Books
Suite 012 *Lemarchand Mansion*
11523 - 100 Avenue
Edmonton, Alberta
Canada
T5K 0J8

Printed and Bound in Canada

Dedication

To the commissioners of the Canadian Wheat Board, past and present, and to Sarah, whose arrival brightened the final months of this endeavour.

CONTENTS

FOREWORD

Research and compilation of this history was undertaken in 1984 in advance of the fiftieth anniversary of the Canadian Wheat Board, and shortly after I had retired as the editor and publisher of the *Manitoba Co-operator*, a weekly farm newspaper published by Manitoba Pool Elevators. It has been a rewarding and educational experience researching archival material predating my personal experiences as a farm editor. Certainly, my sense of the earlier history of Canada's vital grain industry was enriched by the works of earlier writers in the field. Not only was I privileged to have available, and to draw freely upon, Charles Wilson's published work in *A Century of Canadian Grain*, but I was also fortunate in having access to one of his later unpublished works entitled *C.D. Howe; An Optimist's Response to a Surfeit of Grain*. As a guide to a multitude of sources and insights, Wilson's personal experiences and writings were invaluable. To students of Canadian agriculture and farm policy they are an indispensable and complete source of reference material. Other earlier works, such as D.A. MacGibbon's *The Canadian Grain Trade*, and *The Canadian Grain Trade, 1931-1951*, and the several contributions of Professors Vernon C. Fowke and George E. Britnell of the University of Saskatchewan, through their books on Canadian agriculture, served as further sources of understanding.

It was also my good fortune to inherit some fourteen hours of taped interviews with Mr. George McIvor, the remarkable gentleman who served for almost twenty-one years as chief commissioner of the Canadian Wheat Board. Recorded by David Suderman, director of market development for the Canadian Wheat Board, the tapes provided a first person view of the early years of the board, and the events leading up to its inception in 1935, through the eyes of a pioneer directly and intimately involved in the drama. In addition, I was privileged to interview Mr. McIvor over two days in Calgary, in order to clarify a number of points raised in the earlier tapes. At the age of 90, his faculty of recall was little short of astounding. Names, places and specific events, dating back to before the First World War, related during the taping, were carefully checked back through archival sources. In not one case did they fail to meet the test. I can only hope that I have similarly met the test of imparting some of the zest, color and human involvement inherent in Mr. McIvor's personal anecdotes. The tapes themselves are treasures of western Canadian history in the first half of this century.

Unfortunately, two later chief commissioners, Senator William C. McNamara and Garson N. Vogel, the latter a personal acquaintance dating back to the mid-1930s when we were both sprinters on the track team of Gordon Bell High School, had passed from the scene, and the opportunity of similar recorded insights that might have lent color to the story was lost. I did, however, have the privilege of examining their personal office files and memorandums during their tenures on the Board.

My thanks are extended to the commissioners of the Canadian Wheat Board, who commissioned this work, and who allowed me free and unimpeded access to the files and records of the board. I also have a large number of other people to thank for their assistance and tolerance of my persistent interruption of their normal duties. Numerous members of the staff of the Canadian Wheat Board cheerfully answered my questions and guided me to long forgotten files, even those buried in the oppressive confines of the Wheat Board's basement vault, where I spent many long, perspiration-soaked hours combing through the dusty records. A special note of gratitude goes to the board's librarian, Ruth Reedman, and her assistants, who allowed me virtually to denude sections of their bookshelves and hoard the material away for extended periods. Despite that, they continued to provide statistical material, pamphlets, reports of commissions of enquiry, copies of the Congressional Record of the United States, and a multitude of other pertinent information. Another special thanks is due to Bob Hainstock, who succeeded me as publisher and editor of the *Manitoba Co-operator*, and who provided bound volumes of the paper dating back over the years of this project. I make no apology for making extensive use of references from that publication since, as the editor for an extended period, I had confidence in the accuracy and reliability of the originating sources.

Finally, a special tribute to my wife Geraldine who worked throughout as my research assistant. Not only did she spend many hours in the Manitoba Archives Building, and in the City of Winnipeg and university libraries, checking and rechecking statistics, quotations from the Hansard of the House of Commons and the Senate, and numerous other sources to confirm their accuracy, but she also had to live with my preoccupations and moods at home. That our marriage, of over thirty-five years, survived, is indicative of her tolerance and understanding.

If, in the writing of this book, extensive resort has been made to complete quotations from original sources, which may sometimes interrupt the flow of the reading, it has been done in a quest for accuracy, and as a guide to future chroniclers of western Canadian history.

W.E. Morriss
Winnipeg, April 18, 1986

INTRODUCTION

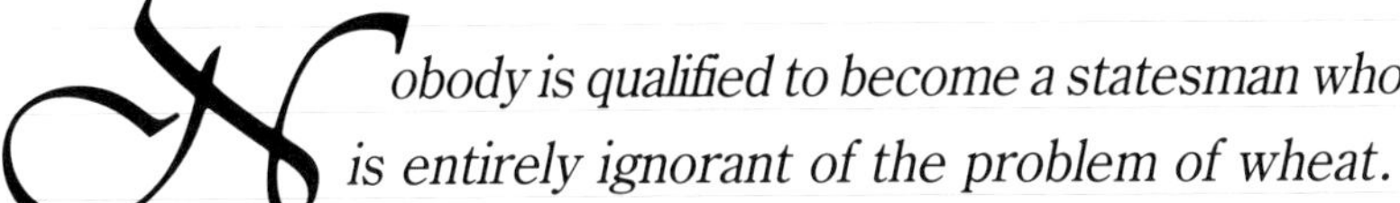

Nobody is qualified to become a statesman who is entirely ignorant of the problem of wheat.

— Socrates

■

The Canadian Wheat Board, which marked its fiftieth anniversary in 1985, is the most widely known but sometimes least understood agricultural marketing agency in Canada. Certainly the board's role in marketing western Canada's wheat and coarse grains on export markets is appreciated and accepted, but there are common misconceptions as to how, and through what legislative parameters, it fulfils its role.

Since the marketing of grains, both in the export and domestic markets, remains the dominant factor in the over-all economic well-being of the Prairie Provinces—as well as making one of the largest contributions to the nation's balance of payments—the day-to-day operations and decisions of the Canadian Wheat Board are commented upon and followed closely, not only in the board's designated area, but across the other diverse regions of the nation and in foreign marketplaces.

Yet even in Winnipeg, the home base for the Wheat Board's global operations and where the grain trade has played a key part in the growth and prosperity of the city, a majority of the citizens would express surprise if they were told that the Canadian Wheat Board is not a department of government. Most seem to understand clearly the relationship of other Crown corporations, such as the Canadian National Railway, the Canadian Broadcasting Corporation, or Air Canada, to the central government in Ottawa, but few equate a similar relationship to the Wheat Board.

That misconception springs, in large part, from the custom of formally designating a minister of the Crown to report to Parliament on the operations of the Wheat Board. While similar duties are delegated to other members of the federal cabinet to report on other Crown corporations, they are not, for example, commonly referred to as the "CNR Minister," or the "CBC Minister." Otto Lang, who recorded a long tenure as minister responsible to Parliament for the Canadian Wheat Board, held a number of portfolios over his years in the cabinet while retaining responsibility for reporting on the affairs of the board. Yet, no matter which portfolio he held, he was commonly referred to in the popular media as Wheat Board Minister Otto Lang whenever a Wheat Board announcement was made. It came to be then, in the minds of a large part of the public, that the board was a department of government financed by the federal treasury, rather than entirely by western Canadian farmers. Only on rare occasions—and normally as the result of a deliberate policy decision by cabinet—has a board deficit been paid out of the federal treasury.

That, in part, may account for another common misconception that, when final payments are announced for payout to farmers following the end of a crop year, they are handouts or subsidies to the producer from the federal treasury. Woe betide the farm editor who fails to appreciate the sensitivity of his readership by not spelling out the details involving such payments. Several years ago when a final payment was announced just prior to Christmas, an unfortunate editor failed to catch an overenthusiastic headline on a story which declared: "Farmers Get Xmas Bonus." His farm readers monopolized the phone lines to inform him that it was "no damn bonus," but the balance of their own money owed them on deliveries of grain they had made during the crop year. Sensitivity on that point amounts to paranoia with some farmers.

Confusion also exists both in Canada and abroad as to the role, application, and reason for delivery quotas administered by the Canadian Wheat Board. Even some knowledgeable agricultural reporters in other regions of the nation (and at least one federal agriculture minister) have sometimes failed to grasp the fundamental difference between delivery quotas and the production quotas common to the various supply-management agricultural marketing boards prevalent in Canada. While production quotas enforce market sharing by limiting production within specified areas, thereby effectively constituting a license to produce, delivery quotas constitute no such restriction.

Misapprehension as to the role of the board can extend into the scholarly area. Foster J. K. Griezic, a member of the Department of History, St. Patrick's College, Carleton University, wrote an introduction to Louis Aubrey Wood's *A History of Farmers' Movements in Canada*, an edition published in 1975. He commented, "The Board became the sole wheat marketing agency and in 1949 was given control of Western coarse grains. It has since undergone minor changes and displays a grudging sensitivity to farmers' demands for increased price supports."[1] The point is that the changes since 1949, while apparently minor in terms of fundamental concept, have been significant in the overall achievement of the board's mandate, and, that legislated mandate does not encompass price support under the accepted definition of that phrase. Nor does the function of income or price stabilization, commonly cited as an objective of the board system, fall within the purview of the Canadian Wheat Board in broad terms. Pooling of returns, combined with equalization of delivery opportunities, may result in a limited form of stabilization within a given crop year. However, year-to-year price—and thereby income variations—are governed by fluctuations in a competitive world marketplace. An aggressive sales policy is incompatible with a legislated requirement to insulate the producer from the vagaries of swings in the international market. Evidence that this duty has not been delegated as a function of the board is given by the introduction by the federal government in 1976 of the Western Grain Stabilization Program. That program operates as a separate entity from the Canadian Wheat Board.

This volume will attempt to dispel some of these misconceptions by outlining the history of the Canadian Wheat Board since its inception in 1935. At that time it was intended as a temporary instrument of income stabilization in a critical period of economic distress and environmental disaster in western Canada. Since then, its form and function have changed dramatically to meet changing circumstances and it has become a major competitive force in the world grain trade.

But, more than that, the history of the board is the tale of the evolvement of an alternative marketing system on the northern fringes of the North American Great Central Plain. Born of the roots of agrarian dissent in the early part of this century, it is the tale of an extraordinary and dedicated group of strong men in search of an ideal. Fighting against what they perceived as an unjust monopoly of grain buyers and the railways, they achieved a unique monopoly of a different kind for the producers.

The course toward that legislated monopoly was a progressive one, dictated by circumstance and change on the political, economic, and environmental stage of the regional and world scene. Contrary to some popular perception, it was not a surging groundswell of ideological unaninimity that swept the West toward a new marketing system. The harsh, semi-arid environment of the vast Canadian plains has always bred men of independent thought. But it is individual rather than group independence. Men such as A.E. Partridge, Henry Wise Wood, A.J. McPhail, C.H. Burnell, Paul F. Bredt, T.A. Crerar, L.C. Brouillette, and others, all played prominent and vital roles in the early history leading up to the central board concept.

Like Don Quixote's province of La Mancha, the early West was a vast, empty space that bred strong men. But, if like Don Quixote they were tilting at windmills, as many suggested, they succeeded in revolutionizing western Canada's grain marketing system despite being unhorsed in several jousts along the way. It was not always with unanimity of purpose however. There were clashes on fundamental policy between groups that persist today. Even within individual organizations, policy divisions were sometimes bitter. For a short period in the mid-1920s the evangelistic co-operative oratory of Aaron Sapiro swept the West and almost resulted in the economic fusion of two of the major protagonists, the Prairie Wheat Pools and United Grain Growers. However, while the whirlwind drive of the spellbinding California lawyer diverted the farmers' attention from political action towards co-operative marketing economics and the eventual birth of the Canadian Wheat Board, policy divisions persisted. They still do.

Each then in his own way pursued a self-perceived Holy Grail which would bring a more certain and secure future to the men and women who had flocked into the sparsely populated New West at the beginning of the century. Sometimes self-educated, they were not only devout and dedicated, but in the main men and women of sound and practical business acumen.

It is not the intention here to go into depth on the careers of these pioneers. Their saga of achievements and setbacks has been extensively documented in a number of histories which are recommended to readers who may wish to delve further into the early history of the grain economy of western Canada. (Please refer to the Selected Bibliography at the end of the text.) However, no history of the Canadian Wheat Board would be complete without an understanding of its roots. Those roots go back before the turn of the century and the agrarian revolt which followed the flood of homesteaders into the western plains.

The influx of settlers who saw the population of the Prairie Provinces increase fivefold within thirty years (from 419,512 inhabitants in 1901 to 2,353,529 in 1931) was a direct result of the national policy. That policy had as its goal the expansion of the Canadian economy through establishment of a prairie wheat economy, thereby providing a protected market for the industrial output of central Canada.

Vernon C. Fowke, in his book *The National Policy & the Wheat Economy*, has traced the formulation of that national drive from pre-Confederation years. Its motivations were diverse. They were political, military, and—above all—commercial. The nucleus of the imperial British presence on the North American continent was locked into the St. Lawrence basin following the American Revolution. By the mid-nineteenth century, the commercial interests of the St. Lawrence were looking southwards at the economic expansion and railway building in the United States with apprehension. The American concept of Manifest Destiny, formulated in the 1840s, was cause for concern in the British colonies. Defined by John L. O'Sullivan, in a statement in the New York *Morning News* of December 27, 1845, the concept was, "...the right of our manifest destiny to overspread and to possess the whole of the continent which Providence has given us for the development of the great experiment of liberty and federated self-government entrusted to us."[2]

As commercial ties to Britain began to weaken, the Canadian colonies of the St. Lawrence foresaw the westward sweep of commercial penetration in the United States as a potential forerunner of northern territorial occupation, and they began to formulate plans to combat that eventuality. Passage of the British North America Act of 1867 established the political constitution and the instrument by which a defensive national policy could be carried out.

Briefly summarized, the national policy espoused by the Fathers of Confederation was to unite Upper and Lower Canada with a struggling British colony in British Columbia, thereby creating an anti-American presence on the northern half of the North American continent. While this has been idealized as the national dream, the dream bore with it the commercial aspirations of the merchants and manufacturers already established in the St. Lawrence basin. This observation is borne out by the second salient feature of the national policy: tariffs. Dominion tariffs enacted from 1879 onwards were designed primarily to protect eastern interests rather than to obtain revenues. It is important to note this fundamental element of the national policy in any study of events in western Canada. Protective tariffs, among other perceived injustices, became a *cause-célèbre* in the subsequent agrarian revolt and continue to rankle Prairie farmers today.

The negotiations, failures, and disappointments that led finally to a bridge of steel being flung over a thousand miles of the rugged Precambrian Shield, thence across the sparsely inhabited Canadian desert, and on through the seemingly impassible Rocky Mountain escarpment have been fully described elsewhere. Note however, that by deliberate calculation the route finally chosen for the Canadian Pacific Railway was as close as possible to the United States border. Rather than choosing to cross the Prairies in an arc through the more fertile park belt and through the Yellowhead Pass, the planners drove rail through the heart of the semi-arid plain and on through the more difficult Kicking Horse Pass to reach Pacific tidewater.

While the latter route was more direct, it is obvious that defence against the threat of economic invasion by American railways was the prime motivating force in choosing the more southerly line. Fowke commented, "The projection of the Canadian Pacific Railway through the heart of the Canadian portion of the Great American Desert may be described as a reverse adaptation of the scorched-earth method of defence."[3] That the concern of central Canada was real in this regard is given by a report on Pacific railroads tabled in the U.S. Senate February 19, 1869. The report read in part, "The opening by us of a North Pacific Railroad seals the destiny of British possessions west of the 91st meridian. Annexation will be but a question of time."

The expansionists' ambition to see the American flag float over every square foot of British North American possessions clear to the North Pole, was thwarted by the westward thrust of Canadian rail building. Following hard on that thrust came pioneers seeking land on the new frontier. In their wake came the commercial entrepreneurs. Railway, land, and immigration policies were inextricably interrelated in the creation of the wheat economy.

Three railways, Canadian Pacific, Canadian Northern, and the Grand Trunk Pacific, began a furious spate of rail expansion in Manitoba and the Northwest Territories. Spurred by the federal policy of land grants to finance such building, the railways built or acquired a myriad of branch lines on the Prairies over a span of twenty-five years from 1885 to 1910. These facilitated land settlement and served as a gathering system for shipment of grain to the Lakehead, where the Canadian Pacific had built two terminals which were ready for use in 1884.

The first country grain elevator in Canada was built by Ogilvie Milling Company in 1881 at Gretna, Manitoba, where a settlement of Mennonite farmers had been established. The shape of the round 25,000-bushel structure was dictated by the fact that elevation of the grain was accomplished by horsepower in the literal sense. Blindfolded horses walking in a circle provided the motive power. In 1893 the first line elevator company operating more than one elevator, Northern Elevator Co., was formed. By 1900 the report of a royal grain commission showed that Northern Elevator had 67 standard elevators of 25,000-bushel capacity or more in operation in the West. In addition Northern had 25 elevators of less than 25,000-bushel capacity and 13 flat warehouses. The explosive growth of elevators, in less than a decade, had brought the total of country elevators to 447. Of these 206 were owned by three line elevator companies, Northern Elevator Co., Dominion Elevator Co., and the Winnipeg Elevator Co. In addition the Lake of the Woods Milling Company had 50 elevators, Ogilvie Milling Company 45, Farmers' Elevator Company 26, and 120 were owned by individual millers and grain dealers.

The birth of the Winnipeg Grain Exchange accompanied this surge of economic activity. As early as 1881 a small group of commodity merchants established a grain exchange in the basement of the Winnipeg City Hall, but it failed to survive a series of bad crops in the middle of the decade. In 1887 the exchange was re-established, and, following its incorporation in 1891, began to trade in wheat futures on January 29, 1904. Prior to that time transactions were conducted on cash grain only. Thus, by the early years of the new century, the elements of confrontation that were to lead to the formation, just over three decades later, of the Canadian Wheat Board were in place: concentration of the grain handling system in the hands of private commercial interests (which many farmers saw as an oppressive monopoly in league with the railways), and a marketing system regarded by the farmers as opposed to their interests. E.A. Partridge of Sintaluta, Saskatchewan, a pioneer of the farmers' co-operative grain handling system, after a visit to Winnipeg in 1904, dubbed the exchange as "the house with the closed shutters."

A month of cold shoulders accorded Partridge when he sought information on the grain business as a representative of the Territorial Grain Growers' Association did nothing toward easing the deepening mistrust and antagonism developing between the farmers and the exchange. Hopkins Moorhouse encapsulated the situation in his book *Deep Furrows* when he attributed the following statement to an exchange member who had been asked about Partridge:

> Oh, him! Only that gazabo from Sintaluta whose been nosing around lately. Some hayseeds out the line sent him down here to learn the grain business. They believe that all wheat's No. 1 Hard, all grain buyers are thieves, and that hell's to be divided equally between the railways and the milling companies.[4]

The words of the unnamed grain man epitomized the misunderstanding which hardened between the exchange and a majority of farmers in the West that has never been fully resolved.

The juxtaposition of two circumstances provided the catalyst for the unprecedented agricultural development of the Canadian West and fulfilment of the national policy. From the days of the Selkirk settlers in the early Red River settlement at Fort Garry, the growing of cereal crops had been an uncertain undertaking until the appearance of Red Fife wheat. Developed in the 1840s by David Fife, a Scottish immigrant farmer in Ontario, the hardy variety made its way to Manitoba by way of the United States. Until then the harsh climate, a short growing season, and rust problems had made wheat production hazardous. But despite its adaptability to the area, it was not a desired variety by flour millers. Because of its hardness it was discounted in price as being "flinty," and bypassed in favour of soft white varieties more adaptable to the millstone grinding process.

However, by the middle of the 19th century a revolution was underway in the milling process. In Europe a Frenchman named Perrigault patented a device known as a purifier which allowed separation of the bran from the coarse endosperm particles of wheat by sieving and air flotation. This was quickly followed by adoption of the gradual reduction process of flour milling in which chilled iron rollers were used instead of grinding stones to produce what became known as Patent flour.

The key to opening the Canadian West had been found; the wave of immigrants that had previously swept into the American frontier now began to move north. Suddenly the once downgraded flinty Fife became the most sought-after variety in the world. It was ideally suited to the new process. The hard wheat produced a higher protein flour which resulted in a superior loaf of bread. Formerly preferred soft white wheats were now selling at a discount to Red Fife. A poster circulated throughout Manitoba by the Ogilvie Milling Company in 1882 declared that it was the variety upon which the reputation of the New North West as a wheat producing region would depend. "No soft or mixed wheat is worth as much by 15 cents per bushel, and this difference in price will hereafter be made by the undersigned millers and wheat buyers," read the poster.

By 1876 Manitoba Red Fife was being shipped by river boat south to Minneapolis, which was rapidly becoming one of the greatest milling centres of the world. Drawing upon the plentiful supply of hard red winters in the Dakotas and Minnesota, Minneapolis mills ground 34 million bushels of wheat to produce 7,434,000 barrels of flour in 1890. Those millers first established the reputation and demand for Red Fife grown in Manitoba and by 1880 were offering premiums for it even over Red Fife grown in the Dakotas.

Spurred on by the politicians, bureaucrats involved in furtherance of the national policy quickly seized on the new reputation of Red Fife to increase the swell of immigration. The Board of Agriculture in Manitoba undertook to secure and distribute stocks of Red Fife and encourage its sole cultivation. The federal government waived the duty on stocks of Red Fife seed coming from the U.S., and the Canadian Pacific Railway announced it would move Red Fife seed stocks free of charge. Discrimination against Red Fife in the Inspection Act of 1874, whereby it could grade no higher than No. 2, was removed.

The tide that would establish the western wheat economy as the dominant factor in Canada's political and commercial aspirations over the opening decades of the century was at full flood. In 1901 there were 55,200 farms in the prairie provinces with 3.6 million acres in crop cultivation. That total peaked at 300,500 farms in 1936 with 40.2 million acres under cultivation. The four years from 1909 to 1912, inclusive, saw an average of over 40,000 new homesteads per year established in the West. It was a phenomenon almost without precedent in the history of national development on the world stage. The dynamic influence of the frontier permeated and transformed the Canadian economy, and its vitality spread from the national scene into world commerce. Exports of wheat and flour, which yielded $10.9 million in 1901, soared to $377.5 million in 1921 and to $495 million by 1929.

Agricultural policy, in direct relation to the needs and aspirations of the farmers themselves, was largely ignored in the course of this

A four-horse team provided the power for this binder in the early part of the century in western Canada. Piled sheaves in the foreground waiting to be stooked testify to the bounty of the harvest.

massive and concentrated period of capital and corporate expansion. Professor Fowke, in his admirable *Canadian Agricultural Policy—The Historic Pattern*, has made the point that government assistance has typically been extended to agriculture because of what agriculture was expected to do for other dominant economic interests in return for that assistance, rather than for what such assistance might do for agriculture. In the national scramble to thwart the anticipated commercial and territorial ambitions of the Americans, that was undoubtedly true. Monopoly powers and land grants vested in the railways, as incentives to provide capital formation and investment,

Sheaves and stooked wheat dot the landscape as far as the eye can see as eight horse-drawn binders move across the western plain.

led to settlers' grievances and confrontation with the railways and grain merchants even before the turn of the century.

In the early stages of the agricultural transformation, settlers from Ontario and from the United States predominated. Strong men and women, each seeking a new life, they were familiar with early populist farm movements such as the Grange and the Patrons of Industry. Such men have time to think and brood on real or perceived injustices while plowing a lonely furrow or during the long wagon trek behind a team of horses or oxen to deliver a hard-won load of grain to the nearest railway point. They found much to inveigh against.

To impel the pace of country elevator construction the railways granted what were, in effect, exclusive rights to line elevator companies adjacent to the sidings on railway property. At the same time by means of boxcar allocations and rights of tenure, the railways discriminated against loading platforms and flat warehouses which had dominated in the early years prior to the evolvement of the more efficient standard elevators. Farmers regarded this as a monopoly agreement between the railways and the line elevator and milling companies. They argued that it restricted competitive buying.

Complaints abounded, charging inadequate gradings, improper weighing, excessive dockage taken, boxcar shortages, and favouritism in car distribution. In addition the farmers saw what they regarded as an inordinate spread between the prices they received at the elevators and the eventual selling prices on the Winnipeg Grain Exchange and on the Liverpool Exchange, which was then the principal world buying market. These apprehensions were exacerbated by formation of the North West Elevator Association in 1901 and its reorganization as the North West Grain Dealers Association in 1903. While the objects of the association, formed by a group of elevator companies and grain dealers in Winnipeg, was to promote co-operation in matters such as the purchase of elevator supplies and to pool the cost of daily price telegrams to agents at each shipping point, it quickly became associated in the minds of the producers as a cartel aimed at controlling country grain prices. It was further proof of the existence of a "syndicate of syndicates."

Dispassionate critiques on the substantive accuracy of the multitude of charges are few in the early literature of the period. Chroniclers of the personalities and achievements of some of the early farm organizations accept the validity of all such charges and their continued abuse as doctrine, despite the judgements and findings of numerous royal commissions and public enquiries which, in general terms, absolved the private grain trade of specific wrongdoings. On the other side of the coin, there were equally ardent admirers of the open market system who defended the private trade despite the obvious vicissitudes, hardships, and injustices suffered by the producers of the period. Charles F. Wilson, in his voluminously documented book *A Century of Canadian Grain*, summed up the events prior to 1914 and the onset of the Great War. He appears to take the view that, while many of the transgressions charged existed, they were largely rectified by ongoing legislation:

> In the transition from the first producer reaction to the "syndicate of syndicates" in 1897 to the passage of the grain act in 1912, which roughly coincided with the span of the Laurier administration, the federal government had developed an increasingly sensitive response to producers' representations as reflected in the cumulative progress of the regulatory legislation. Early issues such as the producers' right to freedom of choice among marketing channels, had been resolved. Many of them had disappeared because of increasingly efficient regulation provided by legislation, and also because competition from farmer-owned country elevator systems and their extension into terminal elevator operations effectively removed the earlier but deep-rooted fears of an elevator monopoly. Over the same span, increasing competition among the railway companies and the expansion of their rolling stock had overcome the worst of the evils that arose in the early years of car shortage.[5]

Whatever the root causes or ameliorative reaction by legislators to the farmers' demands, the seeds of mistrust and antipathy sown in that early period toward the railways, the private grain trade, and the Winnipeg Grain Exchange, took root, flourished, and were reborn in subsequent generations of western Canadian farmers. The apochryphal story of the Saskatchewan farmer who, in the midst of the depression and drought of the Dirty Thirties, reached down and picked up a handful of dust from his barren fields, raised his fist to the sky and cursed the Canadian Pacific Railway, bears more than an element of truth.

As noted in *A Century of Canadian Grain*, the first reaction by the grain growers' associations was toward ownership of their own country and terminal elevator systems in competition with the private trade. They sought through political action protective legislation and its enforcement through the courts. In the period extending up to 1935 and the establishment of the Canadian Wheat Board marketing system by legislation, the quest by farmers and their organizations for reform went through a number of phases. Political class action, such as that taken by the United Farmers of Alberta and the Prairie Progressives, resulted in farmer dominated provincial governments in all three prairie provinces for varying periods. In the 1920s the farm-based Progressive Party held the balance of power in a minority government in Ottawa but failed, through lack of party discipline, to take full advantage of the opportunity to exercise their influence.

Farmers' organizations, with often conflicting ideologies, surfaced and disappeared. In the unfolding progression of successes and failures it is interesting to note that, of the early farm movements and organizations, only two survive intact into the present era. Both represent the concept of co-operative commercialism, through which the members hold a direct financial interest. That financial bond may have been the measure of their survival while others foundered on internal friction. But, even between those survivors, the prairie pools and United Grain Growers, there is a divergence of marketing philosophy which will be examined later.

There is not room to document and identify all of the events and participants in the saga of the first three-and-a-half decades of the century in this introduction, but two periods deserve mention. The first is the suspension of futures trading on the Winnipeg Commodity Exchange in 1917 (at the request of the exchange) under the exigencies of wartime conditions. That suspension was occasioned by the predominance of a monopoly buying agency established by Britain, and resulted in the appointment of the Board of Grain Supervisors, an agency of the federal government endowed with monopoly control over Canadian wheat. It was succeeded in 1919 by the first Canadian Wheat Board which retained that monopoly control in the transitionary period following the end of World War I. Dissolution of that first board in 1920, and the subsequent failure of farm organizations to have it reinstituted in 1922, led to the second period of note, which was the spectacular and controversial emergence of the prairie wheat pools.

The pools, based on co-operative marketing principles, were formed in the wake of the farmers' failure to obtain continuation of the compulsory board system. Establishment of their Central Selling Agency gained world-wide attention. Through voluntary contract pooling of grain, direct selling, and establishment of overseas agencies, the Central Selling Agency of the three prairie pools marketed slightly over one-half of all the wheat in the prairie provinces during its years of operations. When it crashed, along with the world-wide economy in the Great Depression, the federal government was constrained to intervene. As a direct result the federal government, from expediency and almost without design, was drawn into a stabilization operation in 1931 which in turn led directly to the Canadian Wheat Board legislation of 1935.

Born as an emergency expedient to meet an unparalleled combination of economic and environmental disasters in western Canada, the board was at best an unwanted child in the eyes of its political father. As in 1917 when emergency conditions prevailed, the government had made the board system its chosen instrument of agricultural policy. In its original form it was a compromise instrument of stabilization based on voluntary participation. The circumstances of its survival and evolution into a monopoly marketing agency is the main thrust of this book.

In a changing world, where a multiplicity of buyers and sellers on the world's grain markets have largely been replaced by a handful of national agencies, the board today fulfils a unique role as a single-desk seller in a marketplace dominated by single-desk purchasers, an eventuality probably unforeseen at its original inception. While the volume of the world grain trade has expanded over the past fifty years, the number of players has been decreasing. At the start of the 1980s the people who control 75 per cent of the selling and buying in the world could be accommodated in one small room.

Ironically, evidence of this consolidation of purchasing entities surfaced as early as 1924 among the major importing countries. They later railed against the pool's Central Selling Agency as an attempt to extort higher prices from them by cornering a major proportion of Canadian wheat supplies for export sale. A.J. McPhail, president of the Central Selling Agency, noted the trend in his diary on September 23, 1924:

> McRae and I had an interview with Dunning [Premier Charles Dunning of Saskatchewan] today. He told us there was an organization among the French buyers of wheat whereby although buyers might buy separately, one man directed the buying policy. The same situation prevails in Holland and the Rhine mills in Germany. He knows that the same arrangement exists between the British millers, Ranks, Shipton and Anderson, Spillers, etc.[6]

Over the years this trend has continued apace with the addition of state buying agencies, or quasi-governmental organizations, to combined purchasing by large milling concerns. In a world market, now heavily dominated by central purchasing agencies, the Canadian Wheat Board has proven to be a chosen instrument ideally suited to deal with them on a one-to-one basis. Some measure of the success of the board selling policy, particularly in periods of tight world marketing, is illustrated by observations made by outside sources.

Tim Josling of the Food Research Institute, Stanford University, in a technical report on intervention in Canadian agriculture in 1981, commented that, "Canadian wheat producers have for many years enjoyed the advantage of having their produce marketed through the Canadian Wheat Board.''[7] He also reached the conclusion that Canadian wheat policy is a clearly positive international force for stability of prices. At the Canadian Agricultural Outlook Conference of 1982 in Ottawa, Patrick M. O'Brien of the Economic Research Service of the United States Department of Agriculture, presented a gloomy picture for the world grain trade in the coming year. He noted however that Canada was in a unique position to minimize the damage and gave as one of the reasons the Canadian Wheat Board's ability to market aggressively.

But it was left to the *Kansas Wheat Scoop*, a newsletter published by the Kansas Wheat Commission, to provide the most succinct comment on the success of the board's selling efforts. In the issue of April 27, 1984, the newsletter noted that in a very competitive marketplace and a reversal in a trend of increasing world trade, U.S. wheat exports in 1982-1983 dropped by 15 per cent from the previous year. In the same period Canada's wheat exports increased by 16 per cent. ''Next year will be the 50th anniversary for the Canadian Wheat Board. They are asking for suggestions on how to celebrate. We wouldn't mind if they just took the whole year off.''

In the 1983-1984 crop year leading up to that fiftieth anniversary, the Canadian Wheat Board moved a record 27,425,000 tonnes of grain into export markets. That is a far cry from the approximately 6,885,000 tonnes of wheat shipped in the first year of operations in 1935. It is light years away from the first commercial shipment of Red Fife from Manitoba just over one hundred years ago. That shipment in 1876, by riverboat to Minneapolis and thence by U.S. rail to Ontario, comprised a meagre 857 bushels (23.32 tonnes).

Accompanying this increased volume of grain exports has been an equally dramatic shift in the pattern of world grain trade and the countries involved on both the import and export sides of the market. In the inter-war years of the 1920s and 1930s, between World War I and World War II, Canada assumed a commanding lead in world wheat trade, supplying 35.3 per cent of world net exports of wheat and flour. In that same period Argentina accounted for 20.1 per cent of global wheat exports, the United States 16 per cent, Australia 14.8 per cent, and all other exporters (including the Soviet Union) accounted for 13.8 per cent. Of particular interest is the fact that the United States suffered domestic grain shortages in both of the world wars and during the dust-bowl period of the 1930s, and became a net grain importer at those times. The United States did not overtake Canada as the major exporter in a greatly expanded world market until after World War II.

Critics of the central agency system have used this belated and massive entry of the U.S. into a rapidly changing and expanding world market to charge that the declining percentage of global trade enjoyed by western Canadian grain is indicative of flaws in the board system. That percentage-related argument ignores statistical evidence of ever increasing tonnages of Canadian grain being exported, despite critical inadequacies in the rail transportation system which restricted movement to export positions.

In the depressed market between 1935-1936 and the onset of World War II in 1939-1940, Canada raised its share of wheat exports to 40 per cent of the world market. But that only amounted to slightly under 5,000,000 tonnes in a 12,437,000-tonne market for all grains. By comparison that world market had expanded in volume by nearly eight times by 1982-1983, when the world wheat trade reached 96,145,000 tonnes. While Canada's share of that market was 22 per cent, as compared to the 40 per cent share above, her volume of exports had jumped over five times to 21,967,000 tonnes.

Equally important has been the shifting pattern of grain importers. Fifty years ago Western Europe, and particularly Britain, dominated the import market. In 1981-1982 the European Economic Community imported only 4,944,000 tonnes of wheat, while at the same time it became the third largest exporter of wheat in the world, exporting 14,085,000 tonnes of wheat to assume 14.65 per cent of world trade. The Soviet Union, which in the earlier period had been a wheat exporter, became the dominant importer by absorbing 20,140,000 tonnes of wheat or 21 per cent of the total market in 1982-83, and the Peoples Republic of China imported 12,936,000 tonnes of wheat. Japan, which also emerged as a major wheat purchaser during her spectacular post-war industrial growth, accounted for imports totalling 5,597,000 tonnes.[8]

This then is a history, not only of a single organization, but of a changing and volatile world market in the most fundamental and important commodity of human existence. Political considerations, both domestic and international, have played a large part in the decades of transition covered in these pages. Not unnaturally the controversy that marked the choice of the Canadian Wheat Board as the principal instrument of national agricultural policy has remained. Intervening as it does in a mixed marketing economy in which centralized and open markets exist side by side, and where a basic conflict of interest exists between grain producers and farmers in the livestock sectors, the Canadian Wheat Board has not escaped criticism.

Despite that, a study undertaken for the Economic Council of Canada published in 1982 reported that "being a government body, it [the Canadian Wheat Board] has strengths in planning and co-ordinating export grain sales that less centralized open market systems do not. Its central and commanding role in regulatory matters in the grains industry, its historical performance, and its wide acceptance by producers makes its disappearance from the scene unthinkable and unsupportable."[9]

Given this milieu it is difficult, if not impossible, for a commentator on agricultural policy in western Canada to remain neutral. As the former editor of a farm publication, the affinity of the author for the centralized board system is recognized. Nonetheless every effort has been made in researching and documenting this book to present the historic events without prejudice. Should it serve to enlighten participants in the ongoing debate on the problems of wheat, and thereby qualify more of them to become statesmen, the objective of this book will have been fulfilled.

THE PLAYERS

As marketing boards go, the Canadian Wheat Board is the most powerful and prestigious in the world. It has an awesome reputation, and its gray stone headquarters in Winnipeg underscores its power and apparent impregnability.

— Dan Morgan, *Merchants of Grain*

▪

The bitter winds that swirl around Winnipeg's Portage Avenue and Main Street in midwinter have earned the intersection an unenviable reputation for being the coldest inhabited corner of the world. No less bitter have been the winds of dissension that have from time to time gusted around this same hub of the grain trade in Canada. Portage and Main is probably unique in its tight concentration of divergent interests and market philosophies within a single industry. The players in the drama are all situated within a stone's throw of the city's epicentre.

Dominating the southwest corner, the thirty-storey Trizec building rises in glazed and painted-panel angularity against the blue prairie sky. It is the new home of the Winnipeg Commodity Exchange, where the last vestiges of a once dominant Winnipeg Grain Exchange carry on a limited trade in grain futures. On the fifth floor, the private traders cluster in the pit to raise the time-honoured pandemonium of shouted bids and offers. That trade is now confined to non-board grains and oil seeds such as rye, flaxseed and rapeseed, and to off-board grains, representing feed grains such as barley, oats, and feed wheats. The latter category of feed grains, traded solely into the domestic market, was restored to the private trade in 1972 after a hiatus of twenty-three years as the result of a still controversial change in Canada's domestic feed grains policy.

On the northeast corner, an austere cube of stone-speckled concrete soars thirty-two storeys over Portage and Main, embellished on the upper reaches by the quietly circumspect logo of James Richardson & Sons Limited, the oldest grain merchandising firm in Canada. James Richardson, who founded the firm in Kingston, Ontario, in 1857, had the distinction of exporting the first shipment of western Canadian wheat to Liverpool via an all-Canadian route to seaboard through Fort William (now Thunder Bay) in 1883. Since those early days, the family-controlled firm has expanded its commercial and investment empire into other areas. It remains, however, as owner of the largest privately-held line of country grain elevators and port terminals in Canada. Through its holdings in Pioneer Grain Company Limited, the Richardson family in 1985 owned 236 primary elevators scattered across the prairies. Additionally, Richardson Terminals Limited operated two export grain terminals, one at Thunder Bay and another at Vancouver. If Winnipeg or western Canada has an aristocracy, then the highly respected Richardson family would rank at the top of the list.

These two dominant edifices are connected by a complicated warren of brightly lit underground walkways, flanked by boutiques, banks, restaurants, and service shops. There, Winnipegers can escape the cold of winter and the sometimes blistering heat of mid-summer. Above them, where horse-drawn street cars once turned north, south, or west at the city's hub, the intersection is now ringed with concrete planters denying surface pedestrian passage. To cross

Portage and Main one must descend by escalator or stairs and ascend on the other side.

Through the underground passages, business-suited participants in the complex grain trade pass from one office to another, protected from the elements as they conduct their interrelated business. They converge from connecting sheltered tunnels or walkways into the climate-controlled environment below. Directors and managers of the prairie pools descend from the Royal Bank Building at 220 Portage Avenue, which connects directly to the Trizec tower. Together, the farmer-owned pool co-operatives handle the largest percentage of prairie grains through their ownership of 1,071 of the 1,940 primary elevators licensed in western Canada. The Saskatchewan Wheat Pool dominates all others with 590 country elevators. It maintains a branch office in Winnipeg. Alberta Wheat Pool, which similarly has a branch office in Winnipeg, operates 324 country elevators; and Manitoba Pool Elevators with head offices in the Royal Bank Building owns 157. Together, the prairie pools also dominate the waterfront at the ports through the ownership of export grain terminals. Saskatchewan Pool owns five of the twelve giant terminals at Thunder Bay and one in Vancouver. Manitoba Pool Elevators operates two of the Thunder Bay terminals and Alberta Wheat Pool operates one at Vancouver.

On any one day the pool men may pause to converse with traders from the largest member of the big league of world grain traders. From the newly completed Cargill Grain Building they pass over the intersection of Fort Street and Graham Avenue on a covered skyway into the Trizec complex. Cargill, with a global command post for a multinational commonwealth of 140 affiliates or subsidiaries in 36 countries in Minneapolis, Minnesota, has maintained a branch office in Winnipeg since the early days of the grain trade. Then, in 1974, Cargill became a member of the big six western Canadian grain handling companies, with its purchase of 195 elevators from the National Grain Company. After consolidation, Cargill was operating 143 of those primary elevators on the Prairies and a terminal at Thunder Bay in 1985, as well as the largest transfer elevator in Canada at Baie-Comeau, which it built in 1960 after the opening of the St. Lawrence Seaway.

While it maintains the largest presence, Cargill is not the only member of the international big league represented in Winnipeg. They are all there. On the ninth floor of the Trizec building, above the Winnipeg Commodity Exchange, is the office of Continental Grain Co. (Canada) Ltd., subsidiary of the Fribourg family firm which dates back to 1830 in Antwerp. Sharing the ninth floor with Continental is Range Grain Company Limited, one of two subsidiaries of Garnac Grain Company, which is in turn the holding company of the Swiss-owned Andre Group. One floor below is the branch office of Louis Dreyfus (Canada) Limited, a family-owned corporation based in Paris, France. From the Trizec complex you can make your way through the underground maze to the old Grain Exchange Building at 167 Lombard Street. There, on the ninth floor, is Bunge of Canada Limited, the Canadian subsidiary of Bunge Corporation based in Curaçao, Netherlands East Indies.

Sharing the interconnected complex with the big league traders are other international grain export companies such as Alfred C. Toepfer (Canada) Limited, subsidiary of a Hamburg-based firm; Mardorf, Peach & Company (Canada) Limited, subsidiary of the Garfield Weston milling interests in Britain; Anglo Canadian Grain Company Limited, a subsidiary of the Spillers milling firm in Britain; and Ranks Hovis McDougall (Canada) Limited, a subsidiary of the Rank milling interests in Britain. Representatives of Canadian-owned grain merchandising firms also mingle and pass in the underground corridors. Northern Sales Limited, operates out of the fifth floor of the Scotiabank Building, connected directly to the Trizec tower. On the ninth floor of the old Grain Exchange Building is Agro Company of Canada Limited, which exports from both coasts. Other grain merchants such as Toronto Elevators Limited, Ogilvie Flour Mills Company Limited, and Robin Hood Multifood Limited operate within the complex in procurement of wheat, feedgrains, and oilseeds for domestic milling, feed compounding, and crushing.

On the eighth floor of the Trizec building is the head office of XCAN Grain Limited, the export arm of the prairie pools, which maintains overseas offices in London and Tokyo. When XCAN was incorporated in 1970, United Grain Growers, the oldest of the prairie grain handling co-operatives, joined the pools in its formation, but withdrew in 1974 when it incorporated its own export subsidiary, Grain Growers Export Company Limited. United Grain Growers, operating 346 primary elevators across the West and two export terminals at Thunder Bay and one in Vancouver, is the only one of the big six Canadian grain handlers whose offices do not connect directly into the underground passages at Portage and Main. The United Grain Growers Building at 433 Main Street is two blocks north of the nearest surface entrance.

Other grain handling companies include N.M. Paterson and Sons

Limited with seventy-four country elevators and Parrish & Heimbecker Limited with forty-six licensed primary elevators and an export terminal at Thunder Bay. All of these diverse organizations have memberships and cross-memberships in the Lake Shippers' Clearance Association, the Shippers and Exporters Association of the Winnipeg Commodity Association, and the Dominion Marine Association.

Many of the shippers, traders, brokers, agents, and the senior personnel of related associations, such as the Canada Grains Council, the Canola Council of Canada, Western Grain Elevator Association, and Winnipeg Commodity Clearing Limited, make their way through the sheltered Portage and Main labyrinth to lunch or to attend grain trade receptions at the Winnipeg Chamber of Commerce. Sometimes they are joined by representatives from the Grain Transportation Authority at 135 Lombard Avenue, across the street from the old Grain Exchange Building. They meet on an historic, but transformed, spot. The tables and padded armchairs of the sixth floor Chamber of Commerce club rooms sit in elegant repose upon what was once the trading floor of the Winnipeg Grain Exchange. From 1908, through the inter-war years and into the early years of World War II, it was a focal point of the world's export grain trade. The lofty ceiling resounded to the pandemonium of shouted bids and takes; smock-clad young men and women scurried along the raised catwalk, chalk in hand, to update quotations from Chicago, Liverpool, and other exchanges on huge blackboards. Now men and women make quiet business deals over lunch and exchange gossip here. Today the ceiling has been lowered to a point below where the blackboards stood, and oak panelling has replaced the row of telephone booths that supported the catwalk. A block and a half away through the tunnels, electronic panels have replaced the chalk and blackboards in the new Winnipeg Commodity Exchange.

A short one-block, open air walk south of Portage and Main brings one to the watchdog over this interconnected conglomerate of diverse grain trade participants. The sixteen-storey Canadian Grain Commission Building at 303 Main Street houses the administrators of the Canada Grain Act, the roots of which go back to the early days of the century. The first Canada Grain Act became law on April 1, 1912, consolidating and amending the General Inspection Act of 1874 and the Manitoba Grain Act of 1900. Headed by a chief commissioner and two commissioners, the legislated mandate of the Canadian Grain Commission, which reports to the federal Minister of Agriculture, is as follows: "The Commission shall, in the interests of the grain producers, establish and maintain standards of quality for grain and regulate grain handling in Canada, to ensure a dependable commodity for domestic and export markets."[1]

To accomplish those objectives, the commission has been given wide-ranging powers and duties under the Act to establish grain grades and standards; implement a system of grading and inspection for Canadian grain; establish and apply standards and procedures regulating the handling, transportation and storage of grain and facilities used in such operations; conduct investigations and hold hearings when required; manage and operate government owned elevators assigned to the commission by the federal government; undertake, sponsor, and promote research in grain and grain products; and advise the federal minister responsible for the commission on matters relating to grain or grain products. In brief, the commission is responsible for quality control of Canadian grain and for the supervision of its handling.

Organized into five divisions, the Canadian Grain Commission employs some eight hundred people in its operations throughout Canada. The divisions include administration and finance, grain inspection, grain weighing, economics and statistics, and a grain research laboratory. Approximately half of the employees work in the vital grain inspection division on a full time basis at seventeen points across Canada, and some two hundred and fifty are employed in the grain-weighing division at nine points in Canada. The commission assesses the quality of each crop, assists plant breeders in the evaluation of the processing and utilization quality of new varieties, publishes statistics, licences grain elevators, supervises the Commodity Exchange under the provisions of the Grain Futures Act, and performs a multitude of other tasks involved in bringing order to the grain industry.

Built up over the years since the turn of the century, the system regulated by the Canadian Grain Commission has won a reputation for Canadian grain throughout the world. Canada is the only country in the world to export grain successfully on the basis of a combined certificate of grade and weight.

On the upper floors of the Canadian Grain Commission is the Canadian International Grains Institute (CIGI), a non-profit corporation which offers instruction in grain handling, transportation, marketing, and technology, and provides market development support for Canada's grain and oilseed industry. It works closely with the

Canadian Wheat Board, the Canadian Grain Commission, the Department of Industry Trade and Commerce, Agriculture Canada, and the grain business and academic communities. The institute provides potential buyers with a better understanding of the world grain industry and contributes to the maintenance and enlargement of markets for Canadian grains and oil seeds. The institute, founded in 1972, is an outgrowth of a program pioneered by the Canadian Wheat Board in the 1950s which brought delegations from countries around the world to view Canada's grain industry first hand. Representatives of more than seventy countries have attended courses held in the Winnipeg facility, and educational courses have been developed to meet the needs of various domestic groups such as farm leaders, journalists, millers, and marketing specialists.

A central feature for the participants of each of the CIGI courses is a walk two blocks north from Portage and Main to visit and observe the operations of the central player in the sale and marketing of western Canada's grain. In the eight-storey, gray stone headquarters of the Canadian Wheat Board at 423 Main Street, the sale of approximately 90 per cent of the total volume of grain exported from western Canada is negotiated and co-ordinated. All prairie-grown wheat, oats, and barley destined either for the export market or marketed for human consumption in Canada is marketed solely by the Canadian Wheat Board. It is accomplished through a tight-knit organization directed by five commissioners appointed to head the Crown corporation by the federal government.

The cornerstone of the board system still remains the concept of price pooling among producers to offset fluctuations within the marketing year in returns to the individual farmer. This concept is a direct descendant of the farmer-led co-operative movement of the 1920s and 1930s. Central to that idea is the delivery quota system used by the board to draw forward the specific types and grades of grain for which there is an immediate market. Delivery quotas match available supplies with sales by regulating the timing of grain deliveries, not the amount or kind of grain grown. There are no restrictions or incentives for the production of any type of grain grown in western Canada. Thus, while all western farmers are free to make their own planting decisions, the quota system ensures that each farmer has access to the elevator system in relation to the assigned acreage in his permit book. As the crop year progresses, the board makes every effort to equalize delivery opportunities across the prairies. While the Canadian Wheat Board does not market rye, flaxseed, or rapeseed, it does establish delivery quotas for these crops to ensure the fair use of space in country elevators for all grains. Similarly, quotas are established for feed grains sold into the open market for domestic consumption.

Out of that basic concept, honed and refined over fifty years to keep pace with changes and evolution in the world grain markets, has grown a unique organization. Given its centralized concept, the question might arise as to what role the majority of the other players centred on Winnipeg's Portage and Main complex have to play other than participation in the limited markets outside of the board's jurisdiction. The answer lies partly in the fact that the Wheat Board building is the only real property owned by the board. It has no elevators or other handling facilities. From its inception in 1935, the board was enjoined under the Canadian Wheat Board Act to employ existing facilities of the trade. In pursuit of that policy, the Wheat Board appoints primary elevator companies, domestic and export merchants, and various processing companies to act as its agents in the handling of board grains. Each year the board enters into handling agreements with these companies, under which they accept deliveries of board grain and forward it to terminal elevators or to processing plants and move grain from Thunder Bay to eastern transfer elevators. The board sells grain directly to processing plants in the West, to domestic merchants at Thunder Bay and to export merchants at port elevators across Canada.

Under the above circumstances, there are two types of Wheat Board sales. Increasingly over the years the major portion of the sales of wheat, oats, and barley have been undertaken by the direct sales between the board and the customer. In other sales the board enlists the services of accredited exporters, such as the multinationals with their worldwide networks of offices and representatives. These indirect sales generally account for 15 to 20 per cent of board sales.

It is not uncommon to have a combination of direct and indirect sales. The Wheat Board sells strictly on an in store, or FOB (free on board) export terminal, basis. For customers that require assistance for shipping from that point, accredited exporters are called upon to handle the details and are able to offer on a landed, or CIF (cost, insurance and freight), basis. Thus, an export customer may deal directly with the Wheat Board to negotiate a grain purchase and then have an accredited exporter arrange ocean freight and insurance. In making such use of the private trade, the board is able to discharge the pricing and marketing functions assigned to it by legislation and, at the same time, to utilize the facilities and expertise of the private trade in the handling and resale of grain.

Since the major long-term contracts entered into by the Wheat Board gain the headlines, such as those with the Soviet Union and the Peoples Republic of China, many people are prone to presume that these constitute the sole activity of the board. An example of this misconception was given in a story, quoting Canadian sources, in a New York paper in late 1985. Stating that Australia had sold wheat to forty-six countries that year and more than half those sales were of fewer than 100,000 tonnes, the report said this was in contrast to Canada which tended to have a small number of large sales of between 2,000,000 and 4,000,000 tonnes. To set the record straight, Esmond Jarvis, chief commissioner of the Wheat Board, noted the facts, which were that the Canadian Wheat Board, either directly or through its accredited agents, shipped wheat and barley to more than sixty countries every year. A map produced by the board in 1985 showed that western Canadian wheat and barley had been sold in virtually every grain importing nation around the world. "The only two big blank spots were Greenland and Australia. We're working on them," said Jarvis.[2] In pursuit of those world-wide sales, the five commissioners of the board and sales personnel travelled to thirty-two countries in the 1984-1985 crop year, and negotiations were carried out with a number of customers who visited Winnipeg.

Another prevalent misconception in some areas is that the major portion of Canadian sales are made under credit terms. The board may offer credit, at commercial terms only, for repayment periods of up to three years. Such credit sales are financed by the board, but credit lines must be approved by the federal government which guarantees credit in the event a customer should default. Despite availability of that credit, 87 per cent of all board sales in the 1984-1985 crop year were for cash.[3]

Long-term bilateral agreements, which the Canadian Wheat Board pioneered in the 1960s, also tend to dominate public attention, primarily because of the large volumes ranging up to 25 million tonnes over a five-year period. Such agreements represent a key weapon in the board's sales arsenal, usually because of the reliability of supply guaranteed to the purchasing nation. Once again there is a common perception, outside of the grain industry, that such undertakings are fixed-price agreements. Rather, they are letters of intent, under which the Wheat Board undertakes to supply and the customer undertakes to purchase a minimum quantity of grain over a certain period. Separate sales contracts, made periodically under the terms of the agreement, fix price, grade, and the time of shipment. Thereby, the price will be fixed at intervals in line with the then prevailing market environment. The board, as sole supplier of wheat, oats, and barley into the export market, is in a unique position to make and fulfill these long-term agreements.

While sales and market development are the ultimate focal point in the operations of the Canadian Wheat Board, that goal could not be achieved without back-up in a number of other vital areas. Within that division, a market analysis section follows developments in the grain industry around the world. Market analysts are assigned to specific areas of responsibility including Western Europe, Eastern Europe, the USSR, Africa and the Middle East, Latin America, and Asia. Developments in competing export countries are followed and analyzed with equal interest.

Because few other countries are confronted with the constraints of climate and geography, and since the Canadian Wheat Board is the largest user of grain elevation and transportation facilities required to move grain to its ultimate destination, the board has been given authority by regulation under the Canada Grain Act to co-ordinate the entire movement of western grain within Canada. That process begins outside of the board at the offices of the Grain Transportation Authority (GTA) on nearby Lombard Street. The GTA negotiates with the railways for the supply of cars that will be made available for shipments to each port, each week, taking into account grain sales, stocks, terminal inventories, and vessel shipments. This process provides the basis for determining how the grain car fleet will be divided in a specific week between grains marketed by the Wheat Board and those marketed by independent shippers. The initial allocation is made between the board and non-board sales commitments. The GTA then divides that portion of the railcar fleet allocated to the movement of non-board grains among the various shippers that have requested cars for a particular week, taking care to not allow unsold non-board grains to accumulate in terminal elevators to the detriment of the total grain movement. The ball then moves to the Canadian Wheat Board's grain transportation division.

The overriding objective in the board's co-ordination of the grain transportation system is the timely movement of the kinds, grades, and quantities of grain required by customers. Before the grain can move, however, there is a lot of work to be done. The supplies of grain the board has available for sale in any crop year must be determined, both by kind and quality. Export sales must be made for shipment in specific periods from the different port areas. The planning and co-ordination department of the board is responsible for most of this work. It maintains a close watch on development of crops in western Canada to assess potential supplies that will be available for sale and shipment in subsequent months. When harvesting is completed, the estimates are refined and a detailed inventory of exportable supplies available in each shipping area is worked out. With this knowledge with respect to supply, the flow of grain can be precisely scheduled to ensure that operations are on target, and the board is able to flag developing risks and opportunities in its sales program.

The flow of grain from the farms in the kinds and grades required at the precise time to meet sales commitments is controlled by delivery quotas initiated by the board's transportation division. These quota recommendations are then approved and announced by the board. When the required grain has been delivered to the primary elevators, its onward movement is controlled with the co-operation of the elevator and railway companies. This is done through a shipping system in which all western railway subdivisions are divided into 196 train runs, which serve as units of elevator handling and car supply. For each train run, six-week car cycles are continuously in effect, with a new cycle initiated each week, and car distribution is planned and finalized with a week's advance notice to each elevator company. Thus elevator managers know a week in advance the number of cars each will receive for loading in the following week, the kinds and grades of grain to be loaded, and the destination to be marked on the cars. After loading, the cars are collected and marshalled into trains routed to the terminals.

Complete oversight and supervision of the transportation movement is assisted by an operations map which shows the position of every railway car in grain service in western Canada and the number of vessels in port at the West Coast, Thunder Bay, and Churchill. Information on cars loaded or about to load, their location, and the kinds and grades of grain loaded in them is continually updated through a central computer, which can trace the movement of every car in the system.

Backing up this co-ordinated system is the country services division which deals directly with the primary elevators and producers. Apart from handling all enquiries from these sources, this division is responsible for the issuance of participation payments to producers, making cash advances against farm-stored grain, and the issuance of permit books which record the individual farmers' transactions. Once again these operations are computerized. The management information services division operates the central computer system and a treasury division is responsible for all of the board's financial transactions. Streamlining of all of these varied and tightly integrated tasks and adoption of advanced computerization methods, which the board pioneered in the grains industry, had reduced the number of permanent employees at the Wheat Board to 498 in 1985, as compared to a high of 724 in 1972.

These then are the players surrounding Winnipeg's Portage Avenue and Main Street. But beyond that hub, stretching across some nine hundred miles of semi-arid plains to the Rocky Mountains, are over 145,000 grain farms upon whose production the whole complex rests. The unique blend of public and private enterprise which marks the Canadian grain industry rests upon the farmers' support and the produce of their labors in an environment which presents special challenges. Besides a sometimes harsh and uncertain climate, there is the task of moving grain to the export markets of the world. It is a challenge of sheer distance faced by no other exporting nation. The mid-point in western Canada is about 1,450 kilometres from Vancouver, and about 1,300 kilometres from Thunder Bay at the head of the Great Lakes. Grain for export from St. Lawrence River ports must go first by rail to Thunder Bay, and then travel another 2,000 miles through the Great Lakes and the St. Lawrence Seaway before it is in export position. That latter route is shut down by ice for at least three months of the year. Access to the year-round west coast ports at Vancouver and Prince Rupert is through one of the world's most difficult mountain ranges. Routes through Churchill and the Atlantic ports are relatively small and used only a few months of the year.

Despite these challenges of climate and distance, Canada has maintained a reputation on world markets for uniform and high quality grain and assurance of reliable supply. Central to that world-wide reputation are the sales and transportation responsibilities of the Canadian Wheat Board, which have made it one of the nation's top ten corporations and, in most years, Canada's largest exporting company. In 1985, the board's ability to assess grain supplies accurately, develop marketing programs and then co-ordinate deliveries and shipments to ports as needed made it the key player in a mixed marketing grain industry. Its transition to that role was a slow and sometimes uncertain one in a continually changing political and economic environment on the national and world scene. To follow that progress and transition, let us turn back to the dust, depression, and despair of the early 1930s, and the birth pains of the Canadian Wheat Board.

BIRTH PAINS

The maintenance of the free market system which has functioned continuously and, on the whole, smoothly, under the abnormal strains of the past three or four years is essential. It is necessary to the retention of the goodwill of importers in the existing markets abroad, and it is only through the development of this goodwill that Canada can maintain or increase her share of the available world markets.

— Statement by the Council of the Winnipeg Grain Exchange, Winnipeg. *Free Press Evening Bulletin, October 28, 1933*

The tall, commanding figure entered the room, flung off the jacket of his expensive suit and slammed the folded copy of the Saturday evening paper down on it. Anger, frustration, and hurt welled up within John I. McFarland, a man normally not given to outbursts. He reached for his ever-present pipe, pulled a plug of tobacco from the side pocket of the jacket, and cut and crumbled the pungent flake into its bowl. After several attempts with the wooden matches the pipe was satisfactorily alight. McFarland loosened his tie, undid the stud on his stiffly starched white collar, and reached again for the paper to reread the statement that had roused his ire.

That Saturday night, October 28, 1933, may well mark the point when the tide of circumstances turned irrevocably toward a government appointed board for the marketing of grain in western Canada.

The box of matches McFarland put on the small table beside the chair where he now sat bore the trademark of the E.B. Eddy Company, the controlling interest of which was in the hands of the Right Honorable Richard Bedford Bennett, Canada's prime minister. In partnership with Bennett, McFarland had some years earlier amassed a substantial fortune in the western Canadian grain trade. As owners of the Alberta Pacific Grain Company they built a line of 301 country elevators scattered throughout Manitoba, Saskatchewan, and Alberta. The company was sold in 1926 for a high figure to Spillers, a large British milling company.

Their relationship began in 1912 when the Calgary and Alberta Grain Company, which McFarland built from a single elevator operation at Strathcona, south of Edmonton, was amalgamated with Alberta Pacific Elevator Company, in which Bennett had an interest, along with his lifelong friend Lord Beaverbrook and Nicholas Bawlf of Winnipeg. Their partnership in the company developed into a close personal friendship, which accounted in large part for McFarland's presence in Winnipeg that Saturday night.

He had come in late 1930, at the request of the banks and with the reluctant consent of the directors of the Canadian Co-operative Wheat Producers (CCWP), the Central Selling Agency of the prairie pools, to conduct a saving operation as manager of that organization. In taking on that task, McFarland had characteristically specified that he would accept the general managership as a public service, would have no salary, and would draw from the pools only the money needed for living expenses. He also imposed the condition that he be given a free hand in disposing of the affairs of what was essentially a bankrupt enterprise. At the outset he was confident that it would take no longer than a year to rectify the affairs of the ailing marketing agency.[1]

Outside the relative Victorian splendor of the Royal Alexandra Hotel on Winnipeg's North Main Street, where McFarland maintained a suite during the extended absences from his Calgary home, the visible manifestations of the conditions which had prolonged his stay for the past three years were heavy in the crisp fall air. All summer long a cloud of dust had periodically darkened and obscured the sky, swept aloft by the hot westerly winds from the parched plain stretching a thousand miles to the foothills of the Rockies. The unprecedented drought, which began at the start of the decade, was deepening. What little rain fell was laden with topsoil. Black droplets smudged the laundry fluttering on backyard clotheslines.

On Main Street, as in other urban areas across the West, the soup lines were lengthening, and the declining numbers of automobiles on dusty streets gave evidence of a concurrent and deepening financial crisis. Worldwide financial chaos, which followed hard on the Black Tuesday stock market collapse of October 29, 1929, withered world markets for wheat. Grain prices plunged and with them went the bright hopes of the wheat pools, each of which had become in the words of Henry Wise Wood, ''as much a religious institution as the church.''

Net farm income in Canada slid to unprecedented lows. With the index set at 100 for the years 1926 to 1929, farm income across the nation had slumped to an all time low of 18.8 in 1933. That told only part of the story in the Prairie Provinces. There, buffeted by a combination of declining wheat prices and markets, the index hit an unbelievable -3.0.[2] In the fall of 1933 a general survey and study of the moisture in the soils and subsoils of thirty-six townships in western Manitoba was undertaken by the soils division of the Manitoba Department of Agriculture to ascertain crop prospects for 1934. Contained among the recommendations was the statement that: ''Fields with dry subsoils (as outlined) cannot be expected to produce a crop next season unless timely rains, and moisture above that of the average, fall during the 1934 growing season. Any crop sown (in the areas outlined) should be sown on summerfallow. All other fields should be fallowed next season or used as pasture (corn or Russian Thistle).''[3]

The timely rains would not come. Crop yields in southwestern Manitoba dropped from below four bushels to the acre in 1933 to below two bushels per acre in 1934.[4]

West of the city where McFarland sat brooding, the combined impact of drought and depression had shattered the wheat economy. Municipal and provincial resources were inadequate to meet social assistance requirements. For the period 1930 to 1937 inclusive, the relief burden amounted to three-fifths of the total ordinary revenues of the provincial and municipal governments in Saskatchewan, compared to one-fifth for the remainder of the Dominion.[5] The federal government had to step in with outright grants to stave off complete collapse. In 1931 the western farmer, for the first time, became a direct beneficiary under the federal government. In July, Prime Minister Bennett announced that his government would adjust freight rates by absorbing five cents per bushel of the rate on all wheat exported during the year to be paid directly to the farmer. This bonus, described by D.A. MacGibbon as a ''modest, not to say parsimonious,'' contribution to to the western farmer's income, amounted to $12,720,121.[6]

Considering that the gross value of agricultural production in the Prairie Provinces, which approximated a billion dollars in 1926 and 1927, had progressively fallen to a meagre $163 million by 1933,[7] the federal bonus did little to alleviate a disastrous deficit in farm income. The West, which had long been a magnet for land seekers from far and near, became an area of net emigration. Proud men and women, who had left their roots and endured hardship and toil to establish their independence as homesteaders on the new frontier, left their farms to the dust, tumbleweed, and grasshoppers. Pitiful caravans of destitute families, carrying the remnants of their belongings, trekked away from shattered dreams. For some the outward journey was made in once-cherished automobiles or trucks. Now, lacking the money to buy gasoline, they had been converted to ''Bennett buggies'' drawn by horses hitched to makeshift harnesses. Over the decade of drought and depression, the Prairies suffered a net exodus of over a quarter of a million people.

A complex man behind his sometimes austere exterior, McFarland felt all of these things deeply. He had learned the grain trade from a bookkeeper's stool in Winnipeg before journeying west to become one of Canada's leading grain traders. George McIvor, who in 1933 was McFarland's principal assistant as sales manager of CCWP, recalled in later years that McFarland had been extraordinarily successful, ''more successful than any other grain man in Canada...he made millions in market operations while he was with Alberta Pacific in Calgary.''[8] Despite this, and his continuing strong adherence to open market principles, McFarland had been a supporter of the co-operative pool movement, at least at the outset. He was one of the prominent businessmen onstage in Calgary's Victoria Pavilion on the historic August evening in 1923 when Aaron Sapiro launched his emotion-charged campaign for organization of the pools. In addition McFarland served on a seventeen-man committee, set up in August 1923, to study formation of the Alberta Wheat Pool. He subsequently resigned because of disagreement over the form of the growers' contract. Despite that he was one of the first to sign a contract with Alberta Wheat Pool for delivery of pooled grain into Alberta Pacific elevators.

John I. McFarland, chief commissioner Canadian Wheat Board, August 14, 1935 to December 3, 1935.

Before McFarland sold his interest in Alberta Pacific Grain Company to Spillers in 1923, he offered to sell the elevators to the Alberta Wheat Pool at a price to be determined by an independent evaluator. He asked nothing for goodwill, since he maintained that any goodwill possessed by Alberta Pacific was contributed by the farmers.[9] The offer was not accepted. Those who knew McFarland testified to his remarkable personal affinity to the problems of farmers through his business interests and that the role of championing their cause came easily to him.

Whatever his sympathies may have been with the farmers' drive to establish their own organizations, it apparently did not extend to bypassing the mechanism of the Grain Exchange by selling directly to overseas purchasers, which the pools had undertaken to do through their Central Selling Agency. His first act, upon assuming control of that agency in 1930, was to terminate direct selling and close the pools' overseas offices. Thereafter McFarland embarked upon a price stabilization operation using the open market skills that had served him so well in establishing his own personal fortune.

Now, over that cool October weekend in 1933, McFarland reviewed the train of events over the three years since he had first taken on his thankless task. On Sunday the temperature rose to thirty-nine degrees (Fahrenheit), the first time it had been above freezing since the start of the week, but he remained in his rooms locked in thought. His faith in the open market and in the private trade to function to the benefit of the farmer and to the economic well being of the country, at least in times of abnormal stress, was faltering. As one of Canada's foremost and respected private traders, John I. McFarland was about to break rank.

His involvement in the wheat crisis actually began the day that his friend R.B. Bennett was sworn into office as prime minister of Canada on August 7, 1930, after the defeat of the Liberal administration headed by William Lyon Mackenzie King. On that same day, Bennett wired McFarland in Calgary, "May require you proceed to Europe re sale of wheat if requested you must not fail me."[10]

McFarland saw little merit in such an expedition. In a return telegram he told Bennett,

> There are few things I would refuse do for you if within my power and while I do not now refuse in this instance yet from my limited knowledge of present situation I would consider it nonsense to go Europe make sale while there is Bull market in Winnipeg and Chicago pits and advantage should be taken of present speculative fever to reduce supplies which have been so burdensome and the best market in the world is now Winnipeg and Chicago kindest regards.[11]

The Winnipeg market in that week had jumped ten cents to bring wheat just over the dollar level, which would prove to be the highest point in the 1930-31 crop year.

Despite that personal reservation, McFarland joined the party of advisers that accompanied Bennett to an imperial conference when they sailed for London on September 23, 1930. The new prime minister, who was to carry the sole cabinet responsibility for his government's wheat policy throughout his tenure in office, had chosen his former partner as his principal adviser. Also accompanying the prime minister was Alexander J. McPhail, president and general manager of the pool's Central Selling Agency. McPhail was to leave the London conference early. The bull market, to which McFarland referred in his reply to Bennett, had been a short aberration in a steadily declining market. The pools and their Central Selling Agency were in a deepening financial crisis and McPhail was needed at home.

On his return to Winnipeg, McPhail wrote in his diary on November 14, "Everything is tottering. Bredt, Findlay and I were called over near midnight and were in meeting until 1:30 with the banks and Premiers. Banks agreed to keep the long position margined until Monday morning, the 17th, on the Premiers signing a document that they would protect the banks against loss on the amounts put up. I also had to sign the same document agreeing to appoint a general manager suitable to the banks."[12]

McFarland meanwhile was en route home from Britain. He arrived in Montreal November 21, to be met by McPhail who asked him to become the general manager of the hard-pressed Central Selling Agency. Evidently taken by surprise, McFarland promised to consider the offer. After two days of talks McFarland accepted the task in light of the crisis which had become a national emergency.

While it was not a government appointment, there was some debate over the circumstances surrounding the choice of McFarland. Bennett, a man of unquestionable integrity, persistently maintained that he had learned of the appointment only upon his return to Canada some time later. T.A. Crerar, a former president of United Grain Growers and a Liberal spokesman, was to declare in the House of Commons that McFarland's appointment was a condition stipulated by the federal government when Bennett was asked to give financial assistance to the pools.

McPhail, who would have preferred the appointment of Alberta Premier John E. Brownlee, apparently was under no illusion as to the necessity of extending the offer to McFarland. He wrote in his diary,

> The bankers are not particularly interested in anything pool officials have to say. They are only interested just now in anything that will help to get the federal Government to protect them against loss. Hence the reason they are so set on McFarland becoming general manager. They know he is one of, if not the most, intimate friend of Bennett's and that if he can be got into the pool it will probably do more than anything else to get the Dominion Government to do something.[13]

It is quite clear that, having accepted the appointment under his own conditions, McFarland, although reporting nominally to the pool directorate, took his directions from the prime minister in his subsequent use of the Central Selling Agency as the instrument of the government's wheat policy over the next four-and-a-half years.

To the chagrin of McPhail and his fellow directors who hoped the pool's loss of autonomy was temporary, the first actions by McFarland were to terminate direct selling and to preside over the end of pooling of deliveries under producer's auspices. In doing so he earned praise from the Grain Exchange and the private trade. The Winnipeg *Free Press*, a stout defender of the Winnipeg Grain Exchange, welcomed McFarland's appointment with a glowing description of his career as "a romance that stimulates young Canadians." The same article concluded, "Mr. McFarland properly may be described as one of the soundest assets of Western Canada and of Canada."[14] It was praise that was soon to change to condemnation.

The Canadian Wheat Pool was at the zenith of its success at the beginning of 1930. The pools were marketing slightly over 50 per cent of the grain produced in the West through their central agency. Half of that was being marketed directly through its overseas agencies, bypassing the commodity exchanges. In the eyes of many observers the time of decision was at hand. Trade on the Winnipeg Grain Exchange had already been hard hit. Could it survive as a viable market if the spectacular success of the co-operatives over the past half-decade continued? Two incompatible marketing philosophies had collided head on. Which one would win?

Swanson and Armstrong, in their book *Wheat* published in early 1930, outlined the question of the time as follows:

> It is clear at any rate that the coming of the Pool into the situation has affected the interests of those engaged in the marketing of grain as a commmercial enterprise, not only to the extent of taking from them a portion of their business, but by threatening their very economic existence. It is also evident that the outcome of the events now under way or shaping in the future are of vital importance to all who directly or indirectly depend on the production or marketing of grain.
>
> The time, therefore, has passed when the situation could be considered as a mere struggle between the producers and the private dealers as to marketing methods. The time has arrived for consideration of the end to which the present course of events would lead.[15]

Even as that book was delivered from the presses the question posed had become academic. The economic arrow of the Depression had struck the Achilles heel of the Wheat Pool. The directorate, rather than hedging deliveries from producer members through the Grain

Exchange, chose to finance those purchases through bank loans in order to make initial payments to the farmers. In 1929 there was confident talk of two dollar wheat and the pool had set the initial payment at one dollar. Terms of the bank loan were that the pool must maintain a 15 per cent margin on the market values of their inventory. In effect, if the market price dropped below $1.15 a bushel while a $1 advance had been made to the farmer on delivery to the pool, the Central Selling Agency would be obliged to put up collateral to insure the banks against loss. The pools were therefore vulnerable to a price drop and in early 1930 the market set into an abrupt decline.

As that decline threatened to penetrate the 15 per cent margin call level on 1929 crop deliveries, the pool directorate sought the assistance of their provincial governments. They were fearful that the banks would require them to liquidate their grain holdings by making sales into the open market to meet their loans, thereby further disrupting an already fragile market. Premiers John Bracken of Manitoba, J.T.M. Anderson of Saskatchewan, and John E. Brownlee of Alberta, all of whom headed farmer-dominated parties, responded with guarantees on the 15 per cent security margin required by the banks. The provincial pools, in return, undertook to repay any losses sustained by the provinces, either by cash or by pledging their physical assets in the form of their country elevator system.

The tide was only temporarily stemmed. Prices continued to slide. For the 1930 crop year, the pool tentatively set the initial payment at seventy cents per bushel. Soon after, at the insistence of the banks which called for a 20 per cent margin guarantee in the absence of any further government guarantees, the initial payment was reduced to sixty cents. The premiers meanwhile sought the intervention of the central government by way of federal guarantees to the banks against the pool's 1930 advances. Bennett, newly elected to office, refused to make a commitment.

But the force of circumstances did not permit him to remain aloof for long. In the opening days of 1930 the cash price of wheat stood at $1.39 1/2. By year end it had fallen as low as 53 1/2 cents. The pool advance payment had been dropped again, this time to 50 cents. Bennett on December 30, in a long speech in Regina said in part, "The government of Canada, acting as trustee for all the people in the face of an admitted national emergency, has taken steps through the extension of credit facilities and by other means to prevent the forced and precipitate liquidation of the 1930 wheat crop."[16]

That undertaking to the banks was, of necessity, provisionary since the prime minister lacked legislative authority to make such a guarantee without Commons approval on a money bill. However, pending a new session of Parliament, Bennett furnished a written provisional guarantee to the Canadian Bankers' Association. The central government in Ottawa had become an active participant in the grain business. Despite repeated attempts to extricate itself, it was never able to withdraw from that involvement.

It was not until September 12, 1931, that an order-in-council, in consequence of the Unemployment and Farm Relief Act, formalized the commitment by providing a guarantee on bank loans made to Canadian Co-operative Wheat Producers Limited against 1930 crop deliveries to the pools. In the interim the pools had gone through a complete transformation, despite several attempts to restore their autonomy over the central selling organization. Against the advice of McPhail, Saskatchewan Wheat Pool sought imposition of a compulsory 100 per cent pool in that province, under which all farmers, whether contract members of Saskatchewan Wheat Pool or not, would be obliged to deliver their grain into a central pool. Militants headed by L.C. Brouillette, vice-president to McPhail, had won delegate support for the proposal. When Premier Anderson put through a bill in the Saskatchewan legislature, sanctioning a compulsory pool, the constitutionality of the legislation was successfully challenged in the Saskatchewan Court of Appeal. An injunction was granted against carrying an appeal to a higher court. The 100 per cent campaign died.

An attempt by McPhail to have the Central Selling Agency replaced by an interprovincial company with the aid of the premiers also failed. Worn out with overwork and anxiety over the future of the organization that had crumbled about him, McPhail fell ill. After an operation in Regina, he died on September 28, 1931, at the age of forty-seven. By August of that year all three provincial pools, led first by Alberta, had withdrawn from the Central Selling Agency. They were in debt to their respective provincial governments for a total of $24.3 million as a result of the deficit on the 1929 crop and the balance of the 1928 crop and were now operating as separate entities.

As individual companies, the pools hedged the grain delivered to them on the Winnipeg Grain Exchange, or operated limited pools on terms negotiated with the banks under federal guarantees. Canadian Co-operative Wheat Producers, which the prime minister regarded as a business in receivership, remained only in order to dispose of the grain delivered to the pools from the 1930 crop and to provide a corporate instrument for conduct of the federal government's market support operation.

While McFarland and Bennett would not have appreciated the reference to speculation, there is valididity in the observation by H.S. Patton that there was "a certain irony in the fact that the pool central agency, which was created as an alternative to organized speculation, should have been destined to become the instrument of speculative support to the futures market."[17] Both Bennett and McFarland publicly denied that the holding operation, conducted through the corporate entity of CCWP, was speculation. Indeed Bennett's first threat to close down the Winnipeg Grain Exchange and create a government wheat board was made as a result of a statement in November 1932, by A.E. Darby, secretary of the exchange, that the government had been speculating in wheat and had lost. Darby made the statement to a Toronto reporter in an ill-guarded moment during a telephone interview.

Although Bennett had previously turned aside every recommendation that came to him in favour of a government wheat board, he was incensed after being cross-examined in the Commons on Darby's statement. The prime minister wrote to McFarland on November 26, saying in part, "He [Darby] has done me great harm and caused me much trouble; and I suppose the proper thing now to do is to create a wheat board, take over the crop, close up the Exchange, and see what we can do, without having to worry with the unfair and unjust criticism of those we have endeavoured to protect from destruction."[18]

As he had done in the past, McFarland wrote back expressing his reservations on creation of a government board, "A wheat board, no matter how constituted, and operated, would by this time have been utterly discredited, besides having cost the country lots of money...." To drive home those reservations McFarland added a postcript to his letter, "PS You mention closing the Grain Exchange and forming a Wheat Board. Don't jump too hastily."[19] Bennett was temporarily mollified.

Paradoxically, while denying that the government was speculating, the method chosen by McFarland to keep the cash price of wheat from dropping below 50 cents a bushel basis Fort William at the outset of his operation, was predicated on his fundamental belief that the Depression had driven the speculators from the market and that it could not operate effectively without them. His philosophy was best exemplified in his letter to Bennett of January 30, 1931:

> I presume you are aware that the farm leaders are agitating for some legislation to control the Grain Exchange or supervise it, or something

of that sort, their idea being to discourage speculation, believing that speculation is injurious; while I, on the other hand, hold just the opposite view, that speculation is what we need in the grain market. The broader the market the better it is when it comes to selling the product of the west. The whole trouble as I see it at the present time, and this condition has existed now for some months, is that the speculators are either broke or discouraged, and one thing that discourages speculation on the grain markets of the North American continent is that the Federal Farm Board in the United States control the wheat of that country and have a large quantity of it in their ownership, while the pools of Canada hold a similar position on this side of the line, and all this wheat is hanging as a threat over the market, the public not knowing when it might be dumped or sold in large volume and cause them heavy losses. This keeps them out of the market. The only speculator of any importance left in Canada is the Wheat Pool. They are holding the wheat.[20]

Since McFarland held unquestioned control of the Central Selling Agency of the Wheat Pool, he, with government support, was in his own words, "the only speculator of any importance left in Canada."

The method chosen by McFarland was to hold back the unsold balance of grain in the pool, which had grown to 76,738,000 bushels by July 31, 1931. In *A Century of Canadian Grain*, C.F. Wilson has outlined precisely how McFarland conducted the government's price support operation. McFarland converted the cash wheat into futures and merged them with his direct purchase of futures into a combined market support operation. Since carrying charges were involved in holding unsold stocks, whether in the form of cash wheat or futures, he chose the less costly way of carrying them by moving the cash wheat into export or milling and taking back the options without selling them. But, as McFarland refrained from selling the futures, in order to reduce pressure on the market, he was simultaneously acquiring a long position. In this practice of taking back the options, the bank would normally have required any commercial company to sell the futures, thereby completing the sale. This is where McFarland required assistance from the federal government, and a special option account was set up. As the Central Selling Agency accumulated futures, the need arose for switching those futures to more distant contracts as the delivery months approached.[21]

In the spring of 1931 "McFarland was unable to spread all his

May futures over to October, and to satisfy the banks he had to obtain Bennett's authorization to take delivery of about 15 million bushels of wheat in store, tendered on May contracts. He made light of the the fact that non-pool wheat was being tendered because he could exchange the cash wheat for futures whenever the export demand might catch up.''[22] As outside pressures on the market continued, McFarland was obliged to repeat his requests to the prime minister for further guarantees to the banks each time he exhausted his successive credit limits in making even larger purchases, thereby extending his long position in the market.

By late November 1932, McFarland held 75 million bushels in the special option account of CCWP, besides the 76,376,000 bushels that represented the unsold balance of the 1930 pool wheat.[23] Even that massive effort had failed to hold the cash price above the fifty-cent level, as McFarland sought to do. Bennett was becoming apprehensive and refused a request for further guarantees against credit. ''We cannot take any more wheat than 75 million bushels. I do not think you have any appreciation of just how Members of the Government feel and how fearful they are that this is going to wreck the Government,''[24] he told McFarland in a letter of November 30. Despite pleas from his beleaguered lieutenant in Winnipeg that the decision was ill-advised, Bennett sailed for Britain December 5, without authorizing further credit guarantees to the banks.

Fifty years later George McIvor was to recall the aftermath of that refusal. McFarland was in Ottawa pleading his case with Sir George Perley, the acting prime minister. Pressure was mounting on the market, and on the morning of December 16, McFarland phoned his chief assistant in Winnipeg:

> The prospect of what was happening was so frightening. This was it. This was the day. R.B. was determined: and I don't know what went along between them [Bennett and McFarland], but the prospect of the thing was so frightening it was terrible. So he said to me ''George what do you think we should do?'' I said to him, well I don't know either Mr. McFarland, but what I would do if I had your responsibility; I would watch the Chicago market for about 20 minutes, and if there is no change in the situation I would get out. Well, he said ''go ahead.'' The Winnipeg market I think was the highest in the world at 50 cents. So I sat there—these are moments in history—and I looked at the ticker tape and Chicago didn't [change]....Well how do you handle a thing like that? So I decided not to cancel an order, but

> I didn't put in any more. One of my friends out on the floor... he told me after, [that] this was a very dramatic thing. He said there was a lapse of maybe seconds, wheat at 50 cents, and somebody said "the government is out." Wheat in a matter of 30 seconds broke 12 1/2 cents a bushel, down to 37 1/2, which was the low point. What happened was—this was a frightful situation—what happened was that any buying that came in from then on...was real buying. It was people who wanted wheat, and it turned. The market turned. It took a couple of days and it got back up to 50 cents again. So this was one of the critical—the critical day of the whole operation.[25]

The price of cash wheat that day was the lowest recorded on the international market in four hundred years. Since the quoted price was basis the Lakehead on the top grade, the farmer would receive very little on delivery to the country elevator after freight, elevation and handling charges had been deducted. Lower grades and feed grains would not fetch anything.

Farmers, recalling the era, still tell the apochryphal story of the farmer who delivered a load of barley to the country elevator and was told that, after deductions, he owed the elevator company money. Having no money, the farmer asked the agent if he would settle the account by accepting one of the chickens he had brought to town to sell. The agent agreed and took the chicken. As the farmer was leaving, he suddenly turned and laid two more chickens on the counter. "What's that for? The account is settled," said the agent. "Well, I'm going to bring in a couple more loads this week," replied the farmer.

In the same vein, Sir Ashley Cooper, governor of the Hudson Bay Company, at the annual meeting of that company in London in 1932, read a letter from a farmer in western Canada, which he described as representing tersely and tragically, but not without humour, the predicament of many farmers in western Canada: "I got your letter about what I owe. Now be patient. I haven't forgotten you. If this was Judgement Day and you were no more prepared to meet your Maker than I am to meet your Account, you sure would have to go to hell. Trusting you will do this."[26]

In late October 1933, McFarland would have found little humour in those stories. He had continued his market support operations after Bennett relented and successively increased the government's guarantees to the banks on lending limits. By October 28, the CCWP holdings had reached 205 million bushels. This, in McFarland's mind, was virtually all of the visible supply of grain in Canada, and he was becoming increasingly frustrated with the open market.

While the support operation was initiated and carried out with an element of secrecy and precise details were not made public until several years later, traders in the pit of the Winnipeg Grain Exchange could not help but be aware of what was going on. The banks knew precisely from day to day. As McFarland grew increasingly disillusioned with the part his former close associates in the Grain Exchange were playing in the market, his criticism became open. He publicly deplored what he saw as a tendency toward short selling by traders taking advantage of the agency's long position.

On the fourth floor at 300 Carlton Street, John Dafoe, the brilliant editor of the Winnipeg *Free Press*, had turned his heavyweight editorial guns on John I. McFarland. Having welcomed him in 1930 with a glowing editorial as the man who was "plowing a lone furrow" with no salary in order to extricate the country from the grain crisis, Dafoe was now defending the Winnipeg Grain Exchange and attacking McFarland. George McIvor recalled that "eventually the thing got so hot politically, the *Free Press* carried on a terrible campaign against John McFarland."[27] Other spokesmen for the private trade also made sniping attacks against him in the press, particularly Major H.G.L. Strange of the Searle Grain Company. "This hurt him terribly underneath, because in his view, and he was right, he was a decent man trying to do a job for the West which he loved. He loved the West and the farmers...and this was the appreciation he got. He had a very lonely job, and I was the only one he could talk to really."[28]

Beset on the one hand by the provincial pools which, led by Brouillette, had increased their pressure for a monopoly government grain board and now under fire from the Grain Exchange through the *Free Press*, McFarland was becoming increasingly frustrated in his lonely task. In addition he sensed an element of strong partisan politics in the mounting attack from the private trade against the program he was administering on behalf of Bennett's Conservative administration. Both McFarland and Bennett were obsessed with the behind-the-scenes activities of James R. Murray. A well known Liberal, Murray had been associated with T.A. Crerar in United Grain Growers Limited. Crerar was born in Ontario in 1876 and arrived in Manitoba with his parents in 1881. A Manitoba farm boy who taught school while putting himself through college, Crerar became president of United Grain Growers in 1907 and retained that post until 1929. First elected to Parliament in 1917, he became a cabinet minister in Prime Minister Borden's Union government. He later led the Progressive Party for a period and, in December 1929, was sworn in as minister of railways and canals in the Liberal government. Though Crerar was defeated in the 1930 election that saw Bennett sweep to power, Bennett and McFarland felt he was still politically active and working through Murray.

Murray had been general manager of United Grain Growers until early 1930, when he left to serve temporarily as secretary of the Winnipeg Grain Exchange. He left that position to become vice-president and general manager of Alberta Pacific Grain Company Limited, formerly owned and directed by McFarland and Bennett. He was now seen as a Liberal policy adviser. In September 1933, he sponsored, through the banks, a proposal that a three-man board be appointed under McFarland to conduct the affairs of CCWP. However, given the source, the proposal failed to win Bennett's approval.

James R. Murray, chief commissioner Canadian Wheat Board, December 3, 1935 to July 1937.

That same autumn McFarland was seeking support for a policy of acreage reduction. A strong proponent of the theory that overproduction had brought about the crisis in world grain markets, McFarland said at the start of his public career, "Our Governments and farming organizations, should take every step to urge acreage reductions upon other countries, while insisting on similar measures at home. While this may be considered impossible, it must be done...."[29] The three prairie premiers had endorsed such a policy and McFarland sought a similar endorsement from the Winnipeg Grain Exchange. The reply to that request had come, not by direct communication with McFarland, but through the pages of the *Free Press Evening Bulletin* which he slammed down in his room on October 28, 1933.

The acreage reduction campaign resulted from the personal initiatives of Bennett on the international scene. He headed a Canadian delegation that attended the Monetary and Economic Conference in London in June and July of 1933. Although it was not on the agenda, Bennett urged the conference to give consideration to the wheat problem. As a result, at the invitation of the governments of Argentina, Australia, Canada, and the United States, a second conference chaired by Bennett and attended by representatives of eighteen European countries was commenced in London on August 21. At the end of the four-day meeting, an International Wheat Agreement was signed. Twenty-two nations were signatories to the pact which established market quotas for the exporting countries in the 1933-1934 crop year. In addition the four major exporters agreed to further limits on exports for the crop year of 1934-1935. Though that international agreement was to collapse when Argentina harvested a bumper crop in 1933 and chose to disregard her obligations to the other exporting countries, a campaign for support in Canada was being pressed, and McFarland sought the co-operation of the Winnipeg Grain Exchange. Their response, couched in the form of a statement by the Council of the Exchange, was a rejection of McFarland's request. It read:

> The impression is abroad that the Winnipeg Grain Exchange is opposed to plans recently adopted with a view to improving the wheat situation. The council of the Exchange feels that this impression should be removed. No statement has previously been made or authorized by the council in connection with the international wheat agreement. Individual members may have expressed opinions but these cannot be taken as representing the views of the exchange as a whole.
>
> The only function of the Winnipeg Grain Exchange is to provide a market place and trading facilities for all those interested in the producing, handling, and marketing of our crops. These facilities are continuous and they are utilized under whatever conditions may from time to time prevail. Under these circumstances it is obvious that the Exchange, as such, cannot undertake to formulate any statement which could reflect the unanimous views of the members.
>
> Without entering into any discussion of the causes which have produced the Canadian wheat surplus, it is a fact that its existence has led to support being given by the government to wheat prices. Many members of the Exchange have regarded this policy as beneficial to the producers and as in the national interest, and any reasonable

measures which may be taken by the Canadian government to reduce or dispose of the surplus will meet with the co-operation of the members of the Grain Exchange insofar as such co-operation is within their power.

> Actions have been taken by importing countries which have led to the use of lands for wheat growing which are more suitable for the production of other commodities. In course of time, with restoration of more normal trade conditions, these lands will revert to more advantageous uses. When this development occurs the market for Canadian grain will again expand. In the meantime, however, government measures which assist in maintaining a free world market for our grain will receive every possible co-operation from members of the exchange.[30]

If that circumlocutionary rejection of support for the acreage reduction campaign incensed McFarland, the final paragraph which introduced this chapter, and which is repeated here, enraged him: "The maintenance of the free market system which has functioned continuously and, on the whole smoothly, under the abnormal strains of the past three or four years is essential. It is necessary to the retention of the goodwill of importers in the existing markets abroad, and it is only through the development of this goodwill that Canada can maintain or increase her share of the available world markets."[31]

Throughout that weekend and during his walk down Main Street to the Central Selling Agency office on Monday morning, McFarland's anger had not abated. He wrote to Bennett enclosing a clipping of the offending statement:

> I had no knowledge of what was going to be in this Resolution until I saw it in the newspaper Saturday night. I may be entirely prejudiced and wrong in my views, but my reaction to this Resolution is that it is just a bunch of dishwater and does not contain a single constructive suggestion. On the other hand, however, the last paragraph is just the kind of stuff which will make the enemies of the Grain Exchange all the more determined to have a Government Wheat Board. The Resolution points out that their Institution has functioned continuously and smoothly under abnormal strains of the past three or four years. This, of course, is untrue. It has neither functioned continuously nor smoothly. The only way it functions smoothly is when it is going down. Most things run pretty well downhill, and it is one of them, and the only thing that has kept it from going out of existence

> has been the fact that the Government operations have taken care of the farmers' hedges, but these men who operate this Exchange are either blind, or determined not to admit anything, although I do think that our friend Sidney Smith will come out with a blast in the other direction. He is past president of the Exchange and a councillor for this year.[32]

Bennett replied in even more explosive terms. His letter of November 2, to McFarland read:

> It is incredible that men should pass such a resolution. I am sending a letter to Mr. Smith, copy of which I enclose herewith. If they are unwilling to be of any assistance at this time, I think it is quite clear that we will have to create a wheat board and close the Grain Exchange. If their idea of running smoothly is to have the Government support the grain business to the extent we are now doing, then all I can say is that, so far as I am able to control it, it will not run smoothly any longer than I can help.[33]

The prime minister's letter of the same date to exchange member Sidney T. Smith contained an angry threat: "The resolution in question is an insult to the intelligence of those who read it and I find it incredible that men charged with serious responsibilities should have passed it. I must say that it is the strongest argument that has yet been presented to me for the creation of a wheat board at the earliest possible moment....P.S. I have instructed the Law Officers to prepare me a memorandum as to just what we can do in the way of a wheat board."[34]

Garry Fairbairn, in his history of the Saskatchewan Wheat Pool, *From Prairie Roots*, has described the offending statement by the council of the Winnipeg Grain Exchange as "one of the worst public relations blunders in the history of the grain trade."[35] That may be an understatement given the political undercurrents flowing at the time. Over the ensuing month, both Sidney T. Smith and James T. Richardson diplomatically sought to sooth Bennett's wrath. However, Smith may have unintentionally added fuel to the fire when he mentioned the role of Murray in the affair in his letter of November 6, to Bennett:

> I am not surprised at your opinion of the resolution that was issued by the Council of the Grain Exchange. I thoroughly agree with every word you say about it being an aggregation of meaningless words. Personally I disapproved of it entirely and drew up a short statement

which I felt would have met the situation positively and clearly in loyal support of you and your policies in connection with the wheat business, but a number of men, including Mr. J.R. Murray, who has some influence in the Exchange, were in favor of the modified statement which they put out.[36]

Acknowledging Smith's reply on November 8, Bennett shot back:

I have heard of Mr. Murray's activities. He is the one man who should have supported us in our efforts to improve prices. That he has not done so indicates, in my judgment, faulty appreciation of the situation. I dislike a Wheat Board more than you do but if the Grain Exchange is working against us in our endeavour to reduce inventories, we will have to provide some other means to deal with the situation; and the jumble of words that was sent by the Grain Exchange has made many people wonder if the Exchange is composed of businessmen or some other class that need not be described.[37]

McFarland, whose letter had precipitated the prime minister's anger, no longer sought to dissuade Bennett from the active contemplation of a government monopoly board. While still counselling caution, he wrote on November 6, to Bennett: "You of course, are well aware that I have been adverse to a Wheat Board just as much as you have been, and if there was any possible way of avoiding a Wheat Board I would still be adverse to it, but nothing short of a miracle between now and the next crop, in my opinion, can avoid the necessity of the formation of such a Board to take charge of the whole operation of the Grain Trade."[38]

From that time forward McFarland, as Bennett's principal and most trusted grain policy adviser, never again counselled the prime minister against formation of a wheat board. His advice from then on was simply a caution against acting too hastily.

By the early summer of 1934 McFarland was depressed and discouraged after trying to "sell a good lot" and "the price fell away." On June 2, he wrote to Bennett:

I am now coming to the conclusion that we are near the end of the road. The wheat we hold creates the price so long as we hold it. The Public and also many otherwise practical men of affairs see the price advance on the blackboards, and they think we could sell out if we so desired, whereas the fact is the opposite. It gives the public a false impression. The fact is the quoted price is a false measuring rod, and

> we are measured by that yard stick. I am therefore putting it up to you as to the advisability of seriously considering a national wheat control board. Brouillette and his followers want it and will not rest until they succeed. Indeed I am not sure they may be right.
>
> I am sure you think I am against a Board, and it is true I have been, but from here on in I have no argument against it.[39]

Publicly McFarland's criticism of the Winnipeg Grain Exchange, as doing little to assist him in the load the government was carrying while upholding the virtues of the futures mechanism, had become more strident. He alleged that foreign interests had made a "bear raid" on the Winnipeg market by selling short to the detriment of the government's stabilization effort, and he called for supervision of the Winnipeg Grain Exchange. It was particularly galling to McFarland, having for years deplored the absence of speculators from the market and having welcomed the purchase of seats on the Winnipeg Exchange by Chicago traders, to find that the speculators were now coming in on the wrong side thereby jeopardizing his efforts.

The exchange fought back against McFarland and, in early November 1934, issued a statement denying an organized bear raid on the Winnipeg market. Referring to a newspaper article presumed to have originated from an interview with McFarland, the statement said, "The article is inaccurate and misleading: there was no condition existing in the trading on the Winnipeg Grain Exchange that would justify such a story. It reads like fiction, and to the best of our knowledge that is just what it is."[40] The exchange offered to provide facilities for an investigation of the charges and declared it would lend all possible assistance to a government supervisor of the kind recommended. There was no acceptance of the offer. Events were moving inexorably toward government intervention which would make supervision of the Grain Exchange unnecessary.

In his fourth year of office, Bennett had foregone an election after taking soundings on his administration's prospects following defeat of the provincial Conservative governments in Ontario and Saskatchewan. In addition he was locked in a misunderstanding with one of the ablest members of cabinet, Minister of Trade and Commerce H.H. Stevens. In the ensuing split, Stevens broke from government ranks to lead a renegade Conservative following. He established a new group, known as the Reconstruction Party, to contest the forthcoming election. By the beginning of 1935 a general election had become mandatory and, in preparation for the last session of Parliament before going to the country, Bennett had a draft bill drawn up to establish a monopoly grain board.

On June 10, 1935, the prime minister introduced the following resolution in the House of Commons:

> That it is expedient to bring in a measure to establish a board to be known as the Canadian grain board, with power to purchase, receive and take delivery of wheat, oats, barley, rye and flaxseed, or any one or more of such grains for marketing, and to sell, store, transport and market such grains, and to provide for the appointment of such clerks, employees and assistance as may be necessary, and to provide for their remuneration and for the expense of, and arising out of, the operation of the board.[41]

As the election approached, McFarland became a political adviser and public speaker in the undeclared election campaign. His principal preoccupation was with the movements of Murray on behalf of the Liberals. In the spring, however, he fell victim to the strains of his sustained effort to support the market. McFarland took ill, and when the grain board legislation was introduced, he was in Winnipeg General Hospital recovering from a serious heart attack. He was not to be in Ottawa when the Liberals and the private trade, with the active participation of Murray, launched a campaign in committee against the wide-ranging terms of the proposed legislation.

That, however, is for the next chapter. The chain of circumstances that led to introduction of the Conservative legislation represents a remarkable period in the history of western Canada. The saga was set against a backdrop of events and forces on the international and domestic scene, so immense and overwhelming, that in retrospect, it is doubtful the participants fully grasped their signifigance.

McFarland, for his part, began his unpaid task with the conviction that overproduction was the malaise afflicting the grain economy and the consequent plunge in prices. He was supported in that premise by many others, including prominent economists. If production could be cut back then prices would rise. However, when the deepening drought of the decade decimated crops, making legislated acreage reductions academic, prices did not rise appreciably. He was forced to continue his market support operations. McFarland's final loss of faith in the open market system's ability to ease the plight of the farmer and to serve the national interest, despite massive government support of prices through the holding operation, was a remarkable conversion to monopoly state intervention.

For Bennett the conversion was equally dramatic. It was ironic that a Conservative government, noted for its true-blue Tory principles, was constrained to introduce legislation regarded in many quarters at the time as going beyond socialism to border on communism. Caught in the calamitous world economic crisis, Bennett sought first to achieve trade treaties and promote co-operation between the major exporters and importers on the international scene. His efforts toward an international wheat agreement, while achieving what appeared to be a measure of success in the initial stages, were bound, once again in retrospect, to fail. Nations, obsessed with the impact of the Depression on their own domestic scene, withdrew behind a wall of destructive isolationism. Those that had been major grain importers imposed tariffs and paid subsidies to their own producers which stimulated increased production within their own borders. World trade, already faced with reduced consumption due to stringent economic circumstances, stagnated under the impact of these measures. As these forces tightened about him, Bennett became increasingly disillusioned with the intransigence of the private trade, represented by the Grain Exchange, and its failure to recognize his predicament.

The private trade was unwilling, or unable, to admit that abnormal circumstances could arise in peacetime which would render the futures trading system inoperable. While that admission had been made by the Winnipeg Grain Exchange in 1917 during World War I when faced with a major monopoly purchasing agency in Great Britain, the traumatic confrontation with the prairie pools during the late part of the 1920s was too recent to permit such a concession. Having gained a respite in the battle when the pool Central Selling Agency collapsed in 1930, the members of the exchange would not admit the conditions that precipitated that collapse could similarly affect their own trading. Their insistence that laissez faire economic theories and the law of supply and demand would restore order to a world thrown into chaos denied reality. Even more strange was that John Dafoe, the respected editor of the Winnipeg *Free Press*, should ascribe to the same theories and support the exchange viewpoint.

For the farmers who had flocked to the Prairies seeking homesteads over the first three decades of the century it went beyond the shattering of dreams. Caught in the dust of the drought and the destitution brought about by the Depression, there were no dreams left to die. It was enough just to survive from day to day and from season to season in a world which promised little prospect of change. For those who remained, locked by penury onto their farms and with little social contact, it is no wonder that their minds cast about seeking an answer to their misfortune. In the perception of many, the source of their predicament rested in the speculators who controlled the price of their meagre harvests on world exchanges. As their minds cast back to the relative prosperity of 1919, when a Wheat Board handled their grain, and the subsequent collapse of prices when that Board was disbanded, the answer was clear. The system must change.

On the farm organization front there was, strangely, a near vacuum. The Canadian Council of Agriculture, "The Farmers' Parliament," foundered on the rocks of direct class political action and died along with their Progressive Party. The prairie pools, which had shown such spectacular promise, were vociferous and active, but regarded by government as an enterprise in receivership. United Grain Growers, because of the direct political affiliation of their former long-time president T.A. Crerar with the Liberals, was regarded with distrust by the Conservative administration. Bennett chose to call upon the provincial premiers to fill the gap, and having direct farm affiliations, they performed that advisory role ably. However, with taxation resources strained to near breaking point at the provincial and muncipal levels, the premiers could offer little by way of direct relief to the hard-pressed farmers.

Yet, in the midst of this catastrophe, a group of remarkable men, few of them seeking personal material reward, still cast about for answers. Unyielding and uncompromising in their firmly held beliefs and perceived solutions, they clashed constantly. In June 1935, the battle was not yet over.

VICTORY IN DEFEAT

The atmosphere of political partisanship in which the Canada Grain Bill has been enveloped threatens to become so dense as to prevent anybody seeing the subject clearly and discussing it in a healthy manner.

— *The Manitoba Co-operator, June 1935*

▪

As the official organ of a group of Manitoba co-operatives, including Manitoba Pool Elevators, the *Manitoba Co-operator* had every reason for alarm over the environment which had enveloped the introduction of the Canada Grain Act in the House of Commons in early June 1935. With a fast approaching federal election, and the House struggling to complete its work in time for an early adjournment, both the Conservative government of R.B. Bennett and the Liberal opposition were seeking advantage in the upcoming campaign.

The infighting was bitter and divisive.

As staunch and persistent proponents of a monopoly grain marketing agency, the prairie pools were clearly caught in the political crossfire. The board of directors of Canadian Co-operative Wheat Producers were compelled on June 17 to issue the following statement:

> Because of the controversy which has already begun over the Canadian Grain Board Bill recently introduced in Parliament, and in view of the statements which are now being made with reference to the Pool in connection with this legislation, the board of directors of Canadian Co-operative Wheat Producers deem it advisable at this time, and before the controversy becomes of a character which will practically preclude them from taking part in it, to make their position clear to the farmers and public.[1]

Decrying the "circumstances which are tending to make it [Bill 98, the proposed grain board legislation] an element of party strife," the Pool board declared:

> As producers' organizations, having Canadian national welfare and interest at heart, we make no apology for urging and supporting legislation for the establishment of a Canadian grain board. We have urged it in the past and we shall continue to do so until the product of our farms is no longer an object for speculators and profit-seekers to play with, but is put into channels of consumption in the most efficient and economical manner to the benefit of both producers and consumers.[2]

As supporters of the all-encompassing compulsory Bill 98, put forward by Prime Minister Bennett on June 10, the pools were a lone voice against powerful forces seeking outright defeat of the bill or, at the least, temporary legislation with less draconian powers which would last only as long as it took to dispose judiciously of the government holdings acquired under the McFarland stabilization operation.

The pools were not the only ones feeling the heat of unsought political involvement. With John I. McFarland recuperating from a massive heart attack in Winnipeg General Hospital, George McIvor, his principal assistant in the four-and-a-half year stabilization effort, was going through a long, hot summer. Called by Bennett to Ottawa to assist in defence of the government's program and to help counter the attack on the legislation by the exchange and the private trade, McIvor was under pressure. He had persuaded Charles Folliott to take over his responsibilities in Winnipeg during his absence and the proceedings in Ottawa were proving to be an ordeal for the young grain trader. In his words, "There I was down before this group, Bennett trying to get something to cling to in regard to the wheat policy, and the Liberals trying to use it as a medium to try and get rid of the Conservative government. I was the jam in the sandwich."[3]

As sales manager of the Canadian Co-operative Wheat Producers under McFarland, McIvor obviously did not share the same rapport with the prime minister as that enjoyed by his senior. Bennett, despite his qualities as a prime minister, was an autocratic taskmaster and his dictatorial interference, in the absence of his friend McFarland, made the enforced duties of McIvor difficult in the months leading up to the introduction of the grain board legislation. Years later, in a speech delivered in Calgary in 1976, McIvor was to recall that in the summer of 1935 his main problem was with the prime minister. "He immediately became heavily involved in the grain business, telephoning me two or three times a week."

McIvor cited an incident in which he had gone to Ottawa in May 1935, and he and the prime minister had agreed that the CCWP would not buy any more wheat under the stabilization program, but that they would sell some if there were any "hard spots" in the market:

> Mr. McFarland had decided in the month of March, 1935, to put a peg in the grain market at 80 cents a bushel, but had agreed with the grain trade that, if the market did decline to 80 cents, the government agency would be prepared to accept sales of futures against any wheat that was bought by the elevator companies from the producers. The market did break to 80 cents, and we started taking several million bushels of wheat. The prime minister phoned me and accused me of breaking my word. I then realized that he knew nothing about the deal between Mr. McFarland and the Grain Exchange, and he said among other things: "You will do as I say, not as you think. I am the prime minister of this country," and told me to give this wheat back. I told him that every elevator company in Western Canada would be broke...The following morning he phoned me back and asked how I was feeling. I wasn't feeling too well really and told him so. He then urged me to take care of my health, and I thanked him, but said: "What about this wheat from the farmers? You know we have to take this wheat." He replied: "Of course you have," and so ended the incident.[4]

Recalling his relations with Bennett even later, McIvor revealed that he sometimes had definite misgivings about him:

> His treatment of me was quite unjustified....''You do as I say, not as you think.'' This was pretty rough stuff. It never happened [to me] under any other prime minister other than Diefenbaker....And I saved his [Bennett's] bacon....He was about to make some of the damndest mistakes. Supposing he had gone on with this crazy idea of giving back all these futures to the elevator companies....You can't do this to people. They would have been broke, and I told him so.[5]

If McIvor and the pools were attempting to extricate themselves from any political involvement in the pre-election jockeying, James R. Murray, the nemesis of Bennett and McFarland throughout the years of the Conservative market stabilization operation, had no qualms about active partisan manoeuvering in the unfolding events.

Murray was known to have a trigger temper and a temperamental instinct never to back away from a fight. He was a member of a powerful delegation from the Grain Exchange that had proceeded to Ottawa prior to the presentation of the proposed grain board legislation in the House. That delegation included Roy W. Milner, president; R.T. Evans; James A. Richardson; Sidney T. Smith; L.W. Brockington, counsel for the North-West Grain Dealers Association; Isaac Pitblado, counsel for the exchange; and A.E. Darby, secretary of the exchange.

Although he was on that committee as an exchange member, Murray had gone to Ottawa primarily to meet with his contacts in the Liberal party. He and his former associate at United Grain Growers (UGG), T.A. Crerar, were now giving active backroom assistance to the Liberal spokesmen in the legislative battle. Both were adamantly opposed to any form of compulsion in Bill 98. While C.F. Wilson describes Col. J.L. Ralston as ''one of the principal architects, if not the key one, of a voluntary—as opposed to compulsory—board,''[6] there appears to be little doubt that Murray deserves equal credit for his backroom contribution to that philosophy.

Murray's early background remains somewhat clouded. It was said that he was educated at an exclusive public school in Britain, but that he never talked about that period of his life. A family problem which caused him to immigrate to Canada was suspected. ''For some extraordinary reason he never wanted to go back.''[7] What is known, however, is that he came to Canada as a young man and took a position as a timekeeper in a lumber camp. John Kennedy, the vice-president of UGG, found the young Irish immigrant at the lumber camp in 1910 and persuaded him to join the staff. He soon proved to be "a live wire of high voltage" and rose rapidly from one position to another. By 1919 he was assistant general manager to Crerar.[8]

In October 1920, Murray was a member of a wheat marketing committee of the Canadian Council of Agriculture which had been given the task of examining whether a co-operative wheat pool could be organized on a voluntary basis. That committee foresaw shortcomings in any provincial scheme which did not enjoy full monopoly control. Murray, who had done most of the work in drafting a plan for a voluntary contract pool, offered to go ahead and organize a wheat pool if it were insisted upon. He declined, however, to take the position of sales manager of the proposed pool when it was offered to him. The proposal stood in abeyance while the grain growers organizations intensified an alternative demand for reinstatement of the 1919 Canadian Wheat Board which had operated for one year.

While they were now on opposite sides of the fence in both political allegiance and marketing philosophy, Murray and McFarland had been linked together on several occasions in the past. Both had been offered the position of sales manager of the proposed, but unimplemented, 1920 wheat pool and had declined the position. In August 1922, the premiers of Saskatchewan and Alberta offered the top positions in a proposed wheat board, to be set up in consequence of federal legislation, to McFarland and Murray. After consulting with some of their grain trade colleagues they declined the offer in a joint letter. In it they said that the board could only succeed if the sympathetic co-operation of the grain trade could be assured. "Our enquiries made since your proposals of yesterday convince us that the Board could not secure sympathetic co-operation in the use of all the necessary facilities."[9]

In a lengthy response to that letter Dr. Robert Magill, secretary of the Winnipeg Grain Exchange, refuted the imputation of lack of co-operation on the part of the exchange and concluded, "The attempt to create a Wheat Board failed, not because the grain trade at Winnipeg opposed it, but because competent grain men knew that the method of marketing proposed would not be as efficient as the existing method, and would not pass the test long, and more particularly would fail in any year when the marketing conditions were unfavorable to the seller."[10]

It is also interesting to note that in November 1923, Murray, on behalf of United Grain Growers, and McFarland, on behalf of Alberta Pacific Grain, were the first to sign elevator contracts with the Alberta Wheat Pool to accept deliveries of pool grain. In September 1924, A.J. McPhail attempted to recruit Murray as general manager of the pool's Central Selling Agency but failed. Later, however, the volatile Murray incurred the wrath of the pools when, in 1931, he called for a commission of enquiry on a series of charges he made against Manitoba Pool Elevators. This resulted in the Williams Commission which confirmed three of the four charges, to the chagrin of the pools.

One of the allegations against Manitoba Pool Elevators was that units of the most expensive system of country elevators ever built in western Canada had been foisted on farmers at many points within the province where they should never have been built and where there was no reasonable chance of their ever being anything but a burden on the local members. The commission ruled that charge to have been "substantially proved."[11] There was no love lost between the pools and Jim Murray, and the pools were now the principal supporters of Bennett in his proposal for a monopoly grain board.

In light of subsequent events, the backgrounds of Murray, McFarland, and McIvor are significant in the unfolding parliamentary drama of 1935. It is particularly significant and fortunate that George McIvor escaped untainted by partisanship in the highly political proceedings.

Given the pre-election atmosphere in which the grain board bill was brought forward, it is valid to speculate on the form in which it first appeared in the House of Commons. C.F. Wilson states that it was modelled on the Canadian Wheat Board Act of 1922, which was not proclaimed.[12] However Bill 98, as first presented, differed widely from the 1922 proposal in several major respects. It was much broader in its application, covering not only wheat, but oats, barley, rye, and flaxseed. Further, it was not dependent on complementary legislation being passed by the Prairie Provinces to assure its constitutionality, a requirement which in large measure contributed to failure of the first federal initiative.

Dealing with the constitutional aspects when introducing the bill for first reading on June 10, Bennett said in part:

> If we conclude, as I believe the House will, that a Wheat Board is essential, then you ask yourself two simple questions: first, what power has Parliament to create such a board; and second what shall be its powers? With respect to the first, there has been a modification of the legal position by reason of the fact that the Grain Act was

> amended when it was decided by the Supreme Court, by a majority with the Chief Justice dissenting, that the Grain Act was *ultra vires* in so far as certain sections of it were concerned; and it was indicated that it could be made *intra vires* if the elevators were declared to be works for the general advantage of Canada. And so, under Section 233 of the Grain Act, as consolidated in 1927, the declaration is made that these elevators, which are usually on the right of way of various railway companies are works for the general advantage of Canada.
>
> The Bill predicated upon this resolution would limit its operation to interprovincial and international trade. It would not seek to deal with purely domestic trade in any one province for that might be entirely beyond our jurisdiction.
>
> The next question is, what will be the powers of the board? The board will be empowered, as the resolution indicates, to deal with wheat as buyers and sellers and the sole marketers of it for the purpose of ensuring that it shall find at least as large a market as possible under the circumstances that now exist.[13]

Note the reference to "Wheat Board" rather than "Grain Board," and that the powers outlined by Bennett referred only to wheat despite the fact that the bill at that stage included other grains in its terms of reference.

Bill 98 differed from the 1922 legislation in another important aspect in that any deficits from operations of the board would fall upon the federal treasury, rather than upon the provincial governments as in the earlier legislation. Thus the first draft provided for a complete federal government grain monopoly, and trading on the Winnipeg Grain Exchange would have been terminated with the board taking delivery of all grains. Further, in its original form, the 1935 Bill envisaged the board as a permanent and ongoing body as opposed to the temporary one-year provisions in the unproclaimed 1922 act.

Did Bennett expect the proposed legislation to go through the House in its original form, or did he deliberately broaden the terms in order to make strategic concessions to the opposition to get Bill 98 passed in the dying days of the session?

Clive B. Davidson, a grain statistician with the Dominion Bureau of Statistics from 1930 to 1935 and a policy adviser to Bennett, wrote: "It was clear that if the prime minister wanted a national board within a few days, he would have to accommodate the official opposition on most of the objections raised by Mr. Ralston. It is also likely that Mr. Bennett was not averse to giving up some of the powers included in Bill 98 especially if it would expedite passage of the Bill."[14]

R.K. Finlayson, Bennett's chief secretary, said:

> R.B.'s idea in the first instance was to make provision for McFarland to continue his stabilization operations as he had been authorized to do under the Unemployment and Farm Relief Act and to merge his personal authority with that of two other members of the wheat board, of which he would be the head. I carried the P.M.'s instructions to Fred Varcoe [deputy minister of justice], an important one of which was that he should so draft a bill that it would not founder on the rocks of divided Dominion-Provincial jurisdiction, as was the fate of the earlier Wheat Board Act of 1922.[15]

Davidson, who at one period was seconded from the bureau to assist McFarland in the stabilization operation, has summarized the events leading up to introduction of the grain board legislation as follows:

> The shocking events of 1929-30 and 1930-31, the stabilization efforts of 1931-35, the first steps in international co-operation and, of course, international happenings in respect to wheat which were generally known but not quite understood, led inevitably to a national wheat marketing plan in mid-1935. There are those who would add that the fast approaching federal election had some part in bringing wheat issues to a head in a rather hurried fashion. Perhaps so, and no doubt the Bennett government thought it had a popular issue in its wheat policies. But the evidence seems to be weighted in favour of the necessity of a major change in wheat policy by the summer of 1935, election or no election. Stabilization policies, never regarded by their authors, their supporters or their detractors as more than short-term measures, had run their course, and the time had come to replace the very informal arrangements with Mr. McFarland and the successive bank guarantees in respect to loans to Canadian Co-operative Wheat Producers Limited with an official government body. That this official government body should take the form of a Wheat Board or a Grain Board was inevitable because the previous Wheat Board in 1919 and the still earlier Board of Grain Supervisors were organizations identified in the producers' minds as successful ventures.[16]

While Davidson says the development came with startling suddeness, the record shows that Bennett placed the resolution calling for a grain board on the order paper March 4, some three months previous to its June 10 introduction.[17] Announcement of the intention to table the resolution was made in Ottawa on February 28. That same day McFarland wrote to Bennett: "The bombshell fell today in the Grain Exchange in the form of your announced intentions of bringing in a measure to provide for the organization of a wheat or grain board. It caused considerable consternation for a time."[18]

The next day the Winnipeg *Free Press* reported that there were conflicting views in Ottawa as to the true significance of the grain board legislation, and that they seemed certain to continue until the text of the measure was available: "One view is that the legislation will merely continue the John I. McFarland operations on a commission basis. The other view is that the legislation provides for a compulsory wheat board along the lines of the one which operated during the war with the additional power to "rationalize" cereal crops in the three prairie provinces. By rationalization is meant the control or regulation of production."[19]

McFarland declined to comment publicly on the reports, but Alberta Agriculture Minister F.S. Griswold commented that elimination of the Winnipeg Grain Exchange through the operation of the proposed board was a possibility.[20] Reviewing the events of the week at the exchange, James McAnsh, who covered the exchange for the *Free Press*, reported in a classic understatement: "Proposals to set up a Canadian Grain Board dominated the market for the past week, temporarily disturbing trading in futures and giving traders much with which to occupy their idle moments. Premier Bennett's resolution set forth only the general purpose of the bill he proposes to introduce."[21]

Unfortunately after McFarland's letter to Bennett of February 28, correspondence between the two friends, which might have provided enlightenment as to the prime minister's thoughts and intentions in the interim between then and when Bill 98 was introduced, fell off. Bennett fell ill and was absent from the House from February 26 to May 20. As the prime minister was recovering, McFarland suffered his massive heart attack.

In his opening remarks, while introducing the Bill for second reading on June 12, Bennett made reference to the delay in acting on the motion on the order paper:

> Mr. Speaker, in rising to move second reading of this bill I am not unaware of the public interest in its contents, nor yet of the fact that complaints have been made that the matter might not have been dealt with at an earlier time in the session. Before I was ill I had placed

> upon the order paper the resolution which was adopted the other day, and on my return, but for the illness of Mr. McFarland who is still confined to hospital, the matter would have been proceeded with more promptly.[22]

As noted above, McFarland had ceased to counsel Bennett against a wheat board after November 1933, but strangely, in his letter of February 28, McFarland told the prime minister that, having received a large number of phone calls from the trade, "I took the liberty of expressing the view that there was no immediate intention of the formation of any wheat board, and in fact, there could be nothing of that nature attempted until the new crop next August. But that in view of the possibility of the necessity of some such board, it was obvious that you were providing for the emergency if it should arise."[23]

McFarland went on to question whether a board might be necessary:

> I can see where the necessity for a wheat board might not materialize, provided the drought is not broken on this continent. On the other hand, if the drought should break and a good crop is in prospect in North America, I can readily convince myself at least, that such a board may be a national necessity. In the meantime, very bad reports are coming in from large areas of the winter belt of the United States. It is also recognized that there is no moisture in the spring wheat territory except a light snow covering, and the prospect for the coming year is far from being promising. If these conditions continue for a time, and it becomes evident that there is not going to be a normal crop in North America, then I can agree that you will see a very big revival in the world's wheat market. It could be such a revival as would result in our clearing up our carryover to such an extent as to make the necessity of a wheat board appear very much minimized. The whole thing is in the lap of the gods....[24]

The gods did not relent. The conditions foreseen by McFarland were to result in clearing up the carryover to a large degree in the 1935-1936 crop year. In light of McFarland's cautionary note on timing, and his assurances to members of the Winnipeg grain trade, what motivated Bennett to proceed as he did, with what many considered draconian legislation?

It is clear that the prime minister was deeply concerned about the health of his friend and wished to lift the heavy load that had brought about McFarland's illness. Establishing a board and apportioning the responsibility among other commissioners would, in large measure, achieve that end. Additionally, bringing forward an all-encompassing bill with monopoly powers over all grain would meet the demands of the pools. He may have expected that concession to such a board would line up their organizations behind the Conservatives when the government went to the country.

In his assessment of the situation, Davidson noted that the pools had been pressing for a board since early 1931 when their own merchandising operations had come to a halt. "Looking back on their own experiences, the Wheat Pools were seized with the idea that only a marketing agency with the resources of the government of Canada at its disposal was strong enough to cope with world market factors on the one hand, and the needs of producers for some sort of price support on the other. Therefore, in their view, a Wheat Board was the only answer and this viewpoint was widely shared in western Canada."[25]

On the eve of the introduction of Bill 98, Winnipeg *Free Press* Ottawa bureau chief Grant Dexter, reported under an eight-column banner headline that:

> Within the past 24 hours a new wheat board bill has been drafted providing for an 100 per cent compulsory wheat pool in the three prairie provinces. In effect, the bill will create a wheat commission which will possess the exclusive right to buy and sell. The Winnipeg Grain Exchange under its terms will cease to function....The new legislation is entirely different from the bill which has been awaiting presentation in the Commons for some weeks and which would have merely set up a commission to carry on John I. McFarland's operation.[26]

Dexter attributed the change to intervention by the pools. "The sudden change in the wheat board legislation occurred after the arrival at Ottawa of Messrs. Bredt, Brouillette and Bennett, representing the wheat pools of the prairie provinces....Apparently the pool men found the first bill not to their liking and strongly advocated a 100 per cent pool."[27]

An element of retribution cannot be ruled out in the drafting of the monopoly bill presented to the House. Bennett was not a forgiving man and he was deeply upset over McFarland's illness. "Mr. McFarland's illness affected Bennett a good deal in a personal way. His greatest friend was in the hospital, very ill. He was a very ill man."[28] It is quite possible that Bennett attributed McFarland's condition to what he perceived as the intransigence of the private trade. On previous occasions his response when angered was expressed in terms of closing down the exchange.

Also, with the mandatory election fast approaching, the search for a grain policy was not the only problem plaguing Bennett. As the grain board bill was being introduced in the House, an army of the unemployed was moving toward Ottawa. Second reading on Bill 98 was interrupted on June 13, on the motion of CCF Leader J.S. Woodsworth who asked leave to move adjournment "for the purpose of discussing a definite matter of urgent public importance, namely, the situation with regard to the relief camp strikers now marching towards Ottawa and, according to reports, to be stopped by orders from Ottawa."[29]

In the ensuing debate Minister of Justice Hugh Guthrie read a statement to the House as follows: "From information which has come to the government, the government is satisfied that the present easterly march of so-called camp strikers from British Columbia, which has now reached Regina, has been organized and is under the direction of certain communist elements throughout Canada and is a deliberate attempt to disturb the peace, order and good government of Canada."[30]

He then confirmed that the Royal Canadian Mounted Police had been called upon to assist in halting the march of the unemployed.

Originating in Vancouver, the army of unemployed had swelled to an estimated fifteen hundred men by the time it reached Regina. "Riding the rods," on freight trains, inside and atop boxcars, and on open flat cars, they were camping out wherever possible in empty buildings and being fed through makeshift soup kitchens and handouts. While there was evidence that minor communist elements on the fringe were taking advantage of the march, the destitute, ill-clad, raggle-taggle army had only one political objective: they wanted assurance of jobs in a world gone awry.

They left Calgary with cheers and thanks for the assistance given them during their three-day stay. While in Calgary they were given food and clothing by the citizens and thirteen hundred dollars was obtained in a Saturday tag day. As well six hundred dollars was supplied by the Alberta government for their weekend meals.[31] The decision to call out the RCMP at Regina was to have tragic consequences.

As the army of the dispossessed moved eastward, swelling in numbers as it came, Bennett's lengthy dissertation during second reading of Bill 98 on the state of the grain economy was being heard in the House of Commons. Well-larded with statistics, his speech filled some seventeen pages of Hansard and at times was highly political. Despite its length, the prime minister's speech shed little light on why such unexpectedly broad powers were sought. Revealing for the first time the extent of the government holdings as a result of the stabilization program, Bennett strongly defended his own actions and those of McFarland as manager of Canadian Co-operative Wheat Producers Limited.

It was not until the end of his presentation that Bennett made reference to the intent of the proposed legislation:

> The bill, the second reading of which I have moved, is one predicated upon the fact that the general manager of this company whose operations have enabled this end to be accomplished is not further able to discharge his duties. I have indicated, therefore, that a wheat board in name—because we have had one in reality during the last two years—that a wheat board in name and reality should be set up. The terms and provisions of the bill are short and simple. It provides for the marketing of the Canadian wheat crop through the channel I have indicated, not through a private enterprise. It is to be done through a public board created by the Dominion of Canada for the purpose of ensuring against the destruction of that measure of economic stability, weak though it may be, that we through our efforts have been able to build up in the last few years.[32]

Clive Davidson noted that the prime minister, in his address, did not take advantage of the opportunity to treat the creation of the grain board as a new and constructive phase in the reconstruction of the wheat industry after the worst of the depression years and as an answer to the near unanimous demand of organized farmers for such a board. "Rather, he tried to relate the proposal for a grain board to what had been accomplished under stabilization proceedings."[33]

In an equally lengthy rebuttal, the Liberal lead-off speaker, Col. J.L. Ralston, a brilliant Montreal lawyer representing the Nova Scotia riding of Shelburne-Yarmouth, indicated that the official opposition would support a board, but only on a temporary basis as an emergency measure and without compulsory powers. He threw back Bennett's final summation of intent by quoting the prime minister's words and declaring, "That does not sound like a permanent policy."[34]

Ralston suggested that the board be given "ample power to liquidate and get the present dangerous overhang [of wheat] out of the way just as soon as it is possible to do it in orderly fashion. I would give them equally ample power at the same time to conduct stabilizing operations when necessary to protect the producer.''[35] In an earlier cruel thrust, Ralston, whose address was interrupted by the debate on the relief camp marchers, asked, ''What is the real problem facing my right hon. friend? Why is this bill being brought down at the last minute to shear Mr. McFarland, whom we all regret to hear is ill, of his authority and replace him with somebody else?''[36]

Ralston bore the main burden of the Liberal opposition to the bill in the House and in committee. He had become the party's critic of the government wheat policy after he made a speech during the budget debate on March 24, 1933, in which he accused Bennett of gambling on wheat as a result of the statement made by Darby, secretary of the Winnipeg Grain Exchange. Ralston was now being carefully coached backstage by Murray and Crerar. He concluded in support of sending the bill to a committee ''without prejudice or to commitment in the start that I wish to make on any of the provisions of the bill... reserving the right to make any amendments, notwithstanding that the bill has had second reading.''[37]

Public interest in the progress of the bill was intense, particularly in Winnipeg where the existence of the Winnipeg Grain Exchange was at stake. The highly partisan Winnipeg *Free Press* reported that Ralston ''performed under great stress due to the fact that Mr. Bennett had made no reference worthy of mention to the terms of the legislation.''[38] In the same week a cable to the *Free Press* from the Liverpool, England, firm of Whitson, Nielson and Francis was given front page prominence. ''It may be of value to your readers to know something of what is being said in British grain trade circles today regarding the endeavors of the Canadian government to further interfere with, and possibly destroy, the normal channels of trade on your side. These efforts are generally described as madness, suicidal, ridiculous and futile.''[39]

Of little note in national affairs, it was reported in the same newspaper on the previous day that, ''graduating students at Gordon Bell High School were let loose on the world Thursday afternoon when they held their closing exercises at Westminster church.'' Among the musical numbers played at those exercises was '''Expectations' by Dolmetsch played by Garson Vogel.''[40] The young Mr. Vogel was, thirty-six years later, to become chief commissioner of the Canadian Wheat Board. He and the author were two of the Gordon Bell students ''let loose on the world.''

Following second reading in Ottawa, with support for the Bennett bill by Co-operative Commonwealth Federation and Progressive members of the Commons, the draft bill was sent to a special committee of nine members which, at its first sitting, elected the prime minister as chairman. It was an unusual procedure for a prime minister to chair a house committee. However, his performance as a committee chairman was in character with the role he had played as wheat-policy maker and he needed now to implement his most important wheat-policy decision.

During the committee hearings, which commenced June 20 and concluded June 29, Bennett came under increasing pressure to divulge precise details of the McFarland holding operations. In anticipation, McIvor and R.C. Findlay, treasurer of CCWP, had been summoned by the prime minister to Ottawa. It was the statistical and precise evidence of Findlay that was to produce the most lurid headlines during the second week of the proceedings.

"Dramatic Story of McFarland Wheat Holdings Revealed; Has 228,000,000 Bus. at 85.9 Cts," proclaimed the Winnipeg *Free Press*. The story, by Grant Dexter, beneath that headline was indeed dramatic:

> Thursday there was unfolded before the special commons committee on the wheat board bill the story of John I. McFarland and Canada's wheat.
>
> From the committee room in the course of the day flashed cables to the distant ends of the earth, bulletins which, through the agency of great news distributing organizations, hit front pages the world over. These flashes told that the Canadian government is holding 228 million bushels of wheat at a price of 85.9 cents per bushel, with a total commitment by the treasury of $197,000,000.
>
> These, however, are but bald facts.
>
> In the committee room, Robert C. Findlay, treasurer of the Central Selling Agency of the pools, of which Mr. McFarland is the general manager, sat in the witness chair, poring over his ledgers and balances, calculating with a sharp-pointed pencil and gradually piecing together a story of sheer romance and drama. Not all the essential facts were disclosed. The human element, the emotional background—the thing that sent millions of bushels of wheat onto world markets or held back millions of bushels from the market—the thing that dictated the utterance of the words "buy" or "sell," this alone was lacking. In a word, Mr. Findlay, the careful, meticulous accountant, told what

> was done. He did not, and could not tell why.
>
> But the facts which found their way through his lips into the Hansard record, revealed the past four years in perspective. One got the picture.
>
> Wheat was, as it were humanized. Out of it all, came the view of Mr. McFarland, the czar of Canadian wheat, the greatest individual factor in world wheat, the man who during these years had his hand on the throttle of the chief article of commerce in the country. He opened the throttle or closed it at will; wheat flowed out to the world or ceased to flow at his command.[41]

Sharing the front page with that inspired prose was another headline of ominous portent for Bennett and his administration in the approaching election: "Mounties Halt Strikers Truck Trek From Regina." In the House of Commons, Justice Minister Guthrie warned the on-to-Ottawa marchers to obey the law or "take the consequences." Events, in both Ottawa and Regina, were moving toward a climactic close.

From Ottawa, Dexter dramatically reported, "Parliament Hill is in the grip of a tempest of party feeling, stirred up by the almost incredible Liberal sweep in the province of New Brunswick. Forty-three Liberals were elected in a legislature of 48 seats; the Tilley government, including the leader, are among the slain."[42] Bennett must have sensed a feeling of foreboding.

On the last day of the committee hearings in Ottawa, McIvor followed Findlay as the final witness. It was left to him to defend McFarland's operations and rebut some of the previous evidence in the brief of the Winnipeg Grain Exchange. He discounted the submission of exchange president Roy W. Milner, that all of the selling on the Winnipeg market could be accounted for by hedges. "My view, after analyzing the figures in the Canadian visible and having in mind the amount of wheat which is on hand for stabilization purposes is that there is no doubt that there is a large short interest in the Winnipeg market and the figures which I have quoted absolutely prove this fact."[43]

However, the thrust of committee infighting centred around the compulsory features of the proposed legislation. These were contained in sections 9, 10 and 11 of the draft bill which would have required every grain elevator to be operated on behalf of the board and would have prevented any railway company from receiving or delivering grain to an elevator in contravention of the Act. Nor could a grade or weight certificate be issued on grain held in such an elevator. With these clauses in force, no elevator could handle grain except as an agent of the board.

The only support for these compulsory measures during the committee hearings came from the pools. Brouillette, Bredt, and George Bennett, representing the three prairie pools, were also the only witnesses to support inclusion of grains other than wheat in the legislation. While F.W. Hamilton stated in his history of Manitoba Pool Elevators, *Service At Cost*,[44] that representatives of the pools and United Grain Growers Limited presented arguments in favor of the bill, the record shows the UGG support was highly qualified.

R.S. Law, president of UGG, called for appointment of a commission through which the government would assume direct responsibility for disposal of government wheat holdings and through which it would take "such further steps as may be required to protect producers from disastrously low prices." Any losses from such a disposal program would be the responsibility of the government. Law also asked that the compulsory features of the legislation be dropped. In addition the UGG brief said a system involving partial payments to farmers and issuance of participation certificates was not practical under the present conditions, and called for exclusion of coarse grains from provisions of the Act.[45]

Law asked, however, for special regulation of short selling in the futures market and recommended the appointment of a government market supervisor. In a final submission, the UGG brief reiterated a previous request for establishment of Canadian Wheat Institute to promote aggressively and enlarge the demand for Canadian wheat.[46]

But it was apparently the argument of Robert McKee, representing the Vancouver Grain Exchange, that turned the tide in favour of a voluntary board as opposed to a compulsory one. Referring to the clauses which would make the line elevators conform, Bennett's chief secretary Finlayson wrote, "The measure was not intended in any way as one of confiscation, but leading grain men claimed that this was just what it was; and when the bill came up for study before a committee of the House of Commons of which R.B. was the chairman, a quiet, impressive type of grain merchant from Vancouver condemned the bill on that score. R.B. turned to me and whispered: 'That bill must be changed.'"[47]

On Friday evening, June 28, the exhaustive committee hearings adjourned until 10:30 AM the following Monday—the July 1 Dominion

Day holiday. Over the weekend the interested parties were all feverishly at work on drafting and acceptance of amendments that would make it possible to get the legislation through the Commons. By now Bennett had been convinced that he would have to come to terms with the Liberal forces led by Ralston or face a delay in the House which he could not afford. The meetings were held in camera and the prime minister swore the committee members to secrecy.

McIvor, who along with the late Errick Willis, assisted Bennett in redrafting the proposed legislation, recalled that they worked virtually all night on the revisions. ''He [Bennett] dictated this thing....It was extraordinary, he didn't even refer it to the justice department, which is usually done. But that was the Act....And it stood in the court for many years.''[48]

A further note has been provided by McIvor with regard to the section dealing with participation certificates to be issued to producers. Copied from the first Wheat Board Act of 1919, the first draft stated that these certificates were transferable. McIvor recalled that, during the tenure of that earlier board, many farmers had little faith that any further payments would be forthcoming from the government after they had received their initial payment on delivery. As things were to transpire there was an interim payment of thirty cents and a final payment of eighteen cents on the certificates, for a total of forty-eight cents over and above the $2.15 per bushel initial price paid to the producer. However, in the interval, some unscrupulous traders went around the country buying up the participation certificates for as little as five cents a bushel. ''My principal contribution was that the words 'non-transferable' went in there. Otherwise transferable would have gone in and the farmers would have lost a lot of money.''[49]

In an inevitable compromise in committee, Bennett conceded that the compulsory sections 9, 10 and 11, as well as the section on coarse grains and flaxseed, should take effect on proclamation, whereas the rest of the Act would come into force upon royal assent. While other important features of the original bill remained unchanged, the compromise drastically curtailed the powers of the board, and it became a wheat board rather than a grain board.

The report of the special committee was submitted July 2, but speculation on its provisions gave way on the front pages of the nation to events in Regina. Stalled for some two weeks in that city, the frustrated army of the unemployed had swelled to some two thousand men and a mass rally was set for Dominion Day. As four van-loads of RCMP officers drew up to the scene of the rally in Regina's Market Street violence erupted. In the ensuing riot a Regina policeman was beaten to death and forty-two other persons were injured. Twenty-five were taken to hospital, four of them in serious condition. There were 113 arrests in the melee which did not subside until midnight. My brother Frank Morriss reported from Regina:

> Screams of women and children, shots, the acid tang of tear gas bombs, and flying bricks and missiles turned Regina's main streets into a scene of terror Monday night, resulting in the death of Detective Charles Miller, Regina city police, and injuries to 42 strikers and citizens. It was a bloody finish to a complex situation that had gripped the capital Saskatchewan city for over two weeks....Street car windows were smashed, store panes went before an onslaught of rocks as fighting became scattered, and bullets flew as arrests were made on many street corners.[50]

The previous night a group of some five hundred relief camp strikers gathered in Winnipeg awaiting the army from the west to join in the "On to Ottawa" march. They occupied a dining hall near Market Square and refused to leave, and Winnipeg police reinforcements had been called out. While issuing an ultimatum for the strikers to vacate the premises, Winnipeg authorities showed restraint when the deadline passed. The incident dissolved as suffocating heat in the crowded building finally forced the strikers out.

With the hands of the Commons clock at five minutes to twelve for his Conservative government, Bennett was now assailed from all sides. Desperately anxious to get the wheat board legislation through before prorogation, the autocratic Bennett was forced to defend the actions of his government in the aftermath of the Regina riot. In a lengthy speech, Bennett reiterated charges that the march of the unemployed was communist-inspired and declared, "that it is not the intention of this government to allow such demonstrations as will interfere with the maintenance of law and order throughout the country."[51] But the Liberal opposition had no intention of letting the events of Dominion Day fade from public memory.

Finally, on July 4, the amended Bill 98 was unanimously passed in the Commons. In what was to be his last substantive speech in the Commons as prime minister, Bennett made a brilliant defence of the legislation in its truncated form. Liberal leader Mackenzie King congratulated him on his performance, and only quarreled with him on his failure to give both parties credit for the revisions that had been made in committee. In the following election campaign, both parties claimed credit for the Wheat Board Act.

The Senate had the final say July 5, as Bill 98 was rapidly given first and second reading in the upper chamber. Former prime minister Arthur Meighen, now government leader in the Senate, had some reservations on the efficacy of the bill, as he gave a short but complete review of its provisions:

> Honorable members, as we all know, this bill has been under review for a long time in a special committee of the other House, and differs substantially from the one originally introduced. I have studied the bill carefully. It provides in effect for the continuation by the new board which is created, of the control now exercised by Mr. McFarland and his staff in respect to the carryover of Western grain. The new board will be empowered to purchase grain, or rather wheat—for the bill no longer applies to grain other than wheat, except in a sense which I shall mention in a moment, and it applies only to the wheat of the four Western Provinces. The board may purchase only from the producer. The term "producer" is carefully defined. If this bill passes, the commission will no longer be able to purchase in the market, as it has done in the past for stabilization purposes....
>
> I cannot help saying that personally I have grave doubts as to whether the board can function without wider powers than those given to it; but, as this matter has been very thoroughly considered, I do not know that I shall press for a change in the bill in this regard. I want to go on record, however, as entertaining some doubt as to whether the board will not, in some way, have to secure wider powers.
>
> As respects grains other than wheat, the new board will not have power to purchase or market except by special provision of the Governor-in-Council.
>
> The bill provides for the payment of a certain price to all producers upon sale of grain to the board. A certificate will be given to every producer entitling him to share, in proportion of his deliveries, in any excess, over and above what has been paid to producers for the same standard of grain. In this respect the bill conforms exactly with the principle of the old Grain Act, with which I had a great deal to do, and which established the Wheat Board in 1919. This measure really returns to the procedure of 1919 in respect to the marketing of Western wheat.[52]

Before returning the legislation to the Commons, the Senate made several minor amendments, one of which was significant. The clause calling for disposal of wheat and contracts for delivery of wheat held by the government through the Central Selling Agency "as speedily" as possible was changed to read that the wheat was to be disposed of "as may be reasonably possible, having regard to economic and other conditions."[53]

That same day, on July 5, 1935, Bill 98 was given royal assent. Immediately afterwards Parliament was prorogued and Bennett prepared to meet the electorate. The Canadian Wheat Board had come into being, but it was a body with emasculated powers facing a precarious and uncertain future.

There appeared to be no illusions as to who had won the bitter political battle, at least in the short term. Referring to changes made in the special committee, C.F. Wilson wrote, "With these changes, Col. Ralston could claim victory in the creation of a voluntary board, and the Liberal party took credit for the amended bill as their act. It was a victory, in fact, for the exchange."[54]

Some years later J.G. "Jimmy" Gardiner, after he had become agriculture minister in the Liberal administration of Mackenzie King, summarized the events of the era in a cabinet document. "The bitterest battle ever waged between the farmers led by the co-operators and the speculators led by the Grain Exchange was from 1929 to 1940....The first part of their battle ended on the floor of the Commons in 1935 when the Wheat Board Act of 1935 was passed. It ended with victory on the side of the Grain Exchange."[55]

D.A. MacGibbon, a member of the Royal Grain Inquiry Commission, 1923-1924, and a member of the Board of Grain Commissioners for Canada, 1929-1949, commented,

> The Wheat Board Act, when it finally passed Parliament, bore all the marks of a compromise measure. The Canadian Wheat Board became part of the federal government's institutional organization for dealing with the problems arising out of the sale of stocks of surplus wheat. The Wheat Board, however, was not looked upon yet as a permanent body, but was to disappear when the situation became normal.[56]

In Winnipeg there was satisfaction that a monopoly board had been fended off. At the regular general meeting of the Winnipeg Grain Exchange on July 16, 1935, it was recorded "that a note of thanks to the president and all members who recently represented the

Exchange at Ottawa'' was moved, and that ''in this motion the members enthusiastically concurred.''[57]

As long-time advocates of a compulsory board, the pools put on a brave face. In a statement given to the Canadian Press on July 9, 1935, the central executive of the Canadian Wheat Pools said:

> Reports in Western newspapers have left the general impression that the amendments made to the Canadian Grain Board bill have been of a very drastic nature and that the provisions supported by the organized producers of Western Canada have been changed materially or entirely omitted. It has even been stated that the Bill as finally passed by Parliament shows a complete reversal of policy, which, of course, is absolutely incorrect. It should, therefore, be made abundantly clear that the so-called compulsory features which were in the original Bill are in the Act as passed by Parliament, but they do not become operative until proclaimed by the Governor-in-Council. There has been no change in the fundamental principles of the Bill which in any way would make it less satisfactory to the producers.[58]

The solace taken by the pools in the unproclaimed sections of Bill 98 was eventually to bear fruit. In the interim the life of the new board, even in its truncated form, was to hang by a thread. Only the whims of man and nature were to assure its continued existence.

Elements of that survival were already making themselves evident. As the Canadian Wheat Board Act came into force, the army of unemployed was dispersing quietly in Regina following an agreement with the Saskatchewan government, which paid their fares back home or to the relief camps from whence they came. But many of them were soon to volunteer for another army. In Europe a ranting demagogue had consolidated his power over Germany. Adolf Hitler that summer scrapped the last clause still intact of the Versailles Treaty and Germany was rearming for war. In western Canada concern was centred on the prolonged and continuing drought. The events in Europe received only scant attention.

WHEAT BOARD IF NECESSARY, BUT NOT NECESSARILY A WHEAT BOARD

So came the Autumn's ruddy prime,
and all my hopes which had no morrow.
Like seawood cast upon the beach,
Like drift-wood barely out of reach
Of waves that were attuned to sorrow,
Lay lifeless on the strand of time.

— George Martin, *Canadian Birthday Book, 1887*

▪

It was midnight when the immaculately attired Richard Bedford Bennett emerged from his East Block office on Ottawa's Parliament Hill to meet the press. The rotund face, framed by the familiar glasses beneath the wide forehead, gave no hint of the traumatic events of the preceding six hours. He appeared to be in excellent health and good spirits as he read a statement congratulating William Lyon Mackenzie King and his Liberal party on their election victory. He hoped that Mr. King would have as much pleasure in the honour of guiding the country as he had enjoyed over the past five years.

The apparent good spirits masked bitter disappointment. Election returns on that Monday night of October 14, 1935, told of a disastrous rout for Bennett and his Conservative government. The Liberals, with 171 members elected to the 245-seat House of Commons, held the largest majority ever given any party in Canada to that time. In a heavy poll, with 75 per cent of the eligible voters casting ballots, there were also 5 independent Liberals elected in Quebec and 2 Liberal Progressives from Manitoba. The Conservative majority of 138 seats following the 1930 election had been decimated. They now held only 39 seats and 11 of Bennett's cabinet ministers had suffered defeat.

For Bennett, and for some of his cabinet ministers gathered in his East Block office, evidence that they were about to reap the bitter harvest of holding office during an unprecedented depression, came early on that bleak evening. Reading telegraphic despatches and listening to reports from the fledgling Canadian Radio Broadcasting Commission, the national broadcasting agency set up by an act of the Bennett government in 1932, they saw and heard the Liberal tide sweep across the country. In the key province of Ontario, the Reconstruction Party, led by Bennett's former cabinet minister H.H. Stevens and composed of renegade Tories, split the Conservative vote in a large number of ridings. The result was that the Conservatives won only 25 Ontario ridings to 55 for the resurgent Liberals.

As later returns came in from the West the results for Bennett were even more shattering. Passage of the Canadian Wheat Board Act had earned Bennett scant reward. Bennett was the only Conservative returned in Alberta, which gave 15 of its 17 seats to the new Social Credit Party, no doubt due to the spectacular rise of William Aberhart who had taken over the government of that province. The United Farmers of Alberta, which had sent 9 members to Parliament in the 1930 election, disappeared. Manitoba and Saskatchewan each yielded only 1 seat for the Conservatives.

In Winnipeg John I. McFarland, now chief commissioner of the Canadian Wheat Board, was desolate. In a handwritten note to Bennett on October 16, he expressed his condolences, "We are all in mourning here. The boys around our office are distressed beyond words. The Grain Exchange is in large degree jubilant. Paul Bredt is heart broken, and cannot understand how it could be so disastrous....The fact is however I do not believe wheat caused the election of the Liberals except to the extent that Liberals claimed credit for the Wheat Board....''[1]

The Grain Exchange had every reason for jubilation in the Liberal sweep. The Exchange members foresaw a short life for the newborn Canadian Wheat Board and the Sanhedrin had been returned to national influence. Named after a supreme council and court of justice in ancient Jerusalem, this inner circle was the source of Liberal party policy and decision making in western Canada. Followers of the Jewish faith would find it ironic that, given the derivation of the name, the Sanhedrin met on occasion for their intellectual discourses in the exclusive, and restricted, red-brick elegance of the Manitoba Club on Broadway in Winnipeg.

Included in the inner sanctum of the Sanhedrin were Edgar Tarr; John W. Dafoe, editor of the Winnipeg *Free Press*; Frank O. Fowler, manager of the Winnipeg Grain and Produce Clearing Association; and T.A. Crerar, the former Liberal cabinet minister and president of United Grain Growers. On the fringes of this inner group were others such as Joseph Harris, head of Canada Packers, and Elmer Woods of Monarch Life Assurance.[2]

Dafoe, as a charter member of the Sanhedrin, expounded their views through the influential editorial page of the Winnipeg *Free Press*. Into this little-known, private conclave flowed all the minutiae and background on the official and unofficial happenings in Ottawa. Gathered by their intelligence agency within the *Free Press* Ottawa bureau, it was forwarded in despatches by Grant Dexter, the bureau chief.

The philosophic and social allegiance of the Sanhedrin think tank was with the Winnipeg Grain Exchange. The voice of the farmer was seldom if ever heard within the hallowed walls of the Manitoba Club. When the Sanhedrin spoke, Mackenzie King was known to listen, be it an appointment to the Bench, the Senate, or formulation of wheat policy.

McFarland's letter of condolence to Bennett ended on a poignant note: ''It's a sorry outcome at best, but I am not ashamed of what I have done, and I shall always treasure the memory of serving under you during your term of office which is about to terminate. If nature again returns world normal crop yields, your successors in office will then gain some appreciation of what you and I have had to contend with on wheat.''[3]

Although it had not yet come home to McFarland, his own term of public office was about to end as the Liberals took over the reins of power. His appointment as chief commissioner of the new Canadian Wheat Board had been carefully weighed by Bennett who was fearful of the strain the position might impose on his old friend in the wake of his recent illness. He first sent his principal secretary, R.K. Finlayson, to Winnipeg to assess the state of McFarland's health. Finlayson reported back on July 31, that "McFarland is looking pretty well and gaining strength quickly. He will have to have some rest, but I have no doubt he expects to be made Chairman of the Board. In fact, if he isn't, I think it will be more detrimental to his health than if he is."[4]

At the same time Finlayson reported to Bennett that McFarland wanted the compulsory clauses 9, 10 and 11 of the Act proclaimed as soon as possible. "He feels he cannot adequately deal with the elevator companies without them. He thinks that the Futures Market should be closed and a great moral issue made out of it."[5]

While he made the appointment of McFarland as chief commissioner official by order-in-council PC 2497 on August 14, 1935, Bennett refrained from proclamation of the compulsory clauses. Rather, during the election campaign, he defended their inclusion in the Act as a big stick to be used if necessary. They were there to assure that the board got a fair deal, and would be invoked if necessary by order-in-council, "and you can call it dictatorship if you like."[6] Appointed along with McFarland were David L. Smith, assistant chief commissioner, and Dr. Henry C. Grant. Smith had formerly represented the Central Selling Agency of the pools in London, England, and Grant was a professor of economics at the University of Manitoba who had collaborated with McFarland during the acreage reduction campaign.

Under the terms of the new Act, an advisory committee of seven members was appointed on the same day by order-in-council PC 2518.

---

p. 81 *This parchment scroll is the letters patent that appointed the first commissioners of the Canadian Wheat Board on August 14, 1935. Handwritten in copperplate, it bears the Great Seal of Canada in the upper left hand corner and the signature of the Earl of Bessborough, Canada's governor general. The original was discovered in a long-forgotten file when research was being carried out on this history. The scroll has now been framed and occupies a prominent place in the Canadian Wheat Board Building in Winnipeg.*

Bessborough

Canada

George the Fifth by the Grace of God of Great Britain Ireland and the British Dominions beyond the Seas King Defender of the Faith Emperor of India.

To John Irvine McFarland of the City of Calgary, Province of Alberta Manager

David Livingstone Smith of the City of Winnipeg in the Province of Manitoba Agent

Henry Clark Grant of the said City of Winnipeg Professor of Economics at the University of Manitoba

Greeting:

W. Stuart Edwards
Deputy Minister of Justice
Canada

Know you that reposing trust and confidence in your loyalty, integrity and ability, We have pursuant to the Canadian Wheat Board Act, 1935, constituted and appointed, and We do hereby constitute and appoint you the said John Irvine McFarland, David Livingstone Smith and Henry Clark Grant to be Members of the Canadian Wheat Board.

To have, hold, exercise and enjoy the said office of Members of the Canadian Wheat Board unto you the said John Irvine McFarland, David Livingstone Smith, and Henry Clark Grant with all and every the powers, rights, authority, privileges, profits, emoluments and advantages unto the said office of right and by Law appertaining during Our pleasure.

And we do further appoint the said John Irvine McFarland to be Chief Commissioner of the said Board.

And we do futher appoint the said David Livingstone Smith to be Assistant Chief Commissioner of the said Board.

In Testimony Whereof, We have caused these Our Letters to be made Patent and the Great Seal of Canada to be hereunto affixed. Witness: Our Right Trusty and Right Well beloved Cousin and Counsellor Vere Brabazon, Earl of Bessborough, a Member of Our Most Honourable Privy Council Knight Grand Cross of Our Most Distinguished Order of Saint Michael and Saint George formerly Captain in our Territorial Army, Governor General and Commander-in-Chief of Our Dominion of Canada.

At Our Government House in Our City of Ottawa this fourteenth day of August in the year of Our Lord one thousand nine hundred and thirty five, and in the twenty sixth year of Our reign.

By Command.

W. P. O'Meara
Acting Under Secretary of State.

They were C.H.G. Short, Sidney T. Smith, and Robert McKee, representing the mills, elevator companies, and exporters respectively, and L.C. Brouillette, Paul F. Bredt, Lew Hutchinson, and Brooks Catton, representing the three provincial pools and United Grain Growers as the required producer representatives on the committee.

First order of business for the new board and the advisory committee was the setting of an initial payment for deliveries from producers. The Act offered no guidance or criteria for establishing the initial payment other than Clause 7 (e), which stated: "....to pay to producers delivering wheat at the time of delivery or at any time thereafter as may be agreed upon such fixed price per bushel, according to grade or quality or place of delivery, as may be determined by the Board with the approval of the Governor in Council...."[7]

T.W. Grindley, later secretary of the board, was to declare that there were several bases upon which the Board could fix the price: 1. It could be a price considered possible of attainment through sales on the market; 2. It could be a price that would enable the farmer, (a) to get by, (b) to cover production costs, or (c) to make a profit; 3. It could be a price calculated to compensate for the farmers' burden through protection of Canadian industries or one that would avoid large governmental expenditures for direct relief. Grindley added, "It is probable that no one of these bases is transcendent at the time of price-fixing and it is also probable that different considerations rule in different years, when the fundamental conditions change so drastically. In looking back upon the 1935 price, it seems reasonable to suppose that the price was based upon the concept of fair market value—a reasonable interpretation of what was considered possible by attainment of sales during the crop year."[8]

Be that as it may, with an election campaign under way, the setting of the first initial payment had distinct political overtones. In addition, by late August 1935, western farmers were under continuing hardship with drought, rust, and frost which took a heavy toll on the crop. The advisory committee met for three days, from August 27 to 29, but were unable to reach a compromise, with McKee proposing eighty cents in light of market conditions and Manitoba Pool Elevator president Bredt proposing ninety-five cents on behalf of producers.

On August 29, the board advised the committee of its own decision to recommend an initial price of ninety cents a bushel. But, since the board's recommendation was six cents above the cash market, which closed at eighty-four cents on August 29, Bennett wired back to McFarland on August 31, "So far as we can ascertain no wheat has been sold for as high as 90 cents in Canada this crop year. There is no authority in the Act to fix a price so out of line with market quotations as suggested by the Board. We will await the receipt of a formal recommendation and thereupon take immediate action, but the Act is neither a relief nor a bonus measure and its terms do not contemplate such action as that indicated by your telephone message."[9]

Correspondence followed among the prime minister, McFarland, and Bredt, with Bennett still demurring on the 90 cent proposal. Finally, on September 6, the Board having revised its recommendation to 87 1/2 cents, Clive Davidson, who had been appointed secretary to the board, wrote a long letter to Bennett. In it he set out the opinion of the board's legal counsel that "the words 'surplus if any' in 7-e and the provisions for participation certificates in that section and section 13 contained clearly indicate that the Act contemplates both deficits and surpluses as a result of the operations of the Board."[10]

This second recommendation was then approved by Bennett, and the initial payment of 87 1/2 cents per bushel, basis No. 1 Northern in store Fort William, was announced September 6. Prices for other grades were announced September 22, and the board commenced taking deliveries of wheat on September 25. However, very few deliveries were made to the board during the election campaign since the cash market price remained above the initial price level until October 26, 1935.[11]

Much greater political significance was given, however, to a later action taken by McFarland in negotiating the take-over of the grain stocks held by Canadian Co-operative Wheat Producers as authorized by the new Act. Those stocks comprised not only the wheat acquired by McFarland to the government account during the support operation, but also the 1930 pool wheat account. In the summer of 1931 McFarland left the unsold balance of 76,376,000 bushels in the 1930 account intact as he commenced buying futures in order to support the market. While, technically, the producers who delivered to the 1930 pool of CCWP should have waited for the ultimate disposition of those stocks before an accounting was made, McFarland proceeded to strike an agreement with the pool directors on an equalization payment.

Describing the general background of the negotiation and settlement that was reached, MacGibbon has implied direct partisan political manoeuvering between McFarland and the pools:

> The western grain growers had suffered so severely from low prices, as well as from drought, that they were in no mood to give the Government credit for what it had done in attempting to meet the situation. However, if Mr. Bennett could win the active aid and backing of the Pools with their network of local organizations, there was the possibility that this support might be the decisive factor in many constituencies on the prairies. A settlement satisfactory to the Pools of their claims against the Government for the wheat which the Government had taken over would be of great importance to them and a probable factor in securing this support.[12]

As talks between the pool directors and the board progressed on the bargain to be struck, McFarland sought to involve Bennett in the negotiations. He wired Bennett on September 10, "Could you arrange a meeting on your private car on way west from Winnipeg with representatives of Canadian Co-op Wheat Producers Company relative to discussion of terms on which the producers' company will turn over their holdings to the Wheat Board."[13]

The pool directors were encouraged by the outcome of that meeting and proceeded to verify their claim. This required a hurried report from the auditors based on records they had already prepared on an arbitrary basis under instructions from the Central Selling Agency. The auditor's report was submitted on October 5.[14] The report was based on the calculation that, by February 29, 1932, some "seventy-six million bushels of wheat had been moved into consumption at identifiable prices, and that producers had a reasonable claim for compensation on that basis...[This]... calculation showed that an average of 60 1/2 cents per bushel, basis No. 1 Northern in store Fort William-Port Arthur, had been realized."[15]

Based on that, the object of the proposed settlement was to equalize the returns to all pool members delivering to the 1930 pool at sixty cents a bushel. Since the prices actually realized by grades were somewhat better than the grade differentials reflected by the initial payments, this meant that producers delivering at the sixty cent initial, as well as those who delivered at the later fifty-five and fifty cent initial prices, would receive small sums as final payment. On this basis an agreement was reached in an exchange of letters signed by McFarland and Brouillette, president of CCWP, on October 8. The polling date was then less than one week away.

In Ottawa the justice department hastily drafted an order-in-council authorizing a settlement to Canadian Co-operative Wheat Producers of $8,262,415. Included in that amount was $862,487 to reimburse the pools for their operating expenses in the 1930-1931 crop year.[16] But with the election campaign in its final days, there was not the required number of cabinet ministers in Ottawa to hold a meeting of council. Finance Minister E.N. Rhodes circulated the draft by messenger to another minister in Ottawa and thence on to Montreal for two more signatures. Finally it was signed by Bennett, who was then in Toronto.

Rumors of the agreement began to circulate rapidly and, on October 10, in a page 3 editorial, the Winnipeg *Free Press* declared that the government was planning "some last minute stroke, which it hoped and expected, would change the political picture in the West to its advantage." The editorial said that cheques had already been written in the pool offices in Winnipeg and Regina awaiting instructions for their release from Ottawa. Government sources kept silent and Rhodes declined to make any statement.[17]

However on Friday, October 10, with voting to take place on the following Monday, Brouillette issued a press statement in Regina. In it he confirmed the agreement and in addition paid tribute to the stabilization program carried out by the government over the previous years. "It is admitted by all competent authorities that the increased price received by wheat producers as a result of these operations amounted to many cents per bushel. And the total benefits to growers have been estimated between $150,000,000 and $200,000,000 as the operations covered the marketing by Canada of close to 1,750,000,000 bushels."[18]

In a radio address on the same date, the manager of Alberta Wheat Pool said that Bennett had "seen fit to settle the issue," and that "the Alberta Wheat Pool would be lacking in spirit and common gratitude if it failed to express on behalf of the 27,000 Alberta wheat growers its appreciation of Premier Bennett and the Canadian Wheat Board in settling this vexed question in a manner reasonably satisfactory to all."[19]

As newspaper reports speculated that the equalization cheques might be mailed out to producers on voting day, Mackenzie King fought back accusing Bennett of attempting to bribe the farmer. In the event that the agreement had been deliberately calculated to sway the voters, the election aftermath proved that it had been of little avail. Immediate distribution of the equalization payments could not have been made. Despite all the haste in drawing up the order-in-council, there is evidence that the finance department officials had developed serious misgivings over the basis of payment they had helped to draft. The departmental officer who took the draft order to Bennett in Toronto had been instructed to persuade him to add a proviso. As a result, and after the other ministers had signed the order-in-council, Bennett added the words "subject to the amount...being verified by auditors' certificates."[20]

Further, some $891,000 had been included in the calculation to cover coarse grains and flaxseed delivered into the pool, and these grains were not covered under the Canadian Wheat Board Act as passed in 1935. It was left to the incoming Liberal government of Mackenzie King to settle the take-over of the CCWP stocks eventually. This was finally accomplished on April 8, 1936, when royal assent was given to the 1930 Wheat Crops Equalization Act, authorizing payment of not more than $6,000,000 from the consolidated revenue fund.[21]

Following the October 14 rout of the Conservative Party, Mackenzie King set about forming his new cabinet. One of his first tasks after being sworn in was assignment of responsibility for wheat policy. Unlike his predecessor who had assumed sole cabinet responsibility in that field with McFarland as his sole advisor, King chose to establish a wheat committee of cabinet. Fortunately, he had a number of ministers with roots in the wheat economy of the West. The committee was formalized by order-in-council P.C. 3455 on October 31, 1935. It consisted of the minister of trade and commerce, who had responsibility to report on the Canadian Wheat Board under the Act, the minister of agriculture, the minister of the interior, and the minister of finance.

Among holders of those portfolios were two former premiers of Saskatchewan, Charles A. Dunning and J.G. "Jimmy" Gardiner, and the veteran grain adviser T.A. Crerar. The only easterner was Trade and Commerce Minister W.D. Euler, who had first been elected to Parliament in 1917 and had served as minister of national revenue from 1926 to 1930. J.L. Ralston, the Liberal wheat critic during passage of the Wheat Board legislation, had not run for office in the election and had returned to his law practice in Montreal. However, he was to reappear on the scene in the near future.

Nor had Dunning or Gardiner run in the 1935 election. Dunning had first risen to prominence as a director of the Saskatchewan Grain Growers' Association and he had organized the Saskatchewan

Co-operative Elevator Company in 1911. Later he became provincial treasurer and then premier of Saskatchewan before joining the King cabinet as minister of finance in 1929. It is interesting to note that he was premier of Saskatchewan in 1922 when that province passed complementary legislation for a wheat board in the abortive attempt to re-establish the 1919 Board. King now opened up a seat for him in the Maritimes and appointed him finance minister in the new cabinet.

Similarly, a seat was opened up for Gardiner in Saskatchewan and he joined the cabinet as minister of agriculture. A short, five-foot-two, bantam-cock of a fighter, Jimmy Gardiner was to establish a reputation as one of the outstanding agriculture ministers of the century. He had been minister of highways in the provincial government of Dunning in 1922 when the Wheat Board complementary legislation was passed. He had declared opposition to the underlying principle of compulsion, but supported the Bill on the understanding it would operate for only one year. When King recruited him for the 1935 cabinet he had been premier of Saskatchewan for one year.

As for Crerar, who had been returned in the Manitoba riding of Churchill and appointed minister of the interior, his antipathy to any form of compulsion, or any permanent form of government intervention in wheat marketing, was a matter of record. The Sanhedrin in Winnipeg again had a member of its inner circle within the policy-making apparatus of government.

There was little doubt that the new administration's policy objective was to attempt an orderly liquidation of the wheat surplus accumulated under the Bennett-McFarland holding operation as soon as possible and to retain the Canadian Wheat Board only for the duration of the crisis. Having extricated themselves from direct wheat marketing responsibilities, the Liberal government would then return it to the private trade and the pools.

Although his impact on federal grain policy was not to be felt for a number of years yet, the voters in Port Arthur had sent a new member to Parliament who was to become a towering influence in national affairs over the next two decades. Clarence Decatur Howe, a craggy-faced engineer with piercing eyes, was well known in the western grain trade. He had built a fortune through his engineering company, which specialized in the construction of grain terminals. He and Dunning had crossed paths as early as 1916 when a contract to build the Saskatchewan Co-operative Elevator's terminal at Port Arthur had embarked the young Howe on his business career.

Construction of the terminal nearly ended in disaster for Howe when winter gales sent waves smashing through the breakwater and swept away the footings on the newly begun project.

However the tenacious Howe, using innovative methods, resumed the job and completed it in time to handle the 1917 harvest. But the project had cost him $400,000 more than the contract provided. It was enough to bankrupt the young engineer, but his bank stood by him and counselled him to carry on. Shortly afterwards, Howe was summoned to a meeting of Saskatchewan Co-operative Elevators, which had had a large stake in the timely completion of the terminal. In appreciation, the directors presented him with a cheque for $400,000.[22] Dunning was then president of Saskatchewan Co-operative Elevators and he and Howe became fast personal friends.

Back in Winnipeg McFarland was apparently anxious to carry on the business of his new board. It did not seem to occur to him that being so closely associated with Bennett as his personal adviser he would be expected to tender his resignation and let the new administration deal with the situation as they saw fit. Rather, as soon as the cabinet committee was formed, he sought their direction on policy.

Rumors were rife that sales would be pressed at sacrifice prices, and he pointed up the need for an early statement and asked for an early meeting of the board with the cabinet committee. Euler, as chairman of the cabinet committee on wheat, immediately responded with a statement to the press. "There are rumors abroad the government intends to direct the western wheat now held by the Wheat Board be sold, even at sacrifice prices. The rumors are without foundation. Under the law the board headed by John I. McFarland has full regard to the selling policy."[23]

While McFarland had evaded the question as to whether the present board should carry on, the statement seemed to imply that it would. Since the cash market was then under the initial price of 87 1/2 cents a bushel, the board was taking deliveries of wheat. But, as he had in the past, McFarland was taking back the options without selling futures. The results of that autumn were summed up two-and-a-half years later in the report of a royal grain inquiry commission. Pointing to prevailing prices, and having in mind heavy deliveries to the board, Mr. Justice Turgeon said it was hard to conclude that the intentions of the Act were carried out, particularly with regard to the requirement in section 8, "to offer wheat continuously for sale in the markets of the world through established channels."[24]

Feeling that it had clearly been the intention of the Act to terminate support measures by the establishment of a government-guaranteed initial payment, the cabinet wheat committee was becoming concerned. On November 13, they reviewed the situation and decided that a change in the personnel of the board was necessary. McFarland was scheduled to meet with the cabinet committee on November 29, but in the interim James R. Murray was invited to Ottawa for discussions.

Murray convinced the committee, which included his former close associate Crerar, that a more aggressive sales policy was feasible because the committee discussed with him the conditions under which he would seek a leave of absence from his present position in order to replace McFarland on the Board.[25] It is obvious that in seeking a leave of absence from Alberta Pacific Grain Murray intended that his stint as chief commissioner would be limited to clearing up the surplus and winding up the affairs of the Canadian Wheat Board, to which he was philosophically opposed. It is equally obvious that the cabinet committee concurred in his objective.

Euler requested that McFarland bring George McIvor, who had been retained as sales manager of the board, to the Ottawa meeting on November 29. That meeting was a traumatic one. Instead of meeting with the committee, McFarland met with Euler in the trade minister's office. McFarland was later to recall that Euler seemed ill at ease, but finally came out and said it was his "painful duty to invite all three members of the board to tender their resignations. McFarland offered to do so, but only if Euler would declare that the resignations had been requested for political purposes." This Euler declined to do.[26] In imposing a politically embarrassing condition upon the requested resignation, McFarland noted that the Wheat Board Act stipulated that cause must be shown before the board members could be retired. Euler replied that there was evidence of resistance to purchase Canadian wheat because of antagonism toward the personnel of the board. Stung by the accusation, McFarland asked for instances and suggested that the man who had made such a statement was Rank, the British miller. He said he would not resign as he wanted to consult with his colleagues in Winnipeg, and he had statistics to show that the so-called sales resistance was a myth.[27]

McFarland returned to his hotel and Euler immediately sent over a letter formally requesting the resignations of the board. In it he said that, "in the opinion of the government, a definite and persistent sales resistance has existed, and does now exist, in world markets, which is based on antagonism to the present Board. For this reason the Government feels that in the public interest the retirement of the present Board is advisable.''[28] Returning to Winnipeg, McFarland responded to that letter on December 2 in a telegram jointly signed by Smith, Grant, and himself. The Board's resignations were offered provided that three conditions were met: the government would: 1) acknowledge its desire to have a board of its own choice, 2) would withdraw the accusation of sales resistance against the retiring board, 3) and would pay an honorarium in lieu of salary they would otherwise have earned.[29]

McFarland continued to marshal evidence to refute the charge of sales resistance, but the cabinet wheat committee settled the issue by order-in-council on December 3. P.C. 3756 retired the existing board and appointed three new board members. The new members were James R. Murray, chief commissioner, George McIvor, assistant chief commissioner, and Alexander Malcolm Shaw, dean of agriculture at the University of Saskatchewan. Crerar was influential in the selection of Murray as chief commissioner and Gardiner sponsored the appointment of Shaw.

Given his long association with McFarland as his chief assistant in the stabilization operation, the offer to McIvor to become assistant chief commissioner came as a surprise. Murray strongly urged the government to approach McIvor with the offer. As a consequence, Euler spoke to McIvor in his office shortly after requesting the resignations of the current board from McFarland. McIvor was tired and deeply upset and didn't want to give an immediate answer. He immediately went to see McFarland in his Ottawa hotel room. Without hesitation, McFarland told McIvor that he should carry on since he had not become involved politically.

Still undecided, McIvor met with Murray in his hotel room where they had a long conversation. He was later to recall, ''There was very little difference between us. We were both sellers, and wanted to be.'' Stopping in Toronto to visit his mother, McIvor was greatly influenced in his decision to accept the appointment by a chance meeting on the train. The porter informed him that there was someone in a private car who wished to speak with him. He found it to be Finance Minister Dunning who told him, ''George, I want you to take that job.''[30]

Returning to Winnipeg, McIvor talked with his wife and then consulted the pools before accepting. It proved to be a fortunate decision.

George McIvor was to preside over some of the most tumultuous years in the history of the Canadian Wheat Board. It was particularly fortunate, as events were to prove, that Bennett had declined to appoint him to the first board in 1935 on the recommendation of McFarland. The prime minister felt that, with McFarland and McIvor on that board, the public would think it was simply a continuation of the stabilization operation of previous years.

While Wilson asserts that the action of the wheat committee was not intended to call into question McFarland's personal integrity,[31] McFarland was cruelly hurt by the preamble to the order-in-council retiring himself and his colleagues. Repeating the allegations of sales resistance, the order-in-council added, "The Minister is of the opinion that it is inimical to the best interests of Canada in the circumstances that the present members of the Canadian Wheat Board should continue in office...."[32]

Having served for five years as a public service with no salary, and at serious cost to his health, McFarland had every reason to expect that the country should honour him rather than castigate him with the allegation that his serices had been "inimical to the best interests of Canada." Not only had he served without salary, but there is evidence to show that his own financial resources suffered during his long absence from his personal affairs. Although he could have retired at the time of his illness, or at the time the Canadian Wheat Board came into being, it had become a matter of personal pride to him that he should bring the operation to a successful conclusion.

His dismissal by the Liberal government had some of the elements of a Greek tragedy in that he left office on the eve of the vindication of the course he had pursued over those long and difficult years. When the Canadian Wheat Board took over the stocks of 205,186,984 bushels of wheat accumulated during the stabilization operation, they were valued for accounting purposes at the market price of December 2, 1935. This resulted in a book loss of $15,856,645.43. But, when the cash grain and futures were cleared through sale, the final statement of transactions completing the marketing of McFarland's holdings showed a net profit of $8,953,343.07.[33]

When the settlement eventually paid to the pools is deducted from that figure, the final outcome for the federal government was a profit of some $2.5 million. That final accounting was for the future to unveil, and in December 1935 John I. McFarland was a sorely wounded and embittered man as he wound up his affairs in Winnipeg before returning home to Calgary. It was left to the farmers, whose welfare he had sought so selflessly to protect, to pay tribute to McFarland for his sacrifices in their interest. On February 14, 1936, some seven hundred people, the majority of them farmers, gathered at the Palliser Hotel in Calgary for a testimonial luncheon. "Snow-drifted roads and arctic temperatures prevented hundreds from attending. Had fine weather been experienced the Palliser Hotel could never have accommodated the crowds."[34]

McFarland, who was overwhelmed by the reception, was given an illuminated address inscribed as follows:

> The grain growers of Alberta assembled here today desire to pay a tribute to your sincere and unselfish action in contributing your services on their behalf for the five-year period from 1930 to 1935, during which you were in charge of wheat price stabilization undertaking at Winnipeg.
>
> We feel that you rendered a real service to the wheat growers of Western Canada. We cannot repay you for your untiring efforts and the sacrifices you have made. But we can at least express our heartfelt appreciation.
>
> In thousands of farm homes in Western Canada your name and deeds are held in the highest esteem. Your devotion to the cause of agriculture in this western land and the contribution you have so generously made will not soon be forgotten.
>
> We trust that satisfaction deep and lasting will be yours.[35]

In a lengthy address delivered at the luncheon, McFarland reviewed his five-years effort at stabilization and lashed out at the Winnipeg Grain Exchange once again. "Theoretically the open futures system is an ideal system for the handling of wheat if it works; but when it fails to function, as it has failed, because of world-wide subsidies, oversupply and absence of speculators to carry the hedges, then my sympathy leans entirely toward the producer and his protection."[36]

Declaring that, under the current Act, the Wheat Board had one hand tied by having to deal through the existing marketing structure, while the Grain Exchange had absolute freedom, McFarland charged that his successors at the Board had allowed the "shorts to escape" when a price surge developed on the market. That charge was to result in yet another royal commission to investigate marketing and would mark the last time McFarland would appear in the wheat policy spotlight when he appeared as a witness.

In his Calgary address, McFarland also revealed that a payment of nine thousand dollars sent to him by the King government as payment for his short tenure as chief commissioner of the new board, had been sent back. Referring to the order-in-council that dismissed him, he bitterly declared, "Since it purports that my services were a menace to the public interests of Canada, I could not be deserving of a gratuity of any description."[37]

Paradoxically, when in May 1937 McFarland appeared as a major witness before the second Turgeon grain inquiry commission, he was to declare against a compulsory grain board and the closing of the futures market. To everyone's surprise, particularly that of the pools, he now recommended a voluntary wheat board with a minimum price and continuation of the open market under regulation, which would provide farmers with the choice of selling through either medium.[38]

McFarland was treated with great deference and respect during his evidence before the commission. It was a strange conclusion to the wheat policy career of the man who can properly be recognized as one of the fathers of the Canadian Wheat Board.

As for his old partner and long-time friend R.B. Bennett, with whom he shared that distinction, there was only a short term in opposition left in his public career. Following that, Bennett retired to Britain where he acquired an estate near that of his friend Lord Beaverbrook and accepted a peerage. As Viscount Bennett, the bachelor ex-prime minister lived out a lonely self-imposed exile. The "Bennett Buggy" became the symbol of his administration.

That is an unfortunate appreciation of a man who, in one short term of office, achieved a remarkable record of advanced legislation. While many historians have concentrated on the disasters of the Depression, Bennett's government passed legislation that had a profoundly positive effect upon the future course of Canada. While this volume has concentrated upon the Canadian Wheat Board Act, which Clive Davidson has described as "the jewel of the government's marketing program," there were other measures in the agricultural field. They included: the Farmers' Creditors Arrangements Act (1934), whereby a producer's debts might be reviewed with creditors under official auspices; the Natural Products Marketing Act (1934), to supplement the powers of provincial marketing boards relating to interprovincial trade; and the Prairie Farm Rehabilitation Act (1935), pioneer legislation which was the forerunner of a series of federal acts designed to assist Prairie provincial governments in meeting the most urgent of Prairie production and farm income problems.

Other measures included the setting up of the Bank of Canada in 1934 as the first central bank, and the Canadian Radio Broadcasting Act (1932), whereby a commission was set up with powers to undertake broadcasting, to build and operate stations, to acquire radio stations by purchase and lease, and to regulate radio broadcasting in Canada. Bennett was also the key architect in the first International Wheat Agreement of 1933 which, although it subsequently broke down, set a pattern for future international co-operation in wheat.

Also, in early 1935, the Bennett government introduced a major piece of social legislation to provide for unemployment insurance. While that legislation was declared *ultra vires* of Parliament by the Supreme Court in 1937, and it was not until 1940 that the British North America Act was amended and another unemployment insurance plan put into effect, the 1935 legislation established a high priority for the measure.

If that were not enough for a five-year stint in office during a depression, it fell to Bennett to deal with the residual problems pertaining to full sovereignty for Canada and the other Dominions in the Commonwealth by the Statute of Westminster (1931). In addition, he secured preferences for Canadian farmers' produce in their largest market, the United Kingdom, which benefited farmers for two generations.

While we have diverted momentarily from our main theme, it is an impressive record of achievement on which to end this chapter.

POLITICS AND FATE

Henceforth it was clearly apparent that the Canadian wheat growers were not willing to rely on the processes of an open world market to reward them for their toil no matter how many royal commissions might tell them that in the long run this was the most efficient method of selling wheat.

— MacGibbon, *The Canadian Grain Trade 1931-1951*

▪

The persistent jangle of the phone awoke George McIvor at his Dromore Avenue home in Winnipeg's River Heights in the early morning of December 13, 1935. Moments after lifting the receiver he was fully awake. The voice on the line brought a dramatic message. Overnight the Argentine government had authorized their national grain board to purchase wheat at the equivalent of about ninety cents a bushel in Canadian funds.

It had been known for about six weeks that the crop in Argentina was short. Now a killing frost had struck. News of the sudden increase in the Argentine price caused wild excitement in the wheat markets of the world and frenzied buying was taking place.[1] The new Argentine price was an increase of thirty-seven cents over the previous minimum of fifty-three cents, and eighteen cents over the Buenos Aires market price of seventy-two cents on December 12.

George H. McIvor, chief commissioner Canadian Wheat Board, July 1937 to April 30, 1958.

McIvor immediately phoned Jim Murray, the chief commissioner, at his home. By 8.30 AM the new board of commissioners, only four days in office, were assembled for their first critical meeting in the Canadian Wheat Board office on Main Street. Murray was clear in his own mind on the strategy for the day, but he turned to McIvor and said, "Well what do you think we should do?" McIvor ventured that the market was sure to go up: "I think we should sell." Dean Shaw, whose previous experience had been at the University of Saskatchewan rather than in the hurly-burly of the market, simply said, "Whatever you two boys decide."[2] The die was cast on a decision that was to obliquely result in a stay of execution for the fledgling Canadian Wheat Board.

Selling on the Winnipeg Grain Exchange that day was hot and heavy. W.C. Folliott, who had been appointed as general sales manager of the board to succeed McIvor, employed between 40 and 50 brokers on the floor of the exchange to sell 11,684,000 bushels of May futures in the pit at 89 7/8 cents a bushel, which represented the three cent limit over the previous day's close. In addition the board sold 861,445 bushels of cash wheat at a related price. The board also sold 7,782,000 bushels to wheat exporters and 901,000 bushels to millers to cover the exceptionally heavy volume of acceptances of overnight offers which had been prompted by the Argentine news. These export transactions were at 87 1/8 cents, or 1/4 cents over the previous day's close. That price was in accordance with an agreement Murray had made with the trade only two days previously.[3]

The board decision to take full advantage of the windfall opportunity to make sales in the light of the bullish news from Argentina resulted in a record sale of a total of 22,025,445 bushels of wheat in one day.

While the decision to sell aggressively was to raise a political storm, it was fully in line with a series of initiatives that the aggressive Murray had set in motion immediately upon his appointment as chief commissioner. When the new board was announced on December 3, Murray was in Ottawa consulting with the wheat committee of cabinet. McIvor was in Winnipeg and Shaw was still in Saskatoon. The advisory committee to the board was dispensed with on that same day by order-in-council since, according to Trade Minister W.D. Euler, the cabinet committee had been established to advise the board on policy and the advisory committee was no longer deemed necessary.

The advice of the cabinet committee was to sell, and sell hard. Murray, by temperament, was only too willing to accept that advice. He and the committee made a realistic assessment of the world grain situation and decided that, in accordance with the terms of the Act, wheat would be kept on offer continuously using all the facilities of the trade. Since seventeen of the best selling weeks of the crop year had already elapsed, they were conscious of the fact that in order to reduce the carryover to a realistic figure by year-end they would have to make weekly sales almost equivalent to the total of weekly world import demand. While world wheat trade was slack, Argentina was known to have little export surplus and the United States was temporarily an importer of Canadian wheat. The only real competition might come from Australia, and Canadian wheat would have to be offered at realistic premiums to meet that competition.

With the board holding 295,376,167 bushels of wheat and wheat futures, and deliveries continuing on the 1935 crop,[4] the board was urged to mend fences with the domestic and overseas trade over the uncertainty surrounding the trade policies of the McFarland board. Murray undertook to consult with the trade in Winnipeg to enlist their support and to send someone overseas to make direct contact with millers and the trade in Britain and continental Europe. That decision was made in light of criticism in the autumn of 1935, that Canadian prices were being held at unrealistic premiums over competing wheat.

Immediately after the cabinet committee meeting Euler issued a statement:

> The concentration of surplus stocks of wheat in Canada during the past few years has created an abnormal situation in the world wheat trade.
>
> Last June this situation was recognized by Parliament as not being in the best interests of Canada or her wheat producers, and the Dominion Government desires to have our surplus restored on a normal basis. To accomplish this the wheat board will seek the goodwill and co-operation of the grain and milling trades in all importing countries.
>
> It is not necessary to have and there will not be any ''fire sale'' of Canadian wheat, but it will be for sale at competitive values and will not be held at exorbitant premiums over other wheats.[5]

On his return to Winnipeg Murray lost no time in preparing his aggressive policy to expedite sales. The new board took office December 9, and held its first meeting. That same day the executive of Canadian Co-operative Wheat Producers Limited called on the board to seek support in its negotiations with the cabinet wheat committee on the basis of settlement with regard to takeover of their holdings. Murray, however, contended that the issue was one between the federal government and the CCWP.[6]

The next day, the board established membership on the Winnipeg Grain Exchange and the Winnipeg Grain and Produce Exchange Clearing Association by purchasing the memberships held by CCWP. On December 11, the board met with a committee representing the shippers and exporters and an agreement was reached in line with the policy of seeking rapprochement with the trade. In a memorandum the board agreed to offer wheat at realistic premiums and, in so far as possible, not to compete unfairly in business with the exporters' own stocks of wheat that they now held east of the lakes. The board agreed to make wheat available to exporters to cover their overnight acceptances during the first ten minutes after the opening of the market at not more than a quarter-cent over the previous day's close. The board reserved the right to have an independent audit to insure that the wheat so priced represented legitimate exports and excluded speculative transactions.[7] At the time, the exchange had in effect a three-cent limit on daily price changes in either direction. Murray was to later testify that the quarter-cent limit was to encourage the exporters to offer wheat more freely by affording them protection if the market were to open sharply higher after they had cabled offers to their overseas buyers at the close of trade each day.[8] The undertaking remained effective until December 22, 1935, when it was withdrawn.

Also, on December 11, the board met with Cecil Lamont who agreed to leave immediately for Britain and the Continent to interview personally the trade and millers to outline the new Canadian Wheat Board policy and seek their co-operation. Lamont left on December 12. Meanwhile, the board decided that, for the present, two-thirds of current sales would be credited to the holdings taken over from Canadian Co-operative Wheat Producers and one-third to the wheat delivered to the board by producers.[9]

During the first few days in office the Murray board had been gingerly making some sales, but all was in readiness for the big push when the Argentine news broke on the morning of December 13. And sell they did. From December 9, when the new board took over, to the end of the month, sales totalled 50,251,008 bushels.[10] The record sales on December 13, however, were to create a political storm and result in another royal grain inquiry commission.

Preparing to leave Winnipeg December 19 to return to Calgary and private business, John I. McFarland alleged in a press interview that:

> Among other things the big speculators and manipulators who had effected enormous short sales in the Winnipeg futures market awaiting a smash in prices because of the vicious propaganda carried on in this country and abroad were caught napping and stood to lose millions of dollars. The public are wondering, and they have a right to know, whether these destructive short sellers were rescued from their predicament by the reported enormous sales made by the Canadian Wheat Board, much of which was sold at less than prevailing pit quotations, and all of it at much less than Argentine values.[11]

When the new Parliament went into session in February, R.B. Bennett, now in opposition, took up McFarland's charge that the board had bailed out the short sellers. In reply to the Speech from the Throne, Bennett castigated the new government for the dismissal of the McFarland board and quoted statistics to refute the theory that there had been sales resistance against Canadian wheat. Labelling McFarland's successor as "Grain Exchange Murray," the former prime minister declared that Murray represented "opposition, violent, unquestioning, to what is known as pool interests in Western Canada." He further alleged that Lamont had been sent to Britain to reassure the trade that the pools would never again function, and attributed his source as an unnamed minister of the Crown.[12]

Replying to the charges of an exchange-dominated board two days later, Trade Minister W.D. Euler identified Bennett's allegation of protection of the shorts as his most serious charge and invited Bennett to request an investigation by a parliamentary committee. Bennett eagerly acted on the invitation. A special committee was appointed in March and commenced public hearings April 21, 1936.

Murray, as the chief witness before the committee, took the stand the next day. Consistent with his Irish background and tough reputation, and aware that he would be under attack, Murray came out fighting. In his opening statement he stung Bennett with several barbs. Bennett was capable of giving back in equal measure that which he received. The cross-examination, conducted principally by Bennett, kept Murray on the stand until April 30. At one point, to the glee of the former prime minister, Murray admitted that one of his failings was to express strong opinions and that he was hard to get along with.

As the hearings before the Commons committee dragged to a close, Murray emerged as the clear winner in the drawn-out battle. Backed by E.E. Perley, the sole Conservative member from Saskatchewan, Bennett sought to demonstrate that Murray had accommodated the shorts by the board actions of December 13. However, the committee ruled there was no evidence produced that would warrant the charge. Perley insisted that the charge stand, because the committee had failed to make a complete investigation. On his last day on the stand, Murray, with the blessing of the cabinet wheat committee, called for a royal commission to make a complete enquiry into the whole area of wheat marketing, including the question of which was the best method of carrying out sales. He had been advocating such an investigation privately for over a year.

On June 11 in its final report, the committee recommended the appointment of a royal commission to make a complete survey of the production, grading, and distribution of Canadian grain, including the methods of marketing. It also recommended that the charge of protection of the shorts be referred to the commission. The committee report was adopted without dissent in the Commons on June 17, 1936.

In the interim, the cabinet wheat committee had persuaded Mr. Justice W.F. Turgeon, of the Saskatchewan Court of Appeal, to act as a sole commissioner of a royal commission. Turgeon had been chairman of a previous royal grain inquiry commission in 1925 that submitted a report concluding that the futures market benefitted producers. He was now appointed, by order-in-council on June 27, to conduct a second inquiry.

If the previous findings of Turgeon, which coincided with the philosophy of the King administration, were instrumental in his choice as head of the new commission, the appointment was to take an unforeseen turn. While he was adjured to report as speedily as possible, it was to be two years before he submitted his final report to Parliament. The government had already appointed him to head an inquiry into conditions in the textile industry, and the grain inquiry had to share time with that previous duty. The delay was to hamper the government's continuing efforts to extricate itself from grain marketing responsibility.

As the second Turgeon commission began its lengthy task, the Murray board was taking full advantage of a fortuitous environment to rid the country of the unwanted surplus that had overhung the market for so long. Besides the Argentine crop disaster, the 1935 Canadian crop again suffered from the prolonged drought. Total country marketings amounted to only 216,273,373 bushels in the 1935-1936 crop year, of which the Canadian Wheat Board received 150,740,226 bushels. The United States was completely out of the market and its winter wheat crop, sown in the fall of 1935, was again hit hard. The result was that, while world wheat trade hit its lowest level in the post World War I era, Canada captured almost half of that reduced market. World trade slumped to only 514,283,000 bushels, but Canada sold 253,417,000 bushels of wheat in the crop year ending July 31, 1936. At year-end the board holdings consisted of a mere 2,030,761 bushels of the 1935 crop, plus 82,667,891 bushels of the holdings taken over from Canadian Co-operative Wheat Producers. Total holdings of the board were thus reduced from 295,376,167 bushels of wheat at the end of November 1935, to 84,698,652 bushels at July 31, 1936.

During the course of the crop year, prices dropped below the 87 1/2 cent initial price level on October 26, 1935. They kept easing down gradually for several months to a low of 73 5/8 cents on May

26, 1936. Then, in response to adverse weather conditions, prices rose above the 87 1/2 cent level in early July, and above the dollar level by the end of that month. Because most of the 1935 crop had already been sold at prices below the level of the initial payment to farmers, the board realized a loss of $11,858,104.18 on disposition of the crop.[13]

In the face of that loss, and with the carryover reduced drastically, the time appeared ripe for the King government to achieve its desired goal of removing itself from marketing responsibility. On June 25, as the crop year drew to a close, Euler wrote to Mackenzie King setting out his views:

> In my opinion, if the government is ever going out of the wheat business, this is the time to do it. If it is delayed, it will become increasingly difficult as the time for an election approaches. I never approved of Mr. Bennett's policy and we should end it as soon as possible. It can be excused only as an emergency measure at best, for it is not only class legislation of the worst kind, but is confined to one class in one particular section of the country. The loss on wheat today is probably in the neighborhood of $40,000,000 and is a heavy burden on the general taxpayers of Canada. In my opinion there should be no fixed price for the coming year, and some arrangement should be made by which the stock now held should be disposed of by a continuing Wheat Board without detriment to the sale of the coming crop, perhaps by a quota allotment each month.
>
> I am sure that such a course will be justified ultimately. If we continue the policy, the demands of the wheat producers for higher prices (fixed) will be augmented. Moreover, with the principle established, the government will probably be forced to yield to a similar policy with regard to coarse grains and then to products of all kinds. That would constitute a very definite advance towards socialism. If the situation is still to be regarded as an emergency, I would favour the lesser evil of granting a bonus, which could be terminated more easily.
>
> Should the government decide on fixing a price for wheat for the coming crop, it should be no higher than 60 cents a bushel, so that possible loss will be definitely limited.[14]

At the time, Trade Minister Euler was preparing to sail for London for a round of talks on a new trade agreement, and Gardiner was also going overseas in search of farm markets. His letter was placed on the cabinet agenda for later decision when the cabinet committee reassembled in August. In the interim, the pool leaders met on July 6, with Gardiner, Crerar, and Minister of National Revenue J.L. Ilsley. They urged that the 1936 initial payment be set at the cost of production.

The hope of the pools for such a formula was to be rudely shattered when the cabinet met in late August to decide on the initial payment for the 1936-1937 crop year. In line with the government's objective of withdrawing from marketing, Mackenzie King and his colleagues came up with an ingenious solution. Armed with advice from the justice department that the government was not obliged to accept the recommendation of the board on an initial price, the cabinet drew Murray into the cabinet discussions. Murray, at the suggestion of cabinet, then recommended that the initial price be retained at the 1935 level of 87 1/2 cents. Cabinet in turn disapproved the recommendation, except in the event the market dropped below 90 cents a bushel.[15]

Since the price had risen above the ninety cent level, the decision, in effect, removed the Canadian Wheat Board from the market. The producer was denied the option of delivering to the board unless the price dropped below ninety cents. The explanation given for not accepting the board recommendation unconditionally was that the Turgeon commission was seized with the question of what form grain marketing should take and had not yet submitted its report. The inference was that, pending the Turgeon report, no action should be taken which might pre-judge the eventual findings.

The pools were outraged and issued a statement which declared that the western grain grower had been denied the right given him by Parliament to deliver his grain to the board. "As matters now stand, the speculative system which we have fought so persistently, remains in possession of the field....Through the decision announced from Ottawa, the alternative system of controlled grain marketing in the interest of producer and consumer alike, has been forced to pause...."[16]

The pool leaders met with Euler, Crerar and Gardiner in Ottawa in an attempt to have the decision reversed, but to no avail. However, confronted by the reaction from their constituents, western Liberal backbenchers began to express their concern. A rift opened between King and W.R. Motherwell, a respected elder statesman in the Liberal grain policy hierarchy. Motherwell, a founding member of the Territorial Grain Growers Association in 1901 and agriculture minister in King's first cabinet of 1921, expressed grave concern and suggested that members of the cabinet wheat committee be sent to the West to explain first-hand what had been done.[17]

Acting on the request, King sent Crerar and Gardiner on speaking tours to defend the government's actions. But when Parliament resumed sittings in January 1937, another political storm erupted, although somewhat less tempestuous than that which marked the 1936 session. Bennett began the attack during the throne speech debate, and he and Perley continued it during the budget debate. To exploit the discomfort of Liberal back-benchers, Perley forced a vote by moving non-confidence in the King government.[18]

In the ensuing clash, Dunning defended the Liberal policy of denying deliveries to the board unless the price dropped below ninety cents, by implying that it would have enabled the pools to reinstitute pooling without any risk of loss to the pools. Queried by Perley, as to when any such offer was made, Dunning replied that no offer was made, but that the order-in-council, establishing the policy, constituted the offer.[19]

C.F. Wilson has pointed out that this explanation was elliptic in the sense that the order-in-council was not sufficient authority for the pools to offer co-operative pooling without risk of loss. Had the pools reinstituted private pooling and offered an initial payment of 87 1/2 cents, there was no government guarantee that if the price fell below that level they would be reimbursed by the government. In the event of such a drop, the guarantee was only available to producers who delivered to the board. An amendment to the Act would have been required to authorize the board to accept redelivery of wheat from the pools at the guaranteed price, plus carrying charges and other pool operating expenses, or to reimburse them directly on losses, in order to insure them against loss.[20]

It can be speculated that what Dunning intended to imply was that if the pools had been willing to negotiate in August 1936, the government would have been willing to accommodate them in reinstituting private pooling by guaranteeing the initial payment. In any event, the Conservative non-confidence amendment was voted down with only one of the Liberal members breaking rank.

As the political storms rose and subsided in Parliament, the Murray board was winding down the remainder of the wheat stocks accumulated during the previous half-decade and conducting promotional campaigns in the European market, particularly in Britain. It will be recalled that Murray had despatched Cecil Lamont to Britain on a fence-mending mission as one of the first moves of the new board. There Lamont attempted to interest the Millers' Mutual Association in Britain in undertaking a joint advertising scheme to promote the use of Canadian wheat, but he was unable to secure their co-operation.[21]

In May of 1936 Murray had not given up on the promotional program and called McIvor into his office. After a short discussion it was decided to contact Harry Cockfield, of Cockfield, Brown and Company, with whom McIvor had made a chance acquaintance on a train. As a result McIvor and Cockfield left for Britain on May 20, taking with them Dr. W.F. Geddes, chemist in charge of the Board of Grain Commissioners research laboratory. George McIvor was later to recall the trip as one of the most trying experiences of his life.

They left armed with speeches and articles prepared by Gratton O'Leary (later Senator O'Leary), of the Ottawa *Journal*; letters of introduction to Lord Beaverbrook; and strict instructions from Mackenzie King, through Murray, that under no circumstances were they to disparage any other country's wheat. It was an admonition that was to result in McIvor feeling that his fledgling career as assistant chief commissioner was about to come to an abrupt and ignominious end.

Shortly after their arrival in London, McIvor and Cockfield made an appointment to meet with Beaverbrook on a Friday night at his home, Stornoway House. Both were highly nervous at the thought of meeting the man who, as head of a newspaper empire, had become a legend in Canada and Britain. They were ushered into a room to await his arrival. When the "Beaver," a short man with pugnacious features, finally came in he brusquely asked, "What do you fellows want?" McIvor recalled that "it wasn't in the script," but he began by noting that he and Lord Beaverbrook had something in common in that his grandfather's home in Kildonan on the outskirts of Winnipeg was also called Stornoway House.

In the subsequent conversation it was revealed that both had grandparents who came from the Island of Stornoway. Beaverbrook then asked whether Kildonan was in the Selkirk settlement and if McIvor knew Whittier's poem "The Red River Voyageur." McIvor learned it in school and quoted from the poem, "The voyageur smiles as he listens/ to the sounds that grow apace;/ well he knows the vesper ringing/ of the bells of St. Boniface...." Beaverbrook was delighted and called in a secretary to take down the words as McIvor repeated them.

The ice broken, they got down to business. McIvor and Cockfield outlined their mission, which was to seek Beaverbrook's support in promoting Canadian wheat. Given the material prepared by O'Leary, Beaverbrook read it over and remarked that it appeared to be all right. McIvor then carefully explained that, if used in his paper, the material should be used as written or not at all. "You can leave everything to me," said Beaverbrook. Recalling the incident some forty-five years later, McIvor said, "His answer was one I wouldn't have taken in a million years today, but I was pretty inexperienced."

The blow fell the next morning when McIvor met Cockfield at breakfast. Cockfield handed him a copy of the *Daily Express*. On the front page was a blaring headline: "Warning to Housewives, Within a Few Weeks Millions of Bushels of Argentine Wheat Will Be Pouring Into This Country: Watch Out For Holes In The Bread." Given the strict instructions from the prime minister not to disparage another country's wheat, they were aghast. "We spent a pretty miserable weekend."

Repercussions followed swiftly on Monday morning in the form of a call from the secretary of James Rank, head of a powerful milling industry in Britain: "Could you come along and see Mr. Rank?" When, in trepidation, McIvor arrived at Rank's office the only thing on his desk was a copy of the *Daily Express*. Rank, a Yorkshireman, turned the air blue cursing out Beaverbrook, whom he had been unable to reach, and asked McIvor what he had to say for himself. Knowing they were in the wrong and there was no use trying to explain, McIvor replied, "Nothing." Momentarily stumped, Rank concluded the interview: "You mean you have nothing to say for yourself? Then I guess our conversation is at an end."

But as he escorted McIvor to the door, Rank took him by the arm and said, "It was a bloody good piece of propaganda." The next Friday McIvor was invited to spend the weekend at Rank's country estate in Surrey. It marked the beginning of a warm friendship that was to pay dividends in the sale of Canadian wheat to Britain in the future. Without intending to do so, Beaverbrook had done McIvor a great favour.

But for McIvor and Cockfield the ordeal was not over. After leaving Rank's office, McIvor was summoned by Vincent Massey, Canada's high commissioner in London, to explain the *Daily Express* story. Feeling that he "might as well go down with my guns blazing," McIvor explained that he had been "double crossed by your friend Beaverbrook," which did not sit well with Massey. McIvor then had to write a long report to Murray in Winnipeg and nervously wait some ten days for a reply. Murray's eventual response came in the form of a cable: "Received your letter. Keep up the good work."[22]

McIvor returned to Britain in October of 1936 to supervise the promotional and advertising campaign that he had recommended following his first visit. At that time, R.V. Biddulph was appointed European commissioner to the board with headquarters in London in order to have a board presence in the world's major import market.

With the closing price for No. 1 Northern remaining above ninety cents a bushel during the 1936-1937 crop year, the board did not take any deliveries after the ninety-cent rule was implemented by the government on August 28, 1936. While 617,655 bushels of 1936 wheat crop had been delivered to the board prior to that date, an opportunity was given to producers to take back title to the wheat or settle at the open market price. As a result producers took back title on 559,664 bushels while 57,991 bushels were settled at the market price.

In the process of handling that limited quantity of the 1936 crop, and for various incidentals, the board incurred a loss of $49,574.88. During the year the board also disposed of a substantial amount of the holdings taken over from Canadian Co-operative Wheat Producers. With 82,667,891 bushels on hand at the beginning of the crop year, only 6,964,000 bushels remained at July 31, 1937. The end result was that the board showed a surplus of $25,485,526.66 from the sale of the stocks taken over from CCWP in December 1935. When the amount of $15,856,645.35, to repay the advance to the board by the government on the CCWP stocks was deducted, it left a net profit of $9,628,881.31.[23] John I. McFarland's stabilization operation had been justified in absentia.

As the 1936-1937 crop year came to a close, the total carryover of wheat in Canada was down to a mere 32,937,991 bushels with another poor crop in sight. The persistent drought of the decade was to take its bitterest toll in 1937. It was the lowest crop since 1914, at a meagre 156.5 million bushels. Saskatchewan was the hardest hit province, with an average yield of only two-and-a-half bushels per acre producing a scanty 37 million bushels. There was not even enough grain in that province for seed to plant the upcoming 1938 crop.

The crop disaster, combined with the political ploy of the Liberal government when setting the 1936-1937 initial payment, was to prolong the life of the Canadian Wheat Board, which now hung by a very slender thread. Having to all intents and purposes eliminated the board from the market by means of the ninety-cent rule, and giving as a reason the desire not to prejudge the findings of the Turgeon commission, the government was caught in a dilemma.

His objective of disposing of the stabilization stocks completed, in early July 1937, Murray submitted his resignation as chief commissioner. McIvor also submitted his resignation. The issue of terminating the board, which the government ardently desired, was again brought to the fore. The matter came to a head at a cabinet meeting of July 14. Minutes, prepared by E.A. Pickering, an assistant private secretary to cabinet, outlined the decision:

> Decided to continue skeleton board. Murray's resignation to be accepted. McIvor to be Chairman; and vacancy to be filled by nominal appointment, without salary, perhaps by civil servant. Arrangements of last year to be continued, price 87 1/2 cents per bushel. Wheat to be taken only when price below 90 cents. Intention of Council to abolish Board altogether when Turgeon report submitted, if report so recommends. Euler to draft statement setting forth decision of Council, and available for giving Press after Council Wednesday. General opinion of government against continuing Wheat Board. Reason for continuing temporarily to enable government to get wheat enough for distribution for seed grain purposes, also to have Board in existence, pending Turgeon report. Ralston and other legal opinion, that nothing compulsory in legislation.[24]

In the interim, McIvor had again gone to Britain to clear up some of the affairs of the board. When he left Winnipeg the crop in the West was deteriorating, but the extent of the disaster was not yet apparent. He had taken his wife with him and, after completing board business, uncertain as to his future plans, they decided to take a holiday in Scotland. Along with Biddulph they motored north and stopped at Preston.

They checked into the hotel the first evening and went down to the dining room where the headwaiter informed McIvor that the telephone operator had been trying to get him. Returning the call from Biddulph's secretary in London, McIvor was told that Euler wished to contact him urgently. When he telephoned Euler in Ottawa, McIvor was informed that the crop had deteriorated to the extent of a national disaster and was asked if he would take over as chief commissioner. He was requested to return to Canada by the first boat and to stop in Ottawa on his way to Winnipeg.[25] The holiday was over before it began. After his return to Ottawa in mid-July, McIvor discussed the situation with the cabinet committee on wheat and agreed to accept the position of chief commissioner.

Since it was apparent that seed would be required over a wide area, it was decided that the board would retain its remaining holdings of 6,964,000 bushels of futures contracts and exchange them for physical wheat for seed purposes. Most of the seed wheat was acquired from southern Alberta, which had not suffered as severely from the drought. Emphasis was placed on acquistion of the newer variety, Thatcher, because of its rust resistance. That decision was fortuitous because Thatcher demonstrated its value in the rust areas in 1938 where other varieties were either wholly or partially destroyed by rust.[26]

Acquistion and distribution of the seed grain constituted the principal activity of the board in the 1937-1938 crop year, since closing prices remained well above the ninety-cent level during the year and no deliveries were made to the board. The board staff had been reduced to some thirty-five employees, and at the suggestion of McIvor, the board's comptroller, R.C. Findlay, was appointed assistant chief commissioner.

In addition to conversion of the futures for seed, the board purchased seed grain from elevator companies wherever possible and sold it to the provincial government in Saskatchewan. A total of 15,659,462 bushels was handled for seed distribution. This included not only spring wheat, but also seed and feed requirements for coarse grains and for purchase and transportation of seed oats to Quebec. The federal government came to the assistance of the hard-hit Saskatchewan government by guaranteeing that province's bank loans for purchase of the seed. The western producers, over time, repaid the loans.[27]

During the year, the board, in co-operation with the Board of Grain Commissioners for Canada, acquired and arranged for the handling and transportation of approximately twenty-four thousand bushels each of Thatcher and Coronation wheat to Britain for milling test purposes. Biddulph handled the program from the London office, and Geddes once more went to Britain to supervise the tests. Despite the fact that the disastrous crop meant little wheat was available for export and that the proportion of Canadian wheat used in the British miller's mix was bound to drop to a very low percentage, the advertising campaign to encourage the use of Canadian wheat in the United Kingdom was continued.

As the rescue operation was being carried out on the drought- and rust-stricken plains, the grain inquiry commission headed by Mr. Justice Turgeon, was sporadically carrying on its investigations. Because Turgeon was also working on the textile industry investigation, the report did not reach the government until May 4, 1938.

As anticipated, the Turgeon report gave the open trade a clean bill of health. In the lengthy report which ran to 264 pages with appendices, Turgeon declared that he was "convinced, from all the knowledge I have been able to acquire on the subject, that the futures trading system, despite its imperfections, is the one best qualified to look after the interests of our producers, at home and abroad."[28]

Turgeon referred at length to the evidence of McFarland that the best policy was to continue the futures market, under supervision, with the present Wheat Board in operation, and to the evidence of Murray, who favoured supervised futures trading and voluntary co-operative pooling. Turgeon wrote:

> I am therefore of the opinion that under what may be called normal conditions—open markets in the United Kingdom, a fair relationship between world supply and import demand, and no danger clouds on the immediate horizon—the Government should remain out of the grain trade, and our wheat should be marketed by means of the futures marketing system (under proper supervision), and encouragement given to the creation of co-operative marketing associations, or Pools.[29]

The report had been completed, however, in the shadow of recurring surplus. While prices had risen to above $1.50 several times during the previous winter, they had begun a decline after Easter. The decline began after the secretariat of the Wheat Advisory Committee in London forecast a declining world wheat trade, which was expected not to exceed 520 million bushels. On the other hand, production had rebounded in the United States, promising to reach 900 million bushels, while crop acreages in Europe had been expanded and total world yield promised to be substantially higher.

Referring to these developments, Turgeon was obliged to look at the near future and add to his report:

> For all these reasons (and notwithstanding the adverse considerations to which I have referred in relation to government Boards) I do not feel that I can suggest the immediate dissolution of the Canadian Wheat Board. There is a strong possibility that conditions may develop which

> will require a measure of assistance in the marketing of the coming crop, and I do not know, of course, how long these conditions may continue after the final chapter of this report is written.[30]

In an appendix to the report, Turgeon finally put to rest McFarland's charge of protection of the speculative shorts. "I find, on the whole of the evidence that the members of the Board cannot be said to have protected speculative short interests in the Winnipeg wheat market in December 1935."[31]

Turgeon's recommendation that the government should remain out of grain marketing when there were "no danger clouds on the immediate horizon," was an ironic note pointing up the isolationist complacency that pervaded the North American scene of the period. As early as January of that same year, the British government was casting an apprehensive eye on the growing militancy of Adolf Hitler and Nazi Germany. The Canadian government was already in possession of a secret memorandum from the British government outlining proposed procedures, including a ministry of food for purchase of imported food supplies for Britain, in the event of war. The secret memorandum pointed out that, in such an eventuality, a food controller would become the sole buyer of wheat and cereals. It posed the question of whether it was possible under these circumstances to suspend private trading on the Winnipeg Grain Exchange, and the possibility that some central authority, such as the Canadian Wheat Board, might have to intervene to undertake the sale of wheat to the United Kingdom.[32]

The memorandum received scant attention in Ottawa, and McIvor was only to learn of its existence in May 1939 while on a visit to London. James Rank gave the chief commissioner a copy of the memorandum and pointedly asked what action the Canadian government intended to take. McIvor submitted a memorandum to Ottawa, outlining possible alternatives on the British request, but it provoked no immediate reaction. Armed with the recommendations it had so ardently hoped for from the Turgeon commission, the King government was apparently too preoccupied with efforts to extricate itself from wheat marketing responsibility to pay heed to the concerns in Britain.

The same circumstances which had persuaded Turgeon not to recommend the immediate dissolution of the board were now plaguing King and the wheat committee of cabinet in reaching a decision on policy for the 1938 crop. The relief seed operation had been successful and nature had relented, resulting in the prospect of the best crop since 1932, but farmers in the West were still in severe economic distress from the impact of the 1937 disaster.

With wheat prices rapidly declining in the face of a record world wheat crop, the government was faced with the question of whether to provide direct relief to farmers in the West, or to continue the Canadian Wheat Board with a guaranteed minimum price which would result in a loss to the treasury. The dilemma was succinctly outlined in an entry of July 19, in King's diary after a visit to Dunning who was ill. "He [Dunning] advised strongly to fix an .80 rate for wheat, saying that anything between .70 and .80 would hardly prove adequate to meet conditions likely to grow out of the enormous world crop of this year. We would be saving relief in the end by giving State help to the producers."[33]

Following the release of the Turgeon report, the prairie pools had indicated their reluctance to reinstitute co-operative pooling without a guarantee of the initial payment from the federal government. They met in July with the wheat committee of cabinet and asked that the Wheat Board be reactivated. The pools requested that it be authorized to accept wheat, irrespective of the market price, and that the initial payment should be not lower than the prevailing market price, which was then above ninety cents.[34]

On July 5, King announced the intention of the government to reactivate the Wheat Board for the 1938-1939 crop year. But, within cabinet there was an East-West cleavage on the rate of the initial payment. At a cabinet meeting on July 26, the eastern ministers generally advocated an 80-cent level, while Gardiner sought retention of the current level of 87 1/2 cents.[35] Euler had earlier requested a recommendation from McIvor who, making a realistic grainman's analysis of market trends, had recommended a 60-cent level.

In his diary King added an interesting notation on the July 26 cabinet meeting. "It was agreed that Gardiner should seek to have the pools ask the Government to legislate respecting the grain exchange, and to peg the price of wheat, each year, leaving the sales to the pools instead of to a Government Board. He believed he can get them to do this, and that the Government should get out of the grain business before another year, in this way."[36]

The final compromise reached by King and his cabinet colleagues was a courageous one. They would set the initial payment level at eighty cents, despite the inevitable prospect of heavy cost to the treasury. In announcing the cabinet decision, King emphasized that "there will be no hoarding...of wheat by the Canadian Wheat Board. It will be sold as fast as delivered, with no restrictions."[37]

There was little criticism in the West, despite the fact that the initial price had been lowered from 87 1/2 cents, but reaction from the East was immediate. Premier Hepburn of Ontario declared the decision to be "absolutely assinine," and called for operations of the Wheat Board to be extended to Ontario. "Certainly. If we are going to be crazy let us be crazy all over the country."[38]

Early estimates of the cost to the treasury ranged from $20 million to $40 million. But given the disparity between the initial price and open market prices, which were well below the initial price, the producers delivered all of their wheat to the board. Deliveries to the board totalled 292,360,030 bushels, of which 86,539,554 bushels remained unsold at the end of the crop year on July 31, 1939. The cost to the federal treasury was a whopping $61,525,691.

As those costs were mounting, Gardiner set about to lobby the pools to put pressure on the government and to prepare legislation for the 1939 session of Parliament which would rid Ottawa of its unwanted wheat marketing responsibility. It was now abundantly clear to the government that a voluntary Wheat Board could have only one result. In outlining a history of the wheat position in later years, Jimmy Gardiner noted that "the trade received the profits—government took the losses," when he wrote:

> The result was that when the Board set an initial payment which turned out to be above the "world price" the Board got all the wheat and paid a subsidy to the producer equal to the difference between the "world price" and the Board payment; when the Board payment was lower than "world price" the Board got no wheat and the trade received all the wheat and hence all the profit.
>
> This resulted in the Treasury covering all the deficits and the trade taking all profits. This is what I mean by saying the legislation obtained in 1935 was a triumph for the advocates of speculation.[39]

As the government prepared to announce the 1938-1939 initial payment, they faced another problem. During the relative inactivity of the previous year, the staff of the Canadian Wheat Board had been decimated, and McIvor, knowing the uncertain future for the board, again indicated his desire to resign. Shaw had already left to accept a position in Ottawa. On the advice of Murray, who was still actively advising the wheat committee of cabinet, Euler, Gardiner, and Crerar undertook to persuade McIvor to remain as chief commissioner. McIvor consented and recommended that W. Charles Folliott, who had been associated with McIvor on the sales staff of the pool's Central Selling Agency, replace Dean Shaw. That appointment was confirmed by order-in-council on August 31, 1938.

Gardiner lost no time in getting down to his task of convincing the pools to resume co-operative pooling. He met in Regina on August 9, 1938, with representatives of the three provincial pools and "candidly informed the Pool directors of the government's dissatisfaction in the way in which the wheat board legislation had worked out, and its awareness that alternative machinery needed to be explored in the search for a permanent policy."[40]

Gardiner pursued the discussions throughout that fall and early winter on the co-operative marketing proposal. But while he was implicitly seeking to terminate the board, the pool directors and delegates accepted his proposal for resumption of co-operative marketing under the protection of a government guarantee only conditionally. That acceptance was given on the understanding that the existing Canadian Wheat Board Act be left on the statute books in order that it could be reactivated in case of an emergency.

In his quest for a permanent policy to replace the board legislation, Gardiner was motivated primarily by what he perceived as an inequity in the distribution of government assistance to producers. He contended that those farmers with good crops benefitted from the guaranteed initial payment, while those hardest hit by drought and rust had no crop to deliver and therefore received little by way of assistance.

When Parliament resumed its session on January 12, 1939, the Speech from the Throne contained a short reference to proposed grain legislation. "Bills will be introduced to regulate grain exchanges along the lines laid down in the report of the royal commission on grain marketing, to revise the Canada Grain Act, and to assist further in the marketing of farm products."[41]

On February 15, Gardiner, who was to pilot the proposed legislation through the House, rose to make his major policy statement in the Commons. The statement indicated the imminent demise of the Canadian Wheat Board and provoked a storm of protest from the West. Gardiner announced that the government intended to introduce legislation which would "as far as possible" carry out the recommendations of the Turgeon commission. This included "First, that the government should remain out of the grain trade and that our wheat should be marketed by means of the futures marketing system; Second, that the grain exchange should be placed under proper supervision; Third, that encouragement be given to the creation of co-operative marketing associations or pools.[42]

In addition, the government would introduce a bill to deal with emergencies "...drafted on the principle that assistance will be given in proportion to need, calculated on an acreage basis...."[43]

Before Gardiner's policy statement, Manitoba Premier John Bracken had called a conference in Winnipeg to discuss the situation facing western agriculture. It was attended by some four hundred delegates who met from December 12 to 15, 1938. The conference struck a powerful continuing committee to give studied attention to western problems as they exist and as they may arise, the western Committee on Markets and Agricultural Readjustment. The committee then held meetings in Regina on January 21, 1939, and in Saskatoon on February 14. The meetings came down solidly for continuation of the Wheat Board for 1939-1940 and called for a guaranteed initial payment of eighty cents a bushel.

In the wake of Gardiner's policy statement, a delegation of twenty-two men representing the committee proceeded to Ottawa to meet with cabinet. Headed by Bracken, it included the top executives of the pools, United Grain Growers, and boards of trade and muncipal organizations. The private trade was also represented, including Mitchell Sharp for James Richardson & Sons, and George Heffelfinger and L.W. Brockington, for the North West Grain Dealers' Association.

On March 1 the Bracken committee met with King and ten of his ministers in the prime minister's East Block office. Brockington read the committee's submission which, in essence, recommended: (a) continuation of the Wheat Board, (b) a guaranteed initial payment of at least eighty cents, (c) subsidiary assistance for coarse grain producers, (d) assistance through crop insurance or other income support to producers adversely affected by crop failure.[44]

Mackenzie King was impressed by the presentation. "It was as fine a delegation as I have ever listened to."[45] Two days later, King received a delegation from the Winnipeg Grain Exchange, "who seemed more favorable to Gardiner's legislation than to the views expressed by the Bracken delegation."[46]

Gardiner, who had continued taking soundings from pool officials and the Saskatchewan government, was now disposed to admit defeat in his attempt to disband the board. In a letter of March 10 to King, he acknowledged the pressure that had built up and how little support he had received on his co-operative wheat marketing project.

Gardiner was now prepared to recommend continuation of the Canadian Wheat Board, but with the subsidy element in the initial payment diverted into an acreage bonus. He would achieve that objective by reducing the initial payment to sixty cents a bushel and by using the federal monies saved by that reduction to institute the acreage bonus. That recommendation was to provoke another storm of protest when the sixty-cent level was incorporated into a bill to amend the Canadian Wheat Board Act, presented for first reading on March 27.

The Saskatchewan Wheat Pool circulated a petition and obtained 155,000 signatures from producers urging retention of the eighty-cent initial payment. As reports of dissatisfaction poured in from the West, the Bracken committee, armed with the petition, took up the cause and once more met with King and his cabinet. Gardiner stuck by his guns, and his determination to retain his legislative program precipitated a head-on clash between Gardiner and Revenue Minister J.L. Ilsley in cabinet, during which Gardiner threatened to resign. It took the intervention of King and Crerar to break up the conflict. A cabinet compromise was reached in the end on Crerar's recommendation of seventy cents for the initial payment.

The bill which finally emerged to amend the Canadian Wheat Board Act was forged in the political atmosphere of a forthcoming general election, but it still did not appease a number of western members of the Liberal caucus. Five of them, including W.R. Motherwell, voted against it on second reading. The Act finally passed on May 15, and was given royal assent on June 3, 1939. The essential features in the Act were: 1) The initial payment of seventy cents a bushel, plus the issuance of non-transferable participation certificates, was made statutory and, for the first time, was based on delivery for No. 1 Northern at Vancouver as well as at Fort William-Port Arthur; 2) the first delivery quota was introduced with a limitation of five thousand bushels to any one producer, beyond which no producer had access to the board's initial payment; 3) the provisions of the Act were extended to the eastern division to accomodate Ontario producers. (The latter clause replaced one which had given the federal cabinet authority to extend the provisions of the Act to oats, barley, rye and flaxseed, which was now repealed.)

Companion legislation passed at the 1939 session included the Grain Futures Act, the Wheat Co-operative Marketing Act, and the

Prairie Farm Assistance Act. It comprised the package that Gardiner had hoped would serve as a permanent policy replacing the Wheat Board.

The Grain Futures Act provided for supervision of trading on the Winnipeg Grain Exchange by the Board of Grain Commissioners for Canada. Although it was proclaimed August 1, 1939, it never came into effect. No supervisor was appointed and the legislation remained dormant.

The Wheat Co-operative Marketing Act, designed to encourage restoration of the co-operative marketing pools, was scarcely less effective. While the three provincial pools, the North West Line Elevator Association, and several individual elevator companies entered into an agreement with the government to institute such pools, they did not prove popular with the farmers who had three delivery options. It was estimated that the trade-operated pools received only one per cent of the deliveries, while 70 to 75 per cent went to the board and the remainder to the open market. When in 1940 the five thousand-bushel delivery limitation to the board was removed, the voluntary pools became dormant.

The Prairie Farm Assistance Act was more successful and provided a much-needed supplementary farm income support against disasters. The Act provided for a one per cent levy on all grain deliveries to which would be added contributions from the federal treasury. In its final form, the Act provided two bases for relief in that it took into account both economic and crop emergency disasters. Cabinet could declare a national emergency if the average price of wheat dropped below eighty cents per bushel. Payments would then be based on a sliding scale, dependent upon the average yield in a given township, on up to one-half the cultivated acreage or not more than 200 acres per farm. The second formula covered crop failure assistance. In any year that the average yield of wheat was five bushels per acre or less in 135 townships in Saskatchewan or 100 townships in Alberta or Manitoba, the area could be declared a crop disaster area. In that event a minimum of $200 and up to a maximum of $500 per farm could be paid out of the fund, depending upon the size of the cultivated acreage.

The legislative package of 1939 was to prove the last time the federal government would make an all-out effort to rid itself of involvement in the marketing of Canadian grain. It had tried and failed. Although the King government would continue to cherish the hope that the status quo prior to 1930 might be returned, it was to prove a vain hope. In Europe, events were moving swiftly toward the cataclysm of the Second World War, and the Canadian Wheat Board was to play a major role in that struggle.

FORGED IN THE FIRE

Although up to this time the Liberal administration had consistently displayed a theoretical bias in favour of the open market system of selling wheat, it found itself at length compelled to go the whole distance and to place sole responsibility upon the Canadian Wheat Board for disposing of Canada's wheat crop.

— MacGibbon, *The Canadian Grain Trade 1931-1951*

▪

Outside in the still unfamiliar blackout, Londoners cautiously edged their way through the drizzling rain of a cold November evening. In the early winter of 1939 the relative peace of the "phoney war" prevailed, but the pleasure seekers in London's West End carried the mandatory gas masks slung over their shoulders—a constant reminder that the calm could be broken by the shrill wail of sirens signalling an air raid.

Behind the blackout curtains in the elegant Carlton Hotel—soon to be destroyed by Luftwaffe bombs—Tom Crerar and George McIvor sat finishing a late dinner in Crerar's room. They, along with a powerful delegation headed by Crerar, had sailed for England on McIvor's forty-fifth birthday, October 20, to attend the first Empire War Conference.[1] One of the objectives of the mission was to establish a compatible working basis with Britain on the shipment of Canadian wheat, following Ottawa's decision to maintain sales through the Winnipeg Grain Exchange.

At the outset of war on September 3, 1939, the Liverpool Exchange was closed. James Rank, head of the British cereals purchasing committee, cabled McIvor to ask what action the Canadian government would take with respect to the Winnipeg Grain Exchange. After consulting with Ottawa, McIvor informed Rank on September 5, that it was the Canadian government's intention that the Winnipeg exchange remain open for the present. The cabinet committee on wheat was reluctant to close the exchange, in part because of the delivery options then open to western producers, who could deliver to the board up to the five thousand bushel limitation, or to the open market or company sponsored pools. Due to the five thousand bushel limitation on board deliveries, those farmers delivering above that amount had to rely on the futures market for hedging sales on the open market.

Thus, the federal government resisted closing down the futures market, despite the urging of the prairie pools to do so. The pools insisted that the initial price of seventy cents was too low in peacetime and far too low in wartime. A committee of their executive met with cabinet and asked that direct negotiations be entered into with the British government on a parity price related to the cost of inputs purchased by the farmers, but the cabinet remained firm in its decision to retain the open market.

The decision to retain the open market through the Winnipeg Grain Exchange rather than to negotiate on an agency-to-agency basis was received coldly in London. For a period, Rank's purchasing committee responded by making no purchases of wheat from Canada, while at the same time purchasing wheat from other sources, including Argentina and Australia. The government also issued orders to British millers that they regulate and decrease the percentage of Canadian wheat used in their grists. While the British had contracted for ten million bushels of wheat, in direct negotiations with the Canadian Wheat Board prior to the outbreak of war, the hiatus in further purchasing posed a dilemma for the Canadian government.

As a series of lengthy telegrams passed between Mackenzie King and Britain's Prime Minister Neville Chamberlain in an attempt to solve the impasse, McIvor, Folliott, and the board's secretary, T.W. Grindley, had been in Ottawa discussing the situation with a newly formed economic advisory committee. As a result, the decision was taken to offer to facilitate purchase by the British of at least sixty million bushels of wheat through the open market. To assure the British authorities that this could be done without too rapid a run up in prices, the Canadian Wheat Board would agree to give exporters overnight protection against half of the sales made each day. This meant that the board would be providing half of the wheat necessary to fill the British order and the other half would be supplied by the trade, particularly by farmers who had wheat to sell over and above what they may have delivered to the Wheat Board. The advantage of the arrangement was that the board would be sharing with others the responsibility of determining the prices at which the British purchases were made.[2]

Feeling that the formula proposed was unnecessary and complicated, the British purchasing agency still held back and asked why it could not buy directly from the board, as it had done for the ten million bushels purchased the previous August. Over several weeks, McIvor relayed messages through the board's London office in an effort to have the British make a firm commitment for sixty million bushels before the close of navigation on the St. Lawrence. But, even if the British had accepted the offer, it could not have been fulfilled that autumn. In proposing such a large offer Ottawa had not taken into account the disruption in shipping occasioned by the onset of war. The German submarine campaign had begun at the outbreak of hostilities and ships had to move in convoy. There were delays in arming merchant ships, and assembly of the slow-moving convoys took further time.

Because of the difficulties over purchasing and shipping, the British cereals board had purchased only seven million bushels of Canadian wheat by November 1 through the open market. There were not enough ships to move this quantity, plus the ten million bushels purchased in August, out of St. Lawrence ports before the close of navigation. It was this situation that prompted the inclusion of McIvor in the Canadian delegation to the Empire War Conference in London. The decision to send McIvor resulted in a change of membership of the board on October 26, when C. Gordon Smith was appointed assistant chief commissioner to replace R.C. Findlay, who remained as comptroller of the board.

Crerar and McIvor met with British authorities for discussions on the shipping problems that arose out of the the congestion at St. Lawrence ports and established a compatible working basis on the purchasing problem. McIvor then remained in London while Crerar accompanied the military delegates to northern France where the allied armies were dispersed behind the presumed security of the Maginot Line. Along with representatives of other Commonwealth countries, and led by Secretary of State for Dominion Affairs Anthony Eden, the party inspected that vast, interconnected series of forts and underground installations stretching across the eastern frontier of France to the border of neutral Belgium. Built at vast expense as a safeguard against German intrusion, it was considered an impregnable rampart against the Nazi military might which had overwhelmed Poland at the outbreak of war in a lightning blitzkrieg.

On his return to London, Crerar, now an elder statesman and deputy prime minister, called and asked McIvor to have dinner with him in his room at the Carlton Hotel on that cold November evening. Crerar showed obvious signs of agitation throughout the dinner. Finally he rose, lit a cigar, and began to pace the room. Pausing, Crerar turned and revealed the cause of his agitation. "George," he said, "I'm only a country boy from Manitoba, but I don't think that Maginot Line is any good. I don't like it, they'll just go round it."[3] While Crerar's concern was with the overall tactical situation, McIvor's grain-trading instincts were immediately alert.

At the beginning of the mission, discussions had been instituted at the British cabinet level on a long-term bulk contract for Canadian wheat. The discussions arose after Sir Norman Vernon, a confidant of Prime Minister Chamberlain and head of a large milling concern in Britain, broached the subject with R.V. Biddulph, the board's European representative, during an evening walk.[4]

Biddulph relayed the proposal for a long-term contract to McIvor, who in turn discussed it with Crerar. As a result, preliminary discussions were held with representatives of the British cabinet. In a cable to Ottawa dealing with the shipping situation, Crerar mentioned that "sources superior to Rank's Purchasing Committee have suggested that the present open market methods be discontinued and bulk contract for year's supply be entered into with Canadian Wheat Board...."[5]

The cabinet wheat committee in Ottawa promptly consulted with J.R. Murray, now a special adviser to the government on grain policy, and with the Wheat Board commissioners in Winnipeg. There were signs of a deteriorating crop in the United States due to drought and the possibility of a consequent strengthening of prices; they were cool to the proposal. Also, the government remained reluctant to close futures trading on the Winnipeg Grain Exchange which a large long-term contract would have necessitated. As a result the negotiations lapsed.

Crerar's expressed fear of an end-run around the Maginot Line triggered an immediate response in McIvor's mind: "If they go round it, gone are all the wheat markets in Europe in one blow." Interrupting Crerar's train of thought, he said, "Let's talk about wheat. I think we should have a contract with Britain. I've changed my mind." When Crerar asked why, McIvor expressed his concern on the loss of all the European markets except Great Britain, "and we still have millions of bushels of wheat back in Canada."[6]

Crerar immediately switched from his former reluctance to enter into a long-term contract. The result was a meeting with other members of the delegation in Britain, which included Lester B. "Mike" Pearson as its secretary. They came to the conclusion that Canada should enter into a long-term contract. Negotiation presented some difficulties since James Rank, chairman of the British Cereals Purchasing Committee, was now satisfied with the arrangements worked out for the use of the open market and was opposed to such a contract. Despite that, an offer was made to the Ministry of Food in London. Details of two alternative proposals made to the British ministry were outlined in a lengthy cable sent by Crerar to Prime Minister King December 2, 1939.

The first proposal involved the sale of between 250 million and 300 million bushels of wheat at one dollar a bushel, basis No. 1 Northern, Fort William, Port Arthur, and the alternative covered the sale of between 150 million to 180 million bushels at a price of 93 1/2 cents. The cable emphasized that it was very important that the offers be kept entirely secret and that any cables from McIvor's colleagues in Winnipeg be directed through the prime minister in Ottawa.[7]

The cable prompted the cabinet committee on wheat to summon Smith, the new assistant chief commissioner, and Murray to Ottawa for discussions. McIvor and Crerar anxiously awaited a reply in London. It came in the form of a cable from Trade Minister Euler on December 5: "At meeting here today attended by Ralston,

Gardiner, Howe, Euler, Smith and Murray opinion unanimous that both proposals your cable number 732 December 2nd unsatisfactory.''[8]

The offer to the British cabinet was withdrawn to the great relief of Rank, who was convinced that the market price would drop. He told McIvor that he was ''relieved that the bloody thing had ended.''[9] Disappointed at the result, the Canadian delegation sailed for home in mid-December. Crerar's premonition and McIvor's concern were shortly to be borne out. On May 10, 1940, Hitler's forces invaded Belgium and the Netherlands. They bypassed the Maginot Line in a lightning campaign. All of the markets of Continental Europe were gone by early summer.

The trip home in December 1939 was to be just one of the many hazardous crossings of the Atlantic that McIvor would undertake during the course of World War II while he was on Canadian Wheat Board business. Some crossings were sixteen-hour flights in bombers, with oxygen masks on all the way. Bundled up against the freezing cold in long johns and flying suits, sitting on the floor, passengers were unable to see the crew for mail piled up in the cabin. On one occasion an engine failure forced a return to Montreal's Dorval airport.[10]

During the return voyage in 1939, the ship zig-zagged across the submarine-infested Atlantic with the added knowledge that the pocket battleship *Graf Spee* had broken free into the ocean shipping lanes. One of the most powerful warships afloat, the *Graf Spee* was preying on merchant shipping. Shortly after sailing, they turned back when a ship with two funnels—a feature of the *Graf Spee*—was sighted on the horizon. When they were fifty miles apart, it was discovered that it was a sister Empress ship, and the journey resumed. Under wireless silence to prevent detection by the roving U-boat wolf packs, they could, however, still receive messages. Half-way across they were relieved to hear that the *Graf Spee* had been scuttled off Montevideo on December 17, after being damaged in an engagement with three Royal Navy cruisers.

When they arrived at St. John's, they found that the wheat market had slumped. While waiting to take a train to Montreal, Crerar drew McIvor aside for a talk: ''George, you and I have got to have an understanding that you're not going to bring up this wheat contract with your colleagues and I'm not going to bring it up with mine. It's finished.'' While in retrospect, and in light of ensuing events, a long-term contract would have proven fortuitous, McIvor later said he attached no blame to anyone: ''It was a case of two different environments. I was in Europe next to the Maginot Line. The advisers in Canada, including my two Board members, were watching the Kansas crop blow up. I don't criticize their judgement for a moment. The environment was so different.''[11]

McIvor has related another sidelight to that frustrating trip. Prior to his departure from England, Major-General Price J. Montague, deputy chief of staff for the Canadian army came into McIvor's hotel room. His wife was dying of cancer in Winnipeg. He threw a parcel on the bed saying, ''Take that home to the old girl, and tell her I still love her.'' Choked with emotion and unable to say more, Montague turned and left.

Mike Pearson then appeared with a large suitcase. He and his family had been on holiday in Canada when war was declared. Pearson returned to his post in London, leaving his wife and children with Mrs. Pearson's parents in Winnipeg. As a consequence, the children's winter clothing was still in England. Pearson hated to ask, but would McIvor take them back with him, as he couldn't afford to outfit them again. ''Of course. I'd be delighted.'' The load was gathering. At the dock Rank's chauffeur appeared with a large box containing a whole smoked salmon as a present for McIvor.

When McIvor arrived home at 6 AM Christmas morning 1939, after catching an overnight air force flight from Montreal, he was carrying a heavy load. His wife met him at the airport. After breakfasting at Childs restaurant, they delivered the Pearson children's winter clothes, to the delight of Mrs. Pearson. Finally, there was the more sombre task of delivering Price Montague's gift to his wife before going home to celebrate Christmas with their own family.

The long-term contract incident, which arose from Crerar's prescience regarding the vulnerability of the supposedly impregnable Maginot Line, eventually faded from the scene. However, the realization that a collapse could occur in Europe was a major factor in the institution of the first acreage-based delivery quotas which remain an essential feature of the Canadian Wheat Board operation today.[12]

Although the initial German offensive had ended with the overrunning of Poland, and the land fighting had settled into the false calm behind the Maginot Line, the Battle of the Atlantic was being waged full scale. Shipping was in short supply and forced to move in time-consuming convoys. McIvor found on his return to Canada that serious congestion in the grain handling system was progressively worsening.

The 1939 crop was the second largest on record, and total

country deliveries reached 416 million bushels during the crop year. Although prices fluctuated above and below the seventy-cent initial payment, the board received the bulk of the marketings with deliveries of 342 million bushels added to a carryover of 86.5 million bushels

Modernization comes to the harvest scene. A McCormick-Deering Harvester Thresher, forerunner of the modern combine, is shown being drawn by an early tractor with steel-lugged wheels.

at the beginning of the 1939-1940 crop year. The slow export movement left Lakehead terminals badly congested, and wheat stored in the St. Lawrence ports had to be diverted by rail to Atlantic ports for winter shipment. With an unsold carryover of 300 million bushels anticipated, it became obvious that a new delivery policy would have to be devised before the start of the 1940-1941 crop year. As planning on new policy went forward, the King government called an election and, on March 26, 1940, the Liberals were returned with a substantial majority of 178 seats in the 245-seat House.

James A. MacKinnon was appointed minister of trade and commerce in the new cabinet succeeding W.D. Euler, who was appointed to the Senate. J.L. Ralston, who had returned to politics on the outbreak of war, was appointed finance minister. They now joined Gardiner and Crerar on the wheat committee of cabinet.

In June, Gardiner, who had been appointed minister of war

services in addition to his agriculture portfolio, made a bid to take over responsibility for the Canadian Wheat Board from MacKinnon. At the same time he suggested that the Winnipeg Grain Exchange be closed, direct contract negotiations be undertaken with the British purchasing agency, and that the initial payment be raised to ninety cents a bushel. He achieved none of those objectives.

In mid-July, MacKinnon had a detailed brief prepared by the Canadian Wheat Board for submission to cabinet. It pointed up the need for additional storage by way of annexes at country elevators, farm storage payments by way of incremental increases in the initial payment during the crop year, and called for elimination of the five thousand bushel limitation and implementation of a system of periodic delivery quotas to relieve congestion in the grain handling system. Cabinet concurrence in the board submission resulted in major amendments to the Canadian Wheat Board Act which were given royal assent on August 7, 1940.

The changes were: the five thousand bushel limitation on deliveries to the board was removed; provision for the making of an interim payment under certain conditions, and when such payment could be made without any possibility of loss or cost to the government; provision for storage payments on farm-stored wheat at a rate not greater than the established country elevator tariff rate; the board was given power to regulate deliveries by producers at country, mill and terminal elevators and loading platforms; the provision that the board sell continuously was deleted from the Act, ("Obviously, continuous sales are not possible under war conditions"); penalty clauses were made more severe; the board was made responsible for collection of a processing levy not to exceed fifteen cents per bushel on wheat utilized for domestic human consumption. The levy also applied to imported wheat and wheat products, which could only be imported by permission of the board, with proceeds of the levy to go into the ordinary revenues of the board.[13]

The amendments also provided for an eleven-member advisory committee in place of the seven members set out in the original Act. The advisory committee, which had been disbanded in 1935, was reactivated on August 27, 1940. The appointments represented a balance between pool and non-pool producers in the West, and also between the pools and the private trade. They included D.A. Campbell, Toronto, Ont., milling interests; Fred H. Clendenning, Vancouver, B.C., Pacific Coast shipping interests; Paul Farnalls, Halkirk, Alta., producers; Lew Hutchinson, Duhamel, Alta., producers; J.A.

McCowan, Summerberry, Sask., producers; D.G. McKenzie, Winnipeg, Man., producers; Rosario Messier, Contrecoeur, Que., Quebec consumers; Fred Pettypiece, Auld, Ont., Ontario producers; R.C. Reese, Winnipeg, Man., exporters; A.C. Reid, Winnipeg, Man., line elevator companies; J.H. Wesson, Regina, Sask., producers.

The amendment, giving the board powers to regulate deliveries, was to result in a profound change in the fundamental operations of the Canadian Wheat Board which, with refinements over the years, still constitutes an integral part of their marketing system. McIvor and the board's secretary T.W. Grindley were called to Ottawa when the new provisions were being drawn up. Told by the cabinet to put in some kind of system that would equalize opportunities of delivery for the farmers, McIvor and Grindley worked most of the night in a bedroom of the Chateau Laurier Hotel.

The system devised by McIvor and Grindley was accepted by cabinet, but it was not until they were enroute home to Winnipeg that the realization struck McIvor as to the profound change that was to take place in the wheat marketing system. Turning to Grindley he said, "Bill, I never thought of this till now, [but] this is going to change the whole grain movement of Western Canada. The guy up in the Peace River is going to be able to deliver just as quickly as the guy in Manitoba."[14]

Authorized by order-in-council PC 3750 on August 7, 1940, the regulations drawn up by the board specified that no wheat, oats, or barley could be delivered without a permit from the Canadian Wheat Board. Permits, obtained from an elevator agent, were not valid until a statutory declaration of the seeded acreage of each of the grains had been sworn before a justice of the peace, notary public, or commissioner of oaths. Distribution of the permit books began on August 7, and on the same date the board announced that the initial delivery quota would be five bushels per seeded acre of wheat, oats, and barley. The quotas were not interchangeable between the grains.

War conditions and the sharp contraction of the Continental market following the capitulation of France in mid-June made the imposition of delivery quotas a justifiable necessity. The situation in Canada was outlined in the August 7, announcement of the board:

> The extreme difficulties of the situation will be apparent when it is pointed out that at July 31, 1940 the carry-over of old wheat in Canada was about 270,000,000 bushels, with a further 20,000,000 or 25,000,000 bushels of Canadian wheat (in transshipment) in the United

States. The new wheat crop in the West is estimated at well over 400,000,000 bushels and there will be about 22,000,000 bushels more produced in Ontario. Our present elevator storage capacity is 424,000,000 but a deduction from this figure is necessary to provide working space. After allowance for temporary elevator annexes, and some additional storage in the United States, it is calculated that the net available storage capacity for the new crop will be 150,000,000 to 160,000,000 bushels.

The first quotas are patterned to fill this space and to enable every producer to deliver a portion of his crop at the outset. As additional storage space becomes available through exports or consumption, the quotas will be extended.[15]

Implementation of the acreage delivery quota system, which applied to all deliveries whether to the board or to the open market, was welcomed by most producers, particularly in parts of Saskatchewan and Alberta where access to Pacific ports had been sharply curtailed. Shipments out of the West Coast had been restricted at the outset of war and the terminals of Vancouver, Victoria, New Westminster, and later at Prince Rupert were utilized primarily as storage. In addition, the federal government's interior terminals at Edmonton, Calgary, and Lethbridge were filled in order to open space at country elevators. However, the quotas did not win universal approval.

McIvor reported that Murray, as a confirmed free trader, was aghast. ''He couldn't imagine the farmers going around with a book. It was just poison to him.'' McIvor, who consulted Murray on a weekly basis, made a point of meeting with him before the announcement was made and it resulted in a morning-long argument in the board offices. However, Murray finally came around and was eventually convinced of the merits of the delivery quotas.[16]

Many Manitoba farmers who previously enjoyed an advantage on deliveries, since the railways distributed box cars to points nearest the Lakehead shipping position at the outset of the season, were less than overjoyed. An indignation meeting was held at a downtown Winnipeg hotel where McIvor was called upon to defend the action of the board in instituting the delivery quotas. Facing the crowded room, and with the situation in Britain very much in his mind, the chief commissioner didn't pull any punches: ''I said that this was a very small price for producers in Western Canada to pay compared to the hardships of the people in the United Kingdom and surely we were all in the war effort together. Someone got up and moved a vote of confidence in the Board and the matter ended.''[17]

Under the impetus of war conditions, the structure of the Canadian Wheat Board was changing rapidly. Despite retention of the open market system, the board was now virtually in full control of all grain marketing. As the German blitzkrieg rolled through the low countries and into France in May 1940, and the remnants of the British Expeditionary Force were being evacuated under fire from Dunkirk, the market went into an abrupt decline. After consultation with Ottawa, the board asked the Winnipeg Grain Exchange to forbid trading in wheat futures below the closing prices of May 17.

The exchange immediately implemented the request. The May future was pegged at 70 3/8 cents, July at 71 3/8, and October at 75 5/8. In June minimum prices were fixed for cash wheat, and elevator companies stopped buying wheat at country points except for board account. In May 1940, the board made a sale of 50 million bushels to the United Kingdom, and in August made a further sale of 100 million bushels. Then, in May 1941, the board made a sale of 120 million bushels of wheat futures to Britain, the largest single wheat transaction in the history of the world's grain trade to that date. The Canadian Wheat Board was handling the bulk, if not all, of the export trade, leaving only domestic sales to the trade through the exchange.

Heavy shipping losses to German U-boats and shortage of shipping, combined with higher charter rates, made it obvious that in order to maintain vital supplies in Britain Canada was the logical source of supply. The shorter Atlantic route also predicated against shipments out of the West Coast and through Churchill, leaving the Lakehead and the Atlantic ports as mandatory shipping points for grain. The only grain moving out of West Coast ports went as ballast in shipments of lumber, and Churchill was used for storage to reduce congestion at other points. With Canada supplying the major portion of all imports into the U.K., British millers were now using 60 per cent, or more, of Canadian wheat in their grists.

Some measure of the perils associated with delivering vitally needed grain to Britain were related by McIvor. During one of his trips to London, the chief commissioner was sitting in the office of James Rank. "He [Rank] said, 'I'm certainly glad to see you. We got four full cargoes of wheat into Hull. We've been trying hard to get it in there, and it's something off my mind.' He hadn't any more than said that when the phone rang and he went to the phone and came back, and said, 'They've sunk them.' The Germans came over on a raid and down they went, all four of them in the harbor.''[18]

In Canada, the problem of storage was somewhat relieved during the 1940-1941 crop year by the building of annexes on country elevators. Generous tax concessions to the elevator companies allowed them to write off the cost of the annexes over two years. The additional space built during the crop year amounted to 97 million bushels. In addition the federal government entered into agreements with the elevator companies for the building of temporary storage space for 50 million bushels at Fort William and Port Arthur. Temporary storage space for another 3 million bushels was built at Sarnia, Ontario, and for 3 million bushels at Three Rivers, Quebec. Also, in accordance with the amendments to the Act, the Wheat Board provided for farm storage payments to producers at the same rate as applied on wheat stored in country elevators, namely 1/45 of a cent per bushel per day. This was accomplished by increasing the 70 cent initial payment by 1/2 cent increments during the crop year to a maximum of 6 cents by year end.

During the same year, the board also administered collection of the processing levy of fifteen cents a bushel on all wheat used for human consumption in Canada. Proceeds from the levy were incorporated into the board pool for wheat for payment to producers. By coincidence, the net revenues from the processing levy at approximately $5.9 million almost balanced the farm storage payments which amounted to $6.1 million.[19]

The increasing load thrust upon the Canadian Wheat Board, through administration of quotas and other legislated programs, resulted in an explosive growth in personnel. From a staff of approximately thirty-five employees at the outset of the war, personnel grew to approximately five hundred during the course of the conflict. Many were recruited from the private trade and co-operatives as the work load grew in conjunction with the ever growing responsibilities. Without a building of its own, the board was forced to seek space wherever it became available. In one case, the Midtown Building, a former automobile dealership on Edmonton Street in Winnipeg, was converted to office space to accomodate the staff increases.

On August 17, 1940, R.M. Mahoney, general manager of Manitoba Pool Elevators, was appointed supervisor of delivery quotas. Clive Davidson was placed in charge of the acreage department and A.L. Dyker, the first solicitor to the board, was named secretary of the newly-appointed advisory committee. (The young lawyer later enlisted in the Royal Canadian Air Force and was tragically killed in a training accident at Regina in June 1943.) Henry B. Monk replaced him as solicitor to the board in October 1942, and was still fulfilling that role when this history was written.

Administration of the new acreage quota system in 1940-1941 was not without incident. Hundreds of investigations were carried out into various transactions of producers, elevator agents, and others. Prosecutions were instituted in about two hundred and seventy cases during the crop year, and convictions were obtained in all but two cases. "The investigations and prosecutions had a noticeably discouraging effect on infractions of the regulations, and in the late winter and spring months few infractions could be found."[20]

More importantly, establishment of delivery quotas and issuance of permit books provided the government and the board with detailed information on the seeded acreages of some 235,000 producers in western Canada. This data proved invaluable, both in determination and administration of future policy, including the realization that quotas could prove to be an indirect, but effective, instrument for regulation of production without involving any compulsory reduction of acreage. As the year progressed, the need for such reduction in the area sown to wheat became apparent.

While quota restrictions on barley and oats were lifted within a few months, when it became apparent that the bulk of these crops would be required on farms for feed, wheat quotas were progressively increased to twenty bushels per acre up to April 17, 1941, after which they were declared open on April 21. Despite that, and the increase in emergency storage facilities, curtailment of wheat production, in some form or another, was clearly indicated by the beginning of 1941. The statistical position indicated a wheat carryover of half a billion bushels by the end of the crop year.

Impelled in part by government minimum price guarantees and other assistance, but probably more by farmers' recollection that the onset of World War I had precipitated demand and higher prices for wheat, wheat sowings had risen to a record 27,750,000 acres in 1940. But while the stalemate in military operations during the winter of 1939 had raised the expectation that demand might parallel that of the earlier war, that expectation was shattered by the lightning thrust of the German army which overran and occupied Continential Europe by June of 1940. This was to be an entirely different kind of war.

Not only had the wheat importing nations of Continental Europe been eliminated from the market by the German successes, but the source of much of Britain's adjacent supply of other agricultural products such as bacon, meats, dairy products, and eggs had been lost as Norway, Denmark, and the Netherlands fell under German domination. To compensate that loss, Canada, as the source of supply on the shortest supply route, would be called upon to increase livestock and dairy production, and hence coarse grains were needed. The structure of Canadian agriculture, both in terms of diversification and regionality, was to undergo a dramatic change.

In advance of the 1941-1942 crop year, urgent meetings in Ottawa produced a number of policy proposals. At the same time, the newly-organized Canadian Federation of Agriculture, the Wheat Board advisory committee, the prairie pools, and other organizations were submitting policy proposals. Speed was essential if the proposed measures were to influence the planting decisions of farmers in the upcoming season. The federal government announced the 1941-1942 crop policy in the Commons on March 12, 1941.

Trade Minister MacKinnon outlined the policy with respect to the Canadian Wheat Board. The dominion government, through the board, would continue to guarantee the initial payment of seventy cents a bushel on wheat but a limit on total deliveries of wheat, either to the board, to the open market or otherwise, would be set at 230 million bushels. The delivery quota system was to be maintained, with quotas based on sixty-five per cent of the 1940 acreage. The first quota was to be a general one, allowing for delivery of the same amount of wheat per acre from every farmer. However, the second and following quotas were to be set on proportions of the yield from the farmer's shipping point with high-yield areas having a higher quota per acre than low-yield areas. While the board would continue to pay storage to producers on the same basis as 1940-1941, it would be paid only on the undelivered portion of the 230 million bushels. No change was made in the fifteen cent per bushel processing levy.[21]

Although announced as part of the policy package, the fifteen cent processing levy was abruptly discontinued by order-in-council on July 31, 1941. The chief reason given was the necessity to forestall a threatened rise in bread prices.[22]

Agriculture Minister Gardiner followed with a policy statement on wheat acreage reduction payments and measures aimed at maintaining western farm income at a level of $325 million as agreed to by cabinet. Compensation was to be given in the form of acreage bonuses for land taken out of wheat and converted to summer fallow ($4 an acre) or to coarse grains or grass ($2 an acre) plus an additional sum of $2 for each acre summer fallowed or sown to coarse grains or grass in 1941 that was in grass or rye on July 1, 1942.[23]

While announcement of the 1941-1942 policy package was divided between the ministers of separate departments, in part because of a backstage power struggle over administration of wheat policy between Gardiner and other members of cabinet, it was significant in the light of the future fundamental role the board was to play in grain marketing. In effect, the board was separated from the responsibility for stabilization, or assurance of farm income when required, leaving it free to concentrate on its role of marketing grain at the best possible prices under existing market circumstances. Secondly, the acreage quota delivery system was to be used for the first time as part of a policy aimed at crop control, or diversification, through encouragement of more coarse grain production.

Given the urgency of that last objective and with the crop planting season fast approaching, the policy package was implemented by orders-in-council under the War Measures Act, rather than by separate legislation through the Commons. Immediately thereafter, a vigorous publicity campaign was carried out utilizing press releases, pamphlets, and advertising in support of wheat acreage reduction. The World War I slogan, "Wheat Will Win the War," was supplanted by "Less Wheat in 1941 Will Help Win the War." [24]

With emphasis now placed on livestock production, the federal government instituted another program in 1941 which, while not directly related to the western policy package, was to have future implications for the Canadian Wheat Board involvement in domestic feed grains policies. To encourage livestock production, particularly in bacon hogs, the government announced a Feed Freight Assistance Program. Under it, Ottawa paid one-half of the freight charges on western feed grains going to those provinces, provided the feed deficiency provinces in eastern Canada paid the other half. In the fall of 1941, it became apparent that feed shortages would present eastern livestock producers with increased difficulties in maintaining production, particularly under a proposed price-ceiling plan. By the end of 1941, therefore, the central government agreed to assume the full freight on the movement of practically all western feed grains moving east from the Lakehead to destinations in any of the eastern provinces and from Calgary and Edmonton west to British Columbia.[25]

As a result of the wheat acreage reduction program, the acreage sown to wheat in the prairie provinces was the lowest in fifteen years. It declined to 21,140,000 acres in 1941 compared to 27,750,000 acres in 1940, a reduction of about 24 per cent. Drought and extremely high temperatures in Alberta and Saskatchewan caused a rapid deterioration in the crop in June and July. Production of wheat dropped drastically to 296 million bushels in 1941, compared to 514 million bushels in the previous year, a reduction of 42 per cent.[26]

Since market prices remained steadily above the board's initial payment of seventy cents throughout the crop year, the board received only 100 million bushels, or 44 per cent, of the total country marketings of 227.9 million bushels. Normally, the open market deliveries would have hampered the board in fulfilling bulk contracts with the British central purchasing agency, but the backlog of stocks in board hands enabled them to carry them out competently. No purchases of futures were required on the exchange in that regard.

The Canadian Wheat Board made two sales of 120 million bushels of futures to Britain in the course of the year, and total exports of wheat and wheat flour amounted to 222,007,141 bushels, principally to the United Kingdom. Delivery quotas increased at a rapid rate following the general five-bushel opening quota, and all delivery points in the West were placed on an open delivery basis by December 4, 1941. Despite the short crop, the wheat carryover at the end of the crop year was only moderately offset, standing at 424 million bushels at July 31, 1942, as compared to 480 million bushels the previous year.

Meanwhile, the course of the war was taking a number of decisive turns. Unable to break the British in their island home by massive air attacks, and thwarted from invasion by the gallant stand of the Royal Air Force in the Battle of Britain, Hitler turned his onslaught against the Balkans. Then, in June 1941, Hitler's forces invaded the Soviet Union. As that fateful year drew to a close, a Japanese carrier force struck without warning at Pearl Harbor on December 7, 1941. The United States officially declared war on the Axis Powers of Germany, Italy, and Japan.

Against this backdrop of expanding global conflict, the Canadian Wheat Board was assuming an ever more complex role as new priorities arose. Impelled by the rapidly changing events, planning for the 1942-1943 crop year began early. The issues at stake were high. The dilemma facing the government was essentially to continue assurance of income to the wheat farmer, without an increase in price to precipitate a corresponding increase in wheat production. At the same time, diversification to feed grains was urgently required to fulfill the priority for meat, bacon, and dairy products. Additionally, spread of the war into the Pacific had cut off vital vegetable oil sources, and the requirement for fats and oils was critical.

Complicating the policy decision was the fact that, with wage and price controls in effect through the Wartime Prices and Trade Board, western grain producers' income was lagging behind that of others in the wartime economy, and manpower requirements were resulting in acute shortages of farm labour. Despite further subsidization of the grain sector by way of a $20 million acreage bonus through the Prairie Farm Assistance Act in late 1941 whereby western farmers were paid seventy-five cents an acre on up to half of their cultivated acreage, farmers' income failed to keep in step with the rest of the economy, and the Saskatchewan Wheat Pool instituted a massive petition. The campaign spilled over into Manitoba and Alberta and 185,000 signatures were obtained on the petition seeking parity prices for prairie farmers. Each farmer signing the petition contributed twenty-five cents toward sending delegates to Ottawa, and in February 1942, 403 delegates, aboard two special trains, descended on Ottawa to meet with the government.

With the farmers' delegation and other commodity organizations, including the Canadian Federation of Agriculture, the pools, United Grain Growers and the advisory committee of the board, seeking a minimum price of one dollar a bushel for wheat, the government, after several months of thorough consideration, introduced a broad-ranging package well in advance of seeding time.

On March 9, 1942, Trade Minister MacKinnon announced that the statutory initial payment for wheat would be raised, effective August 1, from seventy cents to ninety cents a bushel by an amendment to the Canadian Wheat Board Act. However, he began his announcement with an obvious understatement: "wheat production in 1942 cannot be regarded as an extremely urgent matter."[27] In consequence a limit of 280 million bushels was placed on deliveries through the quota system.

To stimulate a much-needed increase in coarse grains and oil seeds, there were further initiatives. The Canadian Wheat Board was empowered to buy Winnipeg barley futures or cash barley at a minimum of 60 cents per bushel, basis No. 1 or 2 Canada Western in store Fort William—Port Arthur, and a ceiling price of 64 3/4 cents was set. Similarly a minimum price of 45 cents and a maximum of 51 1/2 cents per bushel was set for oats.

Later in the crop year, on April 6, 1943, the board was given an additional duty when it was empowered to assess equalization fees against permits issued for the export of oats and barley, based on the difference between domestic prices and prices obtainable in the export market. The arrangement became necessary in the face of demand from the United States, where prices were not subject to control, and because the Winnipeg price had advanced to ceiling levels. The move assured that any disparity between Canadian and U.S. prices, beyond necessary forwarding costs, would not accrue to the trade and would be reflected back to the producers.

Changes in the oil seed sector were even more dramatic. In the face of growing wartime demand, trading in flaxseed futures and cash flax was terminated by order-in-council on August 28, in the first month of the crop year. The Canadian Wheat Board was designated as the only agency to receive flaxseed from producers at a fixed price of $2.25 per bushel, basis the Lakehead on No. 1 Canada Western. The board was also empowered to buy soybeans at $1.95 per bushel for No. 2 Yellow soybeans basis Toronto.

Additional duties imposed on the board did not stop there. Another order-in-council, issued October 16, 1942, charged the board with administration of drawbacks in respect to flour and other human foods containing wheat sold in Canada during the crop year. Events leading up to the drawbacks, which in effect constituted a two-price system for wheat used domestically and export wheat, led to an abrasive confrontation between the Canadian Wheat Board and Donald Gordon, deputy governor of the Bank of Canada, who had been appointed chairman of the Wartime Prices and Trade Board.

Gordon, a strong-willed Scot, ran up against an equally strong-willed Scot in the person of George McIvor. As administrator of the general price freeze, Gordon insisted that wheat for domestic consumption must be set at 77 3/8 cents a bushel, the closing price on the day his mandate came into effect. Feeling the price to be unfair, McIvor, after communicating his feelings to the government, called a meeting of the advisory committee to the Wheat Board against the express wishes of Gordon who forbade him to do so. The advisory committee, in turn, fired off a letter to the government highly critical of Gordon and his stand.

The Wheat Board pressed two compelling arguments against the price freeze. First, it would abrogate the duty of the board, spelled out in the Act, to sell the producers' wheat to the best advantage and would undermine producer confidence in the board. Secondly, the board's method of bulk sales to Britain had already removed a substantial portion of the open market, and if a further 50 million to 75 million bushels of domestic sales were removed, the small volume remaining would render the open market price mechanism unable to operate efficiently. The final decision by the government to reconcile the conflicting stands was to play a large part in the eventual closing of the Winnipeg Grain Exchange.

With the board's stand, that there be no price ceiling on domestic sales, threatening to topple the government's overall price ceiling, the government decided to subsidize domestic consumers. Under the plan, processors of wheat for breadmaking and other domestic purposes paid the prevailing market price for wheat through the open market. The Wheat Board then paid back to the millers the difference between the open market price and the 77 3/8 cent price, set by the Wartime Prices and Trade Board, with funds provided from the federal treasury.

Further, in order that available transportation might be used most effectively in respect to the various grains and grades of grain, the board assumed control of allocation of railway boxcars in the West on October 15, 1942. Duties in that regard fell to W.C. "Bill" McNamara, who joined the staff on loan from Saskatchewan Wheat Pool in September 1942, as supervisor of car supply.

While the federal policy initiatives resulted in a further decrease in wheat acreage in 1942, dropping to 21,586,500 acres as compared to 21,882,200 in 1941, it was a bountiful crop year. With increased yields prairie wheat production rose to 565 million bushels, compared to 296 million the previous year. Production of all grains in the West rose to over 1.3 billion bushels, with oats soaring to 500 million bushels in 1942 compared to 178 million in 1941. Barley production also set a record in 1942 at 241 million bushels, compared to 95 million bushels in the previous year. Flaxseed production rose from 6 million bushels in 1941 to 15 million bushels in 1942.

The Wheat Board reported, "With limited storage capacity and transportation available, grain marketing problems were unprecedented in intensity and in scope, but as the crop year progressed evidence of a basic improvement in the Canadian grain situation [was] clearly revealed."[28]

Early in 1943, the grain problem in Canada entered a new phase as improved demand became a noticeable factor. The emphasis was passing from storage difficulties to problems of meeting increased demand for Canadian grains with limited transportation available for movement of those grains.

Events were now moving rapidly and inevitably toward monopoly control by the Canadian Wheat Board. Forged in the furnace of war by policy considerations taken on an ad-hoc basis to meet emergencies as they arose, the board was fast assuming many of the duties that were destined to become permanent features of grain marketing in Canada.

Ironically, the increased demand that precipitated the final step came from the United States where the open market philosophy dominated and still prevails. The change was sudden and dramatic. By early 1943, it was evident that the American winter wheat crop was being hard hit by adverse weather conditions. Entering their second year of full participation in the war, the "arsenal of democracy" in the United States was under full mobilization, both industrially and militarily. Demands for agricultural production were high, particularly in the livestock sector. In January 1943, American authorities were already anticipating that an abnormal importation of grain would be required for the year.

The tide of events had also started to turn on the global war front. When Winnipeg papers announced the death of John I. McFarland on February 6, 1943, the news of the passing of one of the fathers of the Canadian Wheat Board shared the front page with dramatic events on all fronts. Russian troops had turned back the German army at the gates of Moscow and were counter-attacking on the outskirts of Rostov. Winston Churchill made a triumphal entry into Tripoli to thank the "desert rats" of Britain's Eighth Army and the Allied air forces personally for their magnificent feat in driving the Axis armies from Egypt and Libya. Italy's dictator Benito Mussolini was reported to have made a sweeping cabinet shake-up in an attempt to nip a plan for a separate peace with the Allies by his son-in-law Count Ciano and two other prominent Italians. In the Pacific, an American task force had invaded the Solomon Islands.

Evidence of U.S. import intentions emerged in March. The Commodity Credit Corporation of the U.S. Department of Agriculture began to place orders for wheat through the Winnipeg Grain Exchange, regardless of grade, for distribution to American feed manufacturers. During the month, the Americans purchased 45 million bushels of wheat futures, which the Canadian Wheat Board supplied through the pit.

That march the untimely death of W.C. Folliott was also reported, and his place as a commissioner of the board was filled on June 1 by the appointment of D.A. Kane, formerly general manager of Manitoba Pool Elevators.

McIvor reported to the wheat committee of cabinet in early April that U.S. import demand for all grains might reach 170 million bushels in the 1943-1944 crop year. Meanwhile, open market prices were rising in the face of the new demand. In March they rose substantially over the board's 90 cent initial price, reaching a high of $1.01 3/4. By July, they had risen as high as $1.12 3/8. As a result, country deliveries were going to the trade and bypassing the board.

While MacKinnon had announced a slightly changed grains policy well in advance of the 1943-1944 crop year on January 29, the rapidly changing picture leading up to the August 1 opening of the new crop year was presenting a complex problem for the government. The initial payment had again been set at 90 cents and deliveries of wheat were to be restricted to 280 million bushels, with delivery quotas restricted to fourteen bushels per authorized quota acre to achieve that limit. Western farmers were encouraged to reduce wheat acreage by not less than 3 million acres, and bonus payments for diversion to coarse grains were continued at a slightly reduced rate.

In June 1943, the Board could offer only 40 million bushels of wheat futures to the British because, as noted above, with the rise in prices resulting from the U.S. demand for wheat for feeding and industrial purposes, farmers were delivering to the open market rather than to the board. As early as July 28, McIvor drew the attention of the cabinet wheat committee to the need for considering the open market situation.

As the critical 1943-1944 crop year opened, a number of other forces were at play, not the least of which was a labour shortage at the Lakehead terminals. By 1943 in the days before automatic dumps were in general use, the shortage of labour to undertake the dirty, dusty job of shovelling grain from boxcars had become so acute that an embargo had to be placed on consignment of cars to the terminals. This, in turn, caused a backup and a widening price spread between country elevators and the terminals. Some congestion was relieved by a program whereby American railways agreed to provide an average of 235 cars a day at the border for loading at country points and direct return to the United States.

In addition, a large part of the bumper 1942 crop had been taken off under adverse conditions and large volumes of damp grain necessitated special delivery authorizations. Transportation was further hampered by extreme winter conditions. Thus, despite the increasing demand in early 1943, the carryover of all grains at July 31, 1943, was an all-time record. Wheat alone stood at 594 million bushels with a large part backed up in farm storage. Visible supplies of grain and flaxseed amounted to 453 million bushels and filled the greater part of Canadian grain storage capacity.

This, along with a number of other factors, compounded the dilemma facing the federal cabinet in light of the rising market prices which were now deflecting virtually all grain deliveries to the private trade. In his advice to the wheat committee of cabinet on July 26, McIvor had outlined reasons for keeping the open market situation under consideration.

If the initial payment were to be raised, as sought by the pools, there was a danger in raising it with each rise in open market prices because of the subsequent difficulty in following the market down. McIvor also pointed to the board's position in making sales on a rising market with no replacement grain being delivered to it. Britain's cereals import division had also made enquiries on purchase of a further 40 million bushels of wheat futures, which the board did not consider it was in a position to offer. The alternative was for the British to enter the open market to buy its futures, which would exert further upward pressure on the market.

By 1941, the British had exhausted their source of Canadian dollars and the Canadian government had accumulated some $700 million in sterling exchange which it converted into an interest-free loan for the duration of the war. Then, in 1942, the Canadian government made an outright gift of $1 billion, which Britain used to meet its own Canadian dollar requirements and those of other sterling area countries, such as Australia and New Zealand, as well as providing assistance to the Soviet Union. All Canadian grain to Britain and the Russians was now going forward under this Mutual Aid program. Rising prices now meant that the federal treasury in Ottawa would have to pay much higher prices for wheat to cover Mutual Aid and relief purposes, as well as a higher subsidy on wheat used for domestic consumption. In September, it was estimated that, because of Mutual Aid and the domestic subsidy, each rise of one cent in open market wheat prices was costing the federal treasury $2.5 million.[29]

The urgency of the situation prompted almost daily meetings of the wheat committee of cabinet, and all three Canadian Wheat Board commissioners were called to Ottawa for discussions. Further aggravating the complex situation was the threat to the maintenance of price ceilings on coarse grains as markets in the United States rose steadily above Canadian market prices.

Many of the meetings took place in the sitting room acquired by the Wheat Board commissioners in the Chateau Laurier Hotel.

As the talks progressed, a battle of wills developed between the scrappy Jimmy Gardiner and Finance Minister J.L. Ilsley. Gardiner, as agriculture minister, was seeking to guarantee the best possible income for prairie farmers, sometimes without regard to the impact on the treasury, which was Ilsley's chief concern. As a stalling tactic, aimed at letting the market rise further before a decision was taken, Gardiner failed to turn up at the meetings, raising the ire of the normally moderate Ilsley.[30]

Several plans to peg fixed prices were put forward, but Gardiner and Ilsley could not find common ground. McIvor at one stage deplored the prospect of having to sell at two or three different prices, even if one of the prices were set by government directive. He contended that as long as the participation feature remained in the Canadian Wheat Board Act the board could not accept a directive as to its selling prices. The alternative would force the board to resign.

It was left to Ilsley to suggest the final solution to the impasse on September 24, which was accepted and carried to Prime Minister Mackenzie King and the cabinet for approval. Under the plan, the futures trading on the Winnipeg Grain Exchange would be suspended. Existing stocks of wheat, including the old crop accounts held by the board and the unsold stocks of wheat in the hands of the trade, would be taken over by the government at existing market prices and held in a special account from which Mutual Aid and domestic sales could be made. Apart from that, the board would continue to accept current deliveries from producers at an amended initial price and sell them to best advantage in commercial export markets. Any additional monies, over and above the initial payment, would be distributed by way of participation certificates.

On an ironic note, the prairie pools which had so long and so ardently sought such a transformation were now at odds on closing of the futures market. Throughout the summer of 1943, J.H. Wesson, president of the Saskatchewan Wheat Pool, continued to recommend a compulsory national Wheat Board. But, the boards of Manitoba Pool Elevators, now headed by W.J. Parker, and the Alberta Wheat Pool, under the presidency of Lew Hutchinson, demurred at closing of the market when, for the first time in years, it was clearly operating to the best price advantage for producers.

THE TURNING POINT

Flexibility of sales and price policy under extraordinary demand conditions was made possible by the monopoly of wheat marketing enjoyed by the Wheat Board after September 1943.

— Britnell and Fowke, *Canadian Agriculture In War and Peace 1935-1950*

▪

In the dining room of Ottawa's Chateau Laurier Hotel, George McIvor glanced across the table at his assistant chief commissioner Gordon Smith and at commissioner Dan Kane. McIvor had noted in the evening paper that the Liberal caucus was holding a dinner meeting in the hotel that night. He had a premonition. "I think they are going to close the exchange tonight. It would be a terrible thing if the Board is not there when it closes. They deserve better treatment than that. Just a simple telegram from the minister that the exchange is going to close? They are decent people and we have worked well with them. I can't go, but I think you two fellows should go back to Winnipeg tonight.''[1]

Returning to the Canadian Wheat Board suite, McIvor phoned C.D. Howe's secretary. Arrangements were quickly completed. Two passengers were bumped from a flight returning to Winnipeg that night. Smith and Kane packed and departed for the airport. The abrupt decision was to prove a wise one. McIvor's hunch was about to be dramatically fulfilled late that night of September 27, 1943.

Events had moved swiftly from that morning. The council of cabinet had approved the compromise on the closure of the exchange, which resolved the impasse between Gardiner and Ilsley. But rumors of the pending closure of the exchange had leaked, and on September 23 the Winnipeg Grain Exchange, unable to contact the Wheat Board commissioners who were in Ottawa, wired Trade Minister MacKinnon to express concern and seek an opportunity to present their views. Receiving no positive response, a delegation of the exchange headed by its president Alex Christie, along with George Mathieson and K.A. Powell, had proceeded to Ottawa arriving that morning.

They were unsuccessful in reaching any of the ministers or the board members to present their case. In fact, after the decision of cabinet to close the exchange had been made, elaborate precautions were taken to screen the principles from delegations and the press. The wheat committee of cabinet, was delegated to work out the details. Its secretary, C.F. Wilson, took the precaution of holding the meeting that afternoon in the Canadian Wheat Board's sitting room, rather than in MacKinnon's office.[2]

The meeting was scheduled for 3 PM, and Ilsley, according to Wilson, was ''manifestly upset'' when Gardiner failed to appear on time. McIvor's description of the reaction to Gardiner's non-appearance is a little more colourful. Gardiner was suspected of stalling in order to give the open market a chance to rise even further so that the return to farmers might increase. Ilsley, knowing that every cent rise would add millions of dollars to treasury costs, was equally anxious to move quickly.

Ilsley, a circumspect man with a Sunday-school teacher demeanour, turned first to McIvor and asked him to phone Winnipeg to ascertain what the wheat price level was on the exchange. Informed that there had been another substantial rise, Ilsley blew up. ''Call him up. Get that son-of-a bitch over here....'' That and other expletives split the air as attempts were made to get in touch with

Gardiner.[3] The doughty agriculture minister arrived some half-hour later and the committee got down to details.

With the departure for Winnipeg that evening of Smith and Kane, Wheat Board secretary T.W. Grindley, a man with a constant eye on board expenses, suggested that the sitting room would no longer be required and he would cancel it, but McIvor had a further premonition. To the surprise of Grindley, the chief commissioner vetoed the idea, asking instead that the head bellboy be contacted to send up about twenty folding chairs. "They had no sooner got the whole lot in than I looked down the hall and here comes Willie King and the whole cabinet."[4] The final cabinet decision was about to be taken in the Wheat Board's hotel sitting room. Starting at around 11 PM, the session was to go on for two hours. Still unaware of the final decision, McIvor and Grindley sat in an adjoining bedroom while the cabinet meeting progressed. As a precaution against the expected outcome, they drew up telegrams to the Winnipeg, Vancouver, and Montreal exchanges:

> You are hereby advised that the Government is ordering the discontinuance of wheat trading on the Winnipeg Grain Exchange as of September 27, 1943, with the exception that open trades may be closed out at the closing prices registered on the Winnipeg Grain Exchange Monday September 27th.
>
> Since it will take some time to arrange the final clearing of all the outstanding futures contracts and for the Board to take over all the unsold cash wheat, the final closing out of these contracts will be deferred for several days.
>
> In the meantime, all futures prices and all cash wheat prices are fixed at the closing prices for Monday, September 27th. No purchases or sales may be made at other than these prices. In particular, it must be emphasized that no export sales may be made until further notice.
>
> Another order affects the buying of wheat from producers and it should be drawn to the attention of your members concerned that all purchasing of wheat from producers on an open market basis will also be discontinued as from Monday, September 27th.
>
> For any further clarification of these orders please get in touch with the Canadian Wheat Board.[5]

McIvor and Grindley also drafted a press release in anticipation of the expected outcome, and when an obviously shaken MacKinnon, who favoured the open market system, opened the bedroom door at the conclusion of the cabinet meeting in the small hours of the morning, all was in readiness.

When the telegram was read to exchange members by Vice-President W.J. Dowler at the opening of the Winnipeg Grain Exchange later that morning, Smith and Kane were on hand. It was a fortunate turn of events. The presence on the floor of the exchange of the two commissioners did a great deal toward smoothing out the transition from one form of marketing to another. McIvor has paid tribute to Smith and Kane for the masterful job they accomplished in the takeover of over 200 million bushels of wheat. With thousands of contracts outstanding on grain sold through the futures market, the board's offices were crowded with anxious buyers who wondered whether they were going to get delivery of their grain. Every contract was considered by the board, and after several weeks of almost round the clock operations, the job was completed without one single complaint of unfair treatement.

McIvor later recalled that he made one mistake. Intending to inform the exchange delegation in Ottawa of the decision, he went down to see Mathieson in his room at the Chateau. But on hearing sounds of heavy slumber through the transom decided not to. "Why wake the poor man in the middle of the night to tell him he's out of business. He'll find out in the morning." The Canadian Press were not so considerate. At 4 AM, they phoned Mathieson to get his reaction and gave him the bad news. "He never quite forgave me for that. I thought I did the right thing, but I didn't."[6]

The change in government policy arising from the increase in wheat prices which carried a threat to the government's price ceiling at home and Canadian commitments abroad, had a number of immediate and practical advantages. By taking over the balance of the unsold wheat in the 1940, 1941, and 1942 crop accounts held by the board and all unsold wheat in commercial hands, the government set up a separate crown account administered by the board under government direction. From this stock, acquired at the closing price on September 27, 1943, of $1.23 1/4 cents a bushel, the board now fulfilled Mutual Aid and domestic requirments.

The takeover made possible the closing out of the three producer pool accounts dating back to 1940. A final payment of 6.3 cents was made on the 1940-1941 deliveries, bringing the total payment to farmers to 76.3 cents. For the 1941-1942 account, a final payment of 15.5 cents brought the producer return to 85.5 cents a bushel, and a final payment of 12.6 cents added to the 90 cent initial for the 1942-1943 account raised total returns to $1.026.[7] A combined surplus of $61,080,046.97 was distributed to farmers for payout of the three crop years.

The problems of the government were eased, with Mutual Aid and domestic needs being drawn from the special account acquired at a fixed price. At the same time, the initial payment to producers was raised to $1.25 a bushel and participation certificates were issued on all new wheat deliveries to the board. These current deliveries were used to fulfill export sales to the United States and other areas outside of the Mutual Aid program, and the board was instructed to sell at terms which it considered reasonable, thereby conforming to the terms of the Wheat Board Act to make sales to the best possible advantage of the producer.

As the board was now administering what was, in effect, a two-price program, sales from the government holdings became known as Class I sales and sales from current accounts were known as Class II sales. This made for a more efficient allocation to domestic and export markets and for more effective utilization of storage and transportation facilities.

While creation of the monopoly board was unquestionably necessary to prevent possible inflation in one sector of the economy, to the detriment of the government's overall price controls, closure of wheat futures trading on the exchange was a bitter pill for Mackenzie King and his traditionally Liberal free-trade cabinet to swallow. Evidence of their still cherished hope of a return to the open market system at the end of hostilities was given by the expiry date of August 1, 1945, on the board's monopoly powers contained in the order-in-council suspending futures trading on the Grain Exchange. Due to its complications, the order-in-council, PC 7942, passed October 12, 1943, was drawn up with the assistance of Henry Monk, solicitor to the board.

While the council of the Winnipeg Grain Exchange met and resolved to comply with the order, a letter was drafted to the government taking exception to certain portions of the preamble to the order: "It appears to us that this order-in-council is an historical document which in later years may be referred to before Royal Commissions, Parliamentary Committees, or the Houses of Parliament, or elsewhere, and as it may also be referred to in plans for post-war return to open wheat marketing, it is desirable that there should appear a true picture of conditions existing at the time of its enactment, as well as the full reasons for the Government's action."[8]

Protesting that any idea that the marketing system was responsible for "abnormal buying margins at country points," mentioned in the preamble to the order, the exchange said the blame for any abnormal spreads must be placed squarely on transportation difficulties. It also regretted that it was not clearly stated that one of the main problems of the government centred on the conflict between (on one hand) that of paying the farmer a price representing the true value of his wheat after several years of low income, and (on the other) of protecting the taxpayer from demands on the treasury arising out of the drawback to the mills and the Mutual Aid pact.[9]

The abrupt change in policy after the government had, as late as March 30, relied on its majority to defeat an opposition motion to abolish trading in wheat futures on the Winnipeg Grain Exchange, was marked by an equally dramatic change in the overall situation. Despite the fact that the carryover at July 31, 1943, was the highest in history, that carryover began to look much less formidable in the face of increased demand and declining crop conditions. As the summer wore on, it became apparent that in addition to very poor crops in Ontario and other parts of eastern Canada and the United States, there was a sharply reduced wheat acreage in western Canada and the prospect of the smallest wheat harvest since 1937.

Sown late due to a cool wet spring, on a scant 16,091,000 acres, the prairie wheat acreage was the lowest since 1918. It produced only 268 million bushels compared to 529 million for the previous year 1942. During the crop year about 118 million bushels of feed wheat, oats, and barley were shipped under Freight Assistance to eastern Canada. Total wheat marketings for the crop year amounted to some 325 million bushels, including 160 million bushels to the United States, primarily for livestock feeding.

A major turning point had been reached. Up to 1943 the problems facing the government and the Canadian Wheat Board had been those of surplus, low prices, income subsidies, and the necessity of encouragement to producers to diversify into the production of coarse grains and oil seeds. With the resurgence of wartime demand, the search for storage accomodation to house unexportable surpluses gave way to one of finding transportation to move available wheat supplies to markets anxious to take them. With the initial payment raised to $1.25, plus payout of the participation certificates on the 1940, 1941 and 1942 crops, the pressure upon the government to subsidize farm incomes was relieved.[10]

Despite the improved sales situation, the government remained cautious on any restoration of wheat acreage to earlier levels. In both 1944 and 1945, Gardiner continued to advocate restraint on wheat production and stressed the need to maintain coarse grains production.

In spite of that, prairie farmers, now assured of improved prices and encouraged by the rapid increase in delivery quotas, increased their wheat area by over six million acres in 1944 and followed with another slight increase in 1945.

But in spite of the increase in wheat acreage, crop output in the last two years of the war was affected by adverse conditions and only "normal" wheat crops resulted. Average production of 340 million bushels for the years 1943, 1944, and 1945 represented a decline of 30 per cent from the average over the first four years of the war. At the same time, demand increased so sharply that exports exceeded gross production by a slight margin. In retrospect, the decision by western farmers to increase wheat acreage, despite the cautionary warnings, proved fortuitous. Every bushel was to be required in a world reeling from the aftershock of six years of war.

In 1943 and 1944, railway transport, terminal elevator capacity, port facilities, and ocean shipping were the major factors placing limits on the volume of Canada's surplus stocks which could be moved into export trade.[11] In the spring of 1943, it had become obvious that because of common grain transportation problems closer liaison was required between Canada and the U.S. As a consequence, Bill McNamara, who had served as the board's supervisor of transportation for the past year, was transferred to Washington. R.M. Mahoney assumed the transportation duties in Winnipeg, in addition to his work as supervisor of delivery quotas.

In the wake of the Japanese attack on Pearl Harbor and the American entry into the war, the British and American governments created a Combined Food Board to deal with threatening food shortages and to make the most effective use of available resources. When the cereals committee of the Combined Food Board was formed in 1943, Canada refrained from seeking membership. The Canadian government had a change of heart in 1944, when the committee broadened its scope to consideration of allocations of export wheat and feed grains. In January 1944, McIvor was appointed to the committee and elected as chairman. This required his attendance in Washington on a monthly basis, in addition to his duties as chief commissioner of the Canadian Wheat Board.

McIvor's chairmanship of the cereals committee of the Combined Food Board throughout the war years and its successor, the International Emergency Food Council, earned the confidence of countries requiring wheat supplies. They knew their claims were equitably considered. "In that capacity, McIvor won for Canadian producers a host of international friends by his level-headed and impartial handling of wheat export programs during a period of critical world shortage."[12]

The expertise of the board was also called upon with its membership on the Emergency Grain Transport Committee in 1943. Set up by T.C. Lockwood, the Canadian transport controller, the committee membership included the Canadian Wheat Board, the general transport superintendents of the railways, the Canadian Shipping Board, the feeds administrator, and C.F. Wilson. The work of this committee was to prove invaluable in the heavy shipping program which now faced the board in export and domestic markets. It continued to function to the end of the war and in the critical transportation period immediately thereafter.

In the 1944-1945 crop year, rail shipments to and lake freighter shipments from the Lakehead reached the highest level in the previous history of the grain trade. Total rail and lake shipments from Port Arthur-Fort William reached 518.2 million bushels. Although United States demand subsided to a total of 60 million bushels over the next two years, this was more than offset by pressing requirements of liberated countries in Europe, the Middle East, and the Far East. As a consequence, the record carryover of 595 million bushels of wheat at the end of the 1942-1943 crop year was reduced to 258 million bushels by the end of the 1944-1945 crop year.[13]

In the two crop years ending July 31, 1945, Canada provided importing countries with 687 million bushels of wheat (including flour), or an average of 28.6 million bushels each month from August 1, 1943, to July 31, 1945. The wheat now remaining in the wartime reserve was to play an important part in meeting the urgent needs of the importing countries during the transition from war to peace.

Another of the many ancillary duties thrust on the Canadian Wheat Board during World War II was the introduction and promotion of rapeseed in western Canada. That previously unknown oil seed was fated in later years to become the Cinderella crop on the prairies. Wilson has noted that the circumstances of the inception of the rapeseed industry have been almost forgotten, but that the industry owes a debt of considerable gratitude to Mrs. Phyliss Turner for her initiative in getting it established.[14]

Phyliss Turner, whose son, John, was later to achieve prominence in the Liberal party and succeed Pierre Elliott Trudeau as prime minister in June 1984, was an economist with the tariff board in Ottawa and had been recruited as administrator of oils and fats on the Wartime Prices and Trade Board. After Pearl Harbor and the subsequent curtailment of vegetable oil imports from the Pacific area, Mrs. Turner cast about for acceptable oil seed substitutes that might be grown in Canada. One of the crops which attracted her attention was rapeseed, which at that time produced an inedible oil but which had a specialized use as a marine engine lubricant. The Agricultural Supplies Board purchased, for distribution to Canadian farmers, all supplies of Large Black Argentine rapeseed available in the United States.

Some forty years later George McIvor, who felt at the time that the Wheat Board had more than enough additional responsibilities and wanted nothing to do with the promotion of an unknown crop, was to recall how Phyliss Turner, "a very delightful person," trapped him into taking on the project. On one of his numerous trips to Ottawa, McIvor received a phone call from Mrs. Turner asking him to come and see her. Although he had never met her, the chief commissioner had heard of her work. "I had some friends in Washington and one of them once said to me, 'You keep that woman home.' I said, 'what's she done now?' He said, 'Well, I'm afraid the next time she comes down here she'll take the White House back with her.' I should have known what I was in for."[15]

In her office Mrs. Turner outlined the need to grow oil seeds to replace the copra supplies lost from the Pacific.

> As she went on I could see that the trap was being closed, but it was pretty difficult to withdraw from the conversation at that point. She said we had to grow rapeseed and sunflowerseed. So, I said, "I wish you the best of luck Mrs. Turner," and got up to go. She said, "Just a minute Mr. McIvor, I want you to persuade the farmers to grow this. I asked, "Do you have any idea what you're asking me to do?" She said she did, then picked out my two weaknesses in the government: "I've talked to Donald Gordon and C.D. Howe, and they said if you ask George McIvor to do this, well he will do it for you." Well, the trap was shut right then and there.[16]

McIvor promised to discuss the matter with his assistant chief commissioner, Gordon Smith, who was to arrive in Ottawa the next day. When informed of the request to promote rapeseed and sunflowerseed, Smith bluntly declared, "The Dickens we are. We've got more than enough to do already." McIvor told Smith the decision was up to him. "Anything you do is all right with me." He suggested, however, that Smith go over and talk to Mrs. Turner. Smith consented to go. "But remember we're not handling rapeseed." When the chief commissioner returned at noon, Smith informed him they were in the rapeseed business. "I could have told you that before you left here this morning," replied McIvor who had already been exposed to Phyliss Turner's persuasive charm.

The result was that in early 1943 Bill McNamara was assigned the job of promoting rapeseed production by western farmers. The limitation on available seed resulted in only 19,630 bushels being grown in 1943. By the 1948-1949 crop year, when the government withdrew a support price of six cents a pound, 1,048,230 bushels were produced. From then on production waned until scientists succeeded in homogenizing the oil and rendering it edible. Sponsored and encouraged by the private trade, it was later established on the futures market and became a substantial cash crop for western farmers. During the war years and immediate postwar years, the Canadian Wheat Board resold the rapeseed and sunflowerseed at purchase prices, while carrying costs were reimbursed by the federal treasury.

The accumulation of complex and varied duties, along with the required administration, enforcement, and accounting procedures for the various programs during the war, placed a heavy burden on the board and its staff. The board's annual reports, which contained a scant eight to ten pages prior to the war, became lengthy documents stretching up to thirty-five pages, to which were added some forty pages of statistical and accounting appendices.

The stocks of wheat, taken over in September 1943 and incorporated into the crown account, were sufficient to supply the domestic market, the United Kingdom, and other countries receiving Mutual Aid until the middle of January 1945. From then until the end of Mutual Aid and the closing out of the crown account on September 1, 1945, the board replenished crown stocks by selling wheat from the 1943 and 1944 crops at approximately $1.43 to cover Mutual Aid and $1.25 a bushel to cover domestic sales.

"Sales of nearly 300 million bushels...were made to countries not receiving Mututal Aid and to United Nations organizations operating on a cash basis...at the Board's 'Class II'...price during the crop years 1943-44 and 1944-45. This price, which averaged $1.41 5/8 and $1.47 7/8 respectively in the two crop years, tended to fluctuate with quotations on U.S. markets until it was stabilized by the Wheat Board at $1.55 a bushel after May 15, 1945."[17]

The efficiency with which the Canadian Wheat Board carried out its many duties, and the stature in which it was held by producers, has been described by D.A. MacGibbon. Although a strong advocate of the open market system, MacGibbon wrote:

> By the end of the war the Canadian Wheat Board was established in a position that had every appearance of stability. The producers appeared to be satisfied that they were being dealt with fairly by the Board. Even the difficult task the Board faced in determining the "authorized acres" which were the basis of the producer's deliverable quantity, when limitations were placed upon marketings, was accomplished with practically no complaints of unfair discrimination. Moreover, this was not because of laxity in administration, for the Board was prompt to prosecute attempts at evasion of the limitations imposed.[18]

The legal department of the Board was indeed busy on prosecutions and enforcement of the regulations. During the 1943-1944 crop year 290 prosecutions were instituted and 289 convictions obtained, mostly for over-deliveries of grain and infringement of regulations governing farm-to-feeder transactions. In 1944-1945, the legal department carried out 584 investigations, which resulted in 342 charges being laid. Of these charges 340 ended with convictions.

Only one serious challenge was made to the board's authority. A Manitoba farmer, Arthur H. Oatway, acting on behalf of himself and other producers, issued a statement of claim in Court of King's Bench October 18, 1943, against the Canadian Wheat Board. Oatway, who farmed at Lilyfield in the Rosser district, called for an accounting from the board on its operations for the five years from 1938 to 1943, and claimed he was entitled to a share in the board's operations for each year. In addition to asking for an accounting for the sale price of his grain, Oatway also alleged that the board mixed the grades, did not keep the markets distinct nor market each crop year's wheat separately, did not credit all receipts of grain sold to the proper crop year, and improperly included expenses of operation in the wrong crop years.[19]

The board's solicitors, J.B. Coyne and Henry Monk, sought to have the statement of claim dismissed contending that the board, acting as an agent of the Crown, was entitled to all the Crown's prerogatives and accountable only to the Crown for its public actions. In the Manitoba Court of King's Bench, Mr. Justice Donovan ruled against the board and declined to dismiss the action. With an injunction, or restraining order, now in effect the government and the board were in an embarrassing position, being unable to distribute cheques to farmers for final payment of the 1940-1941, 1941-1942, and

1942-1943 crop years which had been taken over for the Crown account. That dilemma was resolved when the Board appealed the ruling in The Manitoba Court of Appeal on May 9, 1944, and almost simultaneously the government passed an order-in-council on May 12 under the War Measures Act. The order called for distribution of the surpluses in the three previous crop years, and the board immediately commenced to send out thousands of cheques per day to producers.[20]

On October 5, 1944, the appeal court, in a split three-to-two decision held that the Canadian Wheat Board was a servant of the Crown and that the action could not be maintained against it. The case, however, did not end there. Oatway obtained leave to appeal the decision to the Supreme Court in Ottawa. Finally, on February 27, 1945, the Supreme Court quashed the case and declined to hear Oatway's appeal. The court ruled that the orders-in-council under the War Measures Act had disposed of the case and "that no further lis [grounds for litigation] exists between the parties and that they have nothing for [them] to fight over."[21]

In the latter war years there were a number of changes on the board. In December 1944, C. Gordon Smith resigned as assistant chief commissioner. Dan Kane succeeded him, while C.E. Huntting was appointed to fill the vacancy on the board. In September 1945, Kane resigned and Huntting became assistant chief commissioner. Bill McNamara returned from his post in Washington and was appointed as the third member of the board.

In 1944-1945 the operations of the board were being carried out against a dramatic backdrop as allied invasion forces swept ashore, first in Italy and then into the rest of Continental Europe. The annual report of the Canadian Wheat Board set out the urgency of the situation:

> The Board's operations became more complex and more extended as the war progressed; consequently sales and price policy which governed Board operations during 1944-45 should be set forth in some detail.
>
> In regard to sales policy, one basic fact must be emphasized; to the limit of transportation and port capacities available, every demand for Canadian wheat was met during the crop year 1944-45. With due regard to the volume of wheat which was being carried in Canada during the crop year, the Board felt that its duty was to market every possible bushel of wheat which could be sold under existing conditions. This sales policy was more than justified by the fact that in the

final year of the war in Europe demand for Canadian wheat was urgent, and failure to meet that demand would have had far-reaching repercussions. This was the basic factor in the pressing wheat sales policy pursued by the Board in 1944-45.[22]

As the war drew to its cataclysmic close, rapid liberation of the Mediterranean area, Western Europe, and large areas of Asia, revealed depleted food reserves with millions of people in need. While the large and unexpected demand in 1943-1944 from the United States had waned, it was more than offset by the urgent requirements from the liberated regions. Canada's previously onerous wartime reserve dwindled rapidly. As previously noted, by July 31, 1945, the carryover in all positions had dropped to 258,394,518 bushels from the wartime high of 595 million bushels two years previously. Of that stock, only 28,650,000 bushels were left on farms at war's end. Despite that, the surplus psychology that had overhung the western wheat industry almost without respite since 1930 still permeated thinking in both official circles and in the farm organizations. The boom and bust cycle that followed the end of World War I was still fresh in the minds of both legislators and farmers.

The haunting fear was that once hostilities ceased and continental countries resumed peacetime production the spectre of surpluses would once again return to plague the market. This concern was evident in early 1945 as the government received policy recommendations from the pools, the Canadian Federation of Agriculture, the advisory committee to the Wheat Board and from within regulatory agencies of the government itself. It was to colour and influence all of the policy decisions in the immediate postwar period.

Not the least of the government's quandaries in preparation of the policy for the 1945-1946 crop year was the imminent end of the mandate accorded the Canadian Wheat Board. The board had been maintained, expanded, and involved as the government's principle instrument of agricultural policy under the War Measures Act, but in the October 1943 order-in-council, which suspended futures trading in wheat, an expiry date of July 31, 1945, had been set on those powers. As noted above, the mandate of the government itself was also set to expire. Elected in 1940, the government was at the end of its statutory life and needed a fresh mandate if it were to preside over the transition from war to peace. Consequently, the forthcoming election, announced on April 13 by Mackenzie King, to be held on June 11, 1945, undoubtedly influenced cabinet decisions on the grain policy for the coming crop year.

At the Canadian Federation of Agriculture annual meeting in January 1945, Gardiner called for a reduction of from two million to three million acres in wheat for the coming season. He failed to convince CFA president J.H. Wesson, who opposed any reduction. Instead the CFA, after calling for retention of the Canadian Wheat Board as the sole marketing agency for wheat, opted for production control through use of the quota delivery system. The CFA also sought to have the Wheat Board made responsible for marketing coarse grains on the same basis as for wheat, rather than the current method of sales through the open market at a fixed ceiling with the Board supporting a minimum price when necessary through purchase of futures.

While the CFA support for retention of the Canadian Wheat Board was anticipated given the pool and producer representation on that body, the subsequent policy statement by the advisory committee to the Board was more significant. The advisory committee, with equal representation between producer organizations and other interested segments of the trade, unanimously agreed that the board should continue to operate on a monopoly basis to receive producers wheat in the 1945-1946 crop year. Both the CFA and the advisory committee called for the initial payment to be retained at $1.25. Both also called for the board to continue as the sole agent for marketing of flaxseed, with an increase in the fixed price of $2.75 per bushel to approximately $3.24 to encourage further seeding.

At the same time, the advisory committee stressed the importance of a considerable reduction in commercial stocks of wheat. They believed this could be accomplished by limiting producers' marketings to a maximum of fourteen bushels per acre. Once again production control was sought through delivery quotas.

Faced with these recommendations, the wheat committee of cabinet found difficulty in reaching agreement in a pre-election atmosphere. Gardiner, typically the loner in cabinet, was seeking the maximum return possible for the farmer while Finance Minister Ilsley was preoccupied with the overall effect of the policy on inflationary pressures in the economy during the postwar transition.

In the background, Donald Gordon, chairman of the Wartime Prices and Trade Board, was preparing a memorandum expressing his serious concern over production trends in western Canada. His fourteen-page treasury proposals, attributed the maladjustment of production patterns to the wheat policy adopted in September 1943, which raised the initial payment and paid out substantial sums in participation payments.

Gordon and his officials feared that the trend toward more wheat production at the expense of feed grains, would result in too little bacon and dairy products to fulfill contracts with Britain. This in turn foreshadowed reimposition of meat rationing in Canada and a reduction in the butter ration. If price incentives were used to stimulate production of meat and dairy products to meet such a situation they would pose a threat to the government's price stabilization program. The memorandum claimed that high agricultural prices would threaten the operation of a floor price system after the war, weaken Canada's competitive position in world markets, and stimulate an unwanted rise in agricultural land values.

Gordon therefore called for more draconian measures, including a reduction in the initial payment on wheat, limitations on deliveries of wheat, and a scheme of acreage payments on land transferred out of wheat into feed crops and flaxseed. The Wheat Board was not favourable to Gordon's recommendations. Clive Davidson prepared a critical commentary, pointing out that the producers had accepted a controlled price environment for the duration of the war, and in return, expected some form of protection in the postwar years.[23]

The issue then went to cabinet and on March 2 Trade Minister MacKinnon announced the policy for the forthcoming year. The initial payment was to remain at $1.25, and the government would place full reliance on a strictly enforced maximum delivery limitation to keep wheat acreage in check. MacKinnon stressed that "the limitation of marketings to 14 bushels per authorized acre in 1945-46 is final and will not be altered at a later date."[24] The coarse grains program was to remain the same, with minimum and maximum prices and continued equalization payments. The government's policy statement was silent on the future powers of the Canadian Wheat Board following expiry of its monopoly mandate on wheat marketing.

When Canadians flocked to the polling stations on June 11, grain policy had ceased to be a major factor in elections. Other issues, including the still-simmering argument over conscription and the way it had been handled by the King government, played their part in the outcome. The result was a bare majority for Mackenzie King's Liberal government of 125 seats in the 245-seat House. While Manitoba gave ten of its 17 seats to the Liberals, Saskatchewan and Alberta each returned only two Liberals. In Saskatchewan the CCF dominated with 18 of the 21 seats and Gardiner, as one of the two Liberals, was returned only after a recount. Firmly entrenched in Alberta, the Social Credit Party captured 13 of the 17 seats, but MacKinnon won his Edmonton riding as one of the two Liberals elected in that province.

It was ironic that Gardiner, whose persistent interventions on behalf of the farmer had wrung concessions from the treasury time and again, made it back to office by the skin of his teeth in the face of the CCF tide in Saskatchewan. In his near defeat, Gardiner recognized the need of doing something spectacular on behalf of producers to regain his popularity.[25] Crerar, the elder statesman on the cabinet wheat committee, had been appointed to the Senate on April 18, 1945, and his place was later taken by J.A. Glen who was sworn in as the minister of mines and resources. Gardiner was now even more dominant as the principal architect of grain policy.

In that role, the agriculture minister now set about to capitalize on the basic dread of both producers and government that the postwar period would see a return to a surplus and price recession, as it had following World War I. Despite the fact that circumstances now indicated a period of scarcity rather than surplus, that fear had not abated. The result was to be Canada's first long-term grain agreement. But, unlike the future long-term agreements which were to play such a large role in the success of the Canadian Wheat Board, this one was negotiated at the cabinet level almost solely by Gardiner rather than by the commissioners of the board. The end result was an agreement which remains controversial to this day.

Details of the postwar search for stability remain for the next chapter, but its roots go back to the immediate prewar period. At the initiative of the United States, talks were convened in London under the International Wheat Council aimed at securing an international wheat agreement and market sharing by the exporting nations. Canada was a reluctant participant in those negotiations which broke down in August 1939.

Canada was once again reluctantly drawn into the multinational negotiations when talks under the International Wheat Council were reinstuted in Washington in 1941. Aimed at reaching agreement on prevention of chaotic export wheat competition in the immediate postwar period, the talks continued sporadically for some years. The Canadian government expected little of substance from the talks, but participated out of concern that blame for any breakdown of negotiations might rest upon Canada.

Members of the cabinet committee on wheat were also wary of the behind the scenes manoeuvring of an expatriate Canadian, Andrew Cairns. In the history of the search for an international grains agreement there can have been no more persistent and dedicated advocate than Cairns. He first surfaced as the statistician of the Central Selling Agency of the prairie pools in the mid-twenties. Personally convinced that the days of the open market were numbered and that wheat trade in the future would be placed in the hands of an international agency, Cairns was the consummate operator in that cause.

In 1933 he was on the staff of the Empire Marketing Board in London and aided Prime Minister Bennett on the first IWA negotiations in that year. Later he became secretary of the International Wheat Council and nudged, goaded, and cajoled governments at every opportunity towards his personal dream. He was remarkably successful in initiating conferences. When war broke out, he sought British Ministry of Food sponsorship to co-ordinate wheat purchasing through quota allotments among exporters, which earned him the outright distrust of the Canadian cabinet committee on wheat, particularly Gardiner. It was Cairns' initiatives that led to the IWC meetings in Washington during the war. If an effective international grains arrangement is ever achieved in the future, Andrew Cairns will surely have to be its patron saint.

As for the pools and the Canadian Federation of Agriculture, establishment of monopoly powers for the Canadian Wheat Board in 1943 was viewed as but the first step towards achievement of that same goal. As early as 1933 the three basic principles of pool philosophy had been enunciated: firstly, establishment of a national marketing board; secondly, agreement with other exporting countries on export quotas and prices; thirdly, a fixed price above the market for wheat consumed in Canada. At the end of the war they were still pressing for those goals.

As the Washington meetings dragged into the fall of 1945 with shifting attitudes and little agreement on a minimum and maximum price structure, Gardiner became impatient. C.F. Wilson, Canada's representative at the Washington meetings, reported: "Because of the desultory reports sent to Ottawa during the course of that meeting, Gardiner became convinced that the international approach afforded no hope of the postwar assurance of markets and of price stability that western wheat producers so urgently needed. Thereafter he directed his attention to obtaining the same result by other means."[26]

Before examining the results of Gardiner's search for stability, the traumatic situation facing the Canadian Wheat Board on August 1, 1945, at the start of the new crop year should be put into perspective.

The Board was now employing 716 personnel. It had grown from an organization of some 50 people at the outset of the war. There were 672 employees at the head offices in Winnipeg, 27 in Calgary, 13 in Vancouver, 3 in Toronto, 2 in Washington and 2 in London, England. But the future role of this expanded and complex organization was still very much in doubt. Although its current functions had been extended for the duration of the 1945-1946 crop year by an order-in-council passed under the War Measures Act on April 12, 1945, the federal government, which still cherished hopes of a return to the Liberal free trade philosophy of prewar years, had not made a definitive decision on the board's future after July 31, 1946.

Three alternatives presented themselves: dissolution of the board and a return to the exchange system of open marketing, restoration of the board to its former role as an optional standby marketing agency, or continuation of the monopoly marketing role for wheat and/or other cereal grains. As the war emergency wound down, campaigns had already been mounted by the Winnipeg Grain Exchange for return of the futures market and by the pools, who favoured continuation of the monopoly powers over wheat and extension of those powers to other cereal grains.

In the midst of that uncertainty, the board and its staff were seized of an urgent situation. A cold, late spring delayed seeding and then drought struck large areas of western Canada. Crop deterioration was severe throughout the greater part of western Saskatchewan and southeastern, central and northern Alberta by mid-June. The prairie wheat crop was estimated at 282 million bushels, down over 100 million bushels from the previous year's 392 million bushels. The impact of the drought was so severe that an embargo was placed on export of coarse grains in order to maintain livestock production in Canada. Thus, despite the wheat carryover of 258 million bushels at the beginning of the crop year, every kernel was to be urgently required to meet an unprecedented demand.

The preamble to the report of the Canadian Wheat Board for the 1945-1946 crop year dramatically outlined the situation:

> The major task of all wheat exporting countries in 1945-46 was to provide maximum quantities of wheat and flour to assist importing countries through the first full crop year following the end of the war.

> In that effort Canada played a leading part and for the third successive year provided wheat exports (including flour) in excess of 340,000,000 bushels. Into the effort of 1945-46 went the last of Canada's wartime reserves of wheat and in the latter part of the crop year exports were determined by the volume of wheat which producers made available at country elevators.
>
> The exceedingly urgent demand for breadstuffs during the crop year was, in part, a legacy of six years of war and, in part, due to the small wheat acreage seeded in Europe in 1945 and a virtual crop disaster which struck the Danubian area, Greece, Italy and North Africa. Thus, import demands were expressed not only in terms of the normal requirements of importing countries and special demands following the war, but also in terms of the effects of a devastating drought in southern Europe and North Africa.
>
> Wheat production in Europe in 1945 was about 600,000,000 bushels below the pre-war average and this was sufficient in itself to create an acute demand for breadstuffs in Europe. To the effects of reduced production must be added the accumulated food problem following six years of war, and the urgent demands uncovered by the final liberation of Europe and the defeat of Japan. The requirements of India and liberated areas in the Far East were large and urgent.
>
> The full impact of this food position confronted the Cereals Committee of the Combined Food Board early in the crop year. It was evident that Canada and the United States would have to fill the major part of the world import requirements. The severity of the crisis and the threat of mass starvation on a large scale called for a major, coordinated effort on the part of Canada and the United States. The effectiveness of this effort is indicated by the fact that, in the year ending June 30th, 1946, Canada and the United States together exported about 750,000,000 bushels of wheat (including flour) which constituted the largest wheat exports in the history of the North American continent. In addition to these supplies of wheat, both countries supplied quantities of other grains for human consumption.[27]

All of the exports were programmed through the cereals committee of the Combined Food Board, of which George McIvor was the chairman, and were related to programs undertaken by other countries. As the Canadian Wheat Board reported, "There is no doubt that a potential disaster of great magnitude was overcome by exporting countries making available every bushel of wheat and substitute grains which could be made available, and by the co-ordination of exports, particularly on the part of Canada, the United States and Australia.''[28]

In fact, because of the extreme need, Canada, the United States, and Australia over-exported wheat during that critical postwar year. The export effort, and the attempt to meet domestic requirements left Canada with the lowest reserve stocks since 1937. Total carry-over of Canadian wheat in all positions at July 31, 1946, stood at a meagre 69,858,181 bushels and 27,203,000 bushels of that were on farms. Stocks of wheat in export positions were practically exhausted.[29] MacKinnon's statement prior to the opening of the crop year that a limitation on deliveries of wheat of 14 bushels per authorized acre ''is final and will not be lifted at a later date,'' was lifted in October 1945, in the face of the unexpected demand. Delivery quotas were thrown open.

Canadian wheat played a significant part in the winning of the war. Now, in a magnificent effort, it was playing a part in winning the peace. It was not without some sacrifice on the part of Canadian producers and consumers. Prime Minister King announced on March 18, 1946, that the government would reduce the amount of wheat available for domestic milling by 10 per cent over the previous year and the use of wheat for distilling was reduced by 50 per cent.[30]

While the producers were marketing all of their grain to fill the shortage in world wheat supplies which could not under the circumstances be overcome, a ceiling had been placed on the price they received. Up to the spring of 1945, the Wheat Board had been pricing its exports of Class II wheat by using Chicago quotations and deducting the differential which existed between Winnipeg and Chicago futures prices at the time the Winnipeg Exchange was closed.

However, in May 1945, the board faced a pricing dilemma: the United States was matching competition with an export subsidy through its Commodity Credit Corporation. Since the Chicago market was affected more by the American domestic wheat loan policy than by export considerations, the board left the Class II export price to nations outside of the Mutual Aid program at $1.55 a bushel, basis No. 1 Northern, Fort William. Then, by order-in-council on September 19, 1945, Ottawa instituted a unilateral ceiling at that price. To justify the $1.55 ceiling to producers, the government agreed to guarantee a floor price of $1 a bushel over the next five years.

The decision to peg the export price appears to have been a mixture of benevolence and self-interest. On the one hand, Finance

Minister Ilsley shared the opinion of the Wartime Prices and Trade Board that if the price were allowed to rise on such an important commodity as wheat it would be impossible to keep a lid on inflation. At the same time, reports from the International Wheat Council indicated that no accord could be reached on ceiling and floor prices in a multilateral agreement. In announcing the policy in the Commons, Trade Minister MacKinnon stressed more humanitarian reasons for the $1.55 price peg:

> In these extraordinary circumstances, Canadian wheat might well command for a limited period very much higher prices in the world market. The importing countries, nearly all of them our allies in the war, are buying out of necessity and, to a large extent, on credits. They would be compelled to meet through larger credits or through sacrifice of other food and rehabilitation supplies whatever higher price is demanded for Canadian wheat....There is a moral obligation not to take advantage of our recent allies in their time of compelling need.[31]

The pervasive fear of recurring surplus was also on the government's mind: "Higher wheat prices would encourage the importing countries in a hurried return to wheat production and pre-war policies very directly to the detriment of the wheat exporting countries, particularly Canada. Moreover, production in a number of exporting countries would be unduly encouraged."[32]

The $1.55 ceiling, along with the five-year guarantee of a $1 floor in the event of of a recurring world surplus, were the first steps in the search for stability through the postwar transitional period. Agriculture Minister Gardiner, however, was already concentrating on a further step that was to lead to controversy.

When steam was king. A line of boxcars draws up to the station at Homewood, Manitoba. Diesel engines replaced the steam locomotives in the early 1950s.

SEARCH FOR STABILITY

The government of Canada and the government of the United Kingdom, recognizing that their mutual interest in the maintenance of reasonable prices and adequate supplies of wheat for consumers and of steady remunerative prices for producers can best be met by international co-operation in the expansion of world trade and employment, have entered into the following arrangements designed to ensure a measure of security in the supply and of stability in the price of wheat supplied by Canada to the United Kingdom.

— Preamble to four-year agreement between Canada and the United Kingdom, July 24, 1946

The meeting of the cabinet committee on wheat was held on Parliament Hill in Ottawa May 2, 1946. The atmosphere was tense. Jimmy Gardiner had his mind set firmly on the largest of all contracts—a long-term multi-million bushel sale of wheat to Britain. Convinced that multilateral negotiations presented no hope of the postwar price stability he so ardently desired for western farmers, the agriculture minister would accept no roadblocks to his plan.

The modifying influence of T.A. Crerar, now a senator, was absent from the committee and Finance Minister J.L. Ilsley was unavailable for the meeting; the aggressive Gardiner had little trouble in dominating the meeting. Trade Minister MacKinnon, as chairman of the cabinet wheat committee and the only other member present, was no match for Gardiner.

Also in the committee room were a number of advisers who had grave reservations on the course of Gardiner's initiatives toward a massive bilateral agreement. They included the three commissioners of the Canadian Wheat Board, McIvor, Huntting and McNamara, board secretary T.W. Grindley; and M.W. Mackenzie, deputy minister of trade and commerce.[1]

Gardiner had first broached the subject of a five-year wheat agreement with Britain at a previous meeting of the committee in December 1945. After first ascertaining that prospects of agreement in the international price negotiations were bleak, Gardiner noted that he would shortly be heading a delegation to London to renegotiate other food contracts. He suggested that Canada's granting of priority to Britain on wheat sales and the unilateral price peg of $1.55 a bushel be used as levers in the negotiation of a long-term wheat contract.

Gardiner initiated preliminary discussions with the British in late December, and these were followed up in mid-January 1946 when he and MacKinnon went to London on a trade mission. On his return to Ottawa February 7, Gardiner immediately reported to cabinet on the preparatory talks. The negotiations were resumed in March when Britain's Minister of Food, Sir Ben Smith, visited Ottawa to plead for increased wheat production.

McIvor, who had already expressed the board's grave reservations on the terms of the proposed five-year contract, which involved a proposed offer of up to 200 million bushels a year in the initial stages of discussion, was now drawn into the negotiations and followed Smith back to London in April.

During his absence, the board was at work formulating a reply to MacKinnon, who had asked for a study on the merits of the proposed contract. As a result McIvor, after his return from London, forwarded a lengthy confidential memorandum to MacKinnon. While the members of the board had more serious reservations about the wisdom of the contract than their memorandum displayed, their comments were circumspect because they were reluctant to intrude their views upon what was primarily a political decision.[2]

Among other things, the board's memorandum queried the wisdom of tying up too large a portion of Canada's available wheat supplies to one customer, thereby denying contractual access to other traditional customers under similar terms and conditions. It also warned that a long-term contract would necessitate continuation of the monopoly powers of the board and postpone reversion to the government's prewar policy of restoring the open market, or at least, a voluntary board. McIvor had previously sought advice on the future role of the board, but the decision had been held in abeyance by the cabinet wheat committee which shied away from a lengthy debate in the Commons which amendments to the Canadian Wheat Board Act might provoke.

As the May 2 wheat committee meeting got under way, it also faced another pressing issue brought forward by McIvor. The duration of the $1.55 export price ceiling had not been defined. With commercial export prices near the $2 a bushel level, farmers were holding back on their deliveries in the expectation that the ceiling might soon be lifted. With supplies urgently needed, the board sought direction from MacKinnon through the wheat committee.

C.F. Wilson, as secretary to the cabinet wheat committee, has documented the proceedings.[3] The ministers first turned their attention to the export ceiling. They recognized that it was impractical to continue the fixed price on a unilateral basis. With the British contract dominating his thoughts, Gardiner recommended that such a contract supersede the ceiling. Until the contract could be concluded, he recommended that producers be paid $1.55 on wheat delivered into the domestic market rather than the $1.25 they were now receiving. Any change in the domestic price, however, would have to be approved by Ilsley, and that issue, in turn, involved the gradual phasing out of domestic price controls.

Mackenzie, who had been chairing an interdepartmental committee on the broader aspects of Canada's postwar trade policy, warned of dangers in a bilateral agreement, but the warning fell on deaf ears. Huntting and McIvor also expressed reservations on the bilateral agreement, but, despite that, Gardiner was determined that negotiations with Britain proceed. The ministers were forced to face the inevitability that a long-term contract would necessitate retention of the board's monopoly powers. Too thin a trading volume would remain to permit reopening of the futures market for sales outside of the contract. The question of the constitutionality of retaining the board's monopoly powers in peacetime, which had been raised in the Wheat Board's memorandum, was disposed of by deciding that, temporarily at least, the powers could be conferred through the National Emergency Transitional Powers Act.

> Undoubtedly, the decision was eased by the stature the Board had acquired through its competent administration of the complex problems in the war years, and by the current strength of the farm organizations' support for a monopoly Board handling all grains. Nevertheless, the contract had precipitated the issue, and the government's prewar policy of eventual withdrawal from marketing operations and the restoring of them to the Pools and to the private trade was thereby summarily reversed.[4]

Toward the end of the meeting, Gardiner and MacKinnon readily accepted the board's recommendation that the terms of the proposed contract be made subject to any terms that might be negotiated under an international wheat agreement. This was among the many concerns raised in the board's memorandum. While there seemed to be little prospect of a successful outcome, Wilson was given authority to see what could be done to revive the multilateral negotiations.

Finally, it was decided that McIvor should resume negotiations through Sir Andrew Jones, the newly arrived head of the British food mission in Ottawa "who should be advised at once that Canada was prepared to proceed to negotiate a five-year contract on the basis of $1.55 per bushel No. 1 Northern for the crop years 1946-47, 1947-48, 1948-49; not less than $1.00 per bushel for 1949-50 and 1950-51 with the actual price to be determined a year in advance. The quantity involved would be 180,000,000 bushels per year, a stated percentage to be in flour, the actual amount to be subject to negotiation."[5]

A measure of the Wheat Board's reluctance to be associated with the contract negotiations, increasingly directed by Gardiner at the political level, was indicated in their memorandum of April 28: "The contract now under discussion is not a contract as generally understood in the grain trade. It is, in the Board's opinion, in the nature of a treaty between the Government of Canada and the

Government of the United Kingdom.''[6] While Gardiner was later to declare that the farm organizations accepted the agreement for its stabilizing value, in lieu of immediate attainment of an international wheat agreement, and as a bridge to the latter, there were early indications of opposition from that quarter.

On March 28, a delegation of the Canadian Federation of Agriculture, headed by its president, H.H. Hannam, and vice-president, W.J. Parker, had made its annual presentation to the prime minister and cabinet. The federation brief began with a call for the Canadian Wheat Board to be established as the sole institution for the marketing of all Canadian cereal crops. This was supported by all CFA members with the exception of United Grain Growers, who asked that their non-concurrence be recorded.[7]

The principal thrust of the CFA presentation on grain policy dealt, however, with a request for aggressive leadership by the government in working out an international wheat agreement. Parker, as president of Manitoba Pool Elevators, later declared that the principal of a bilateral agreement was discussed at some length to which the federation expressed its opposition, and just as definitely supported a multilateral arrangement embracing all countries, importing and exporting alike.[8]

Evidence of any further discussion with the farm leaders is scant, since most of them left Canada for a prolonged period to attend the founding meeting of the International Federation of Agricultural Producers in London. When they returned the final agreement was a fait-accompli. It is also quite clear that the government did not formally consult with the advisory committee of the Canadian Wheat Board during the contract negotiations. C. Gordon Smith read a prepared statement at the January 9, 1947, meeting of the advisory committee: ''Since V.J. Day, many things have been done by the Board and the government which should have first been referred to this committee, but the most glaring affront to us is evident in the wheat contract with the United Kingdom.''[9]

After transmission of the cabinet wheat committee's proposal to Sir Andrew Jones on May 3 by McIvor, there was a delay in getting the two sides together. Then, in mid-June, a British delegation arrived in Ottawa, followed several days later by Britain's minister of food, John Strachey. At this point, Gardiner's intervention in the negotiations became even more direct. Negotiations between the teams commenced June 14 and made considerable progress by the time Strachey arrived June 18 for a one-day stop enroute to Washington.

Gardiner seized the opportunity to meet with Strachey and one or two of his officials. In their talks, Gardiner and Strachey agreed upon a four-year contract for 160 million bushels of wheat in each of the first two years and 140 million bushels thereafter. The price for the first two years was fixed at $1.55. Floor prices of $1.25 and $1 were agreed to for the third and fourth years.

Since no price ceiling levels were specified for the third and fourth years of the contract, it was agreed between the two ministers that negotiations would be held seven months in advance of each of the final two crop years on the actual prices to apply in those years. Gardiner believed strongly that since Canada would be selling to Britain at below world prices in the first two years any such losses should be added to world prices in the final two years. He discussed that principle with Strachey. Enter now what became the famous, or infamous, "have regard to" clause.

Reporting on the discussions later Gardiner said that when the principle that any advantage gained by Britain in the first two years of the contract would be compensated for in the last two years was raised, "those with whom we were discussing it came right back and said, 'That is absolutely fair. We have no reason for refusing to do it.'"[10] Firmly believing that he had reached a gentleman's agreement, Gardiner left it to the British side to draft a clause giving effect to that verbal understanding. The next morning Sir Andrew Jones handed C.F. Wilson the British draft for consideration by the Canadian negotiators.

Wilson has recorded that "In all probability it had been prepared as a cockshy or try on."[11] Since the draft was precisely written into the final contract as Clause 2 (b), and since it was to become the centre of controversy later, it is reproduced in its entirety here:

> The actual prices to be paid for wheat to be bought and sold within the crop year 1948-49 shall be negotiated and settled between the United Kingdom Government and the Canadian Government not later than 31st December, 1947, and prices for wheat to be bought and sold within the crop year 1949-50 shall be negotiated and settled not later than the 31st December, 1948. In determining the prices for these two crop years, 1948-49 and 1949-50, the United Kingdom Government will have regard to any difference between the prices paid under this Agreement in the 1946-47 and 1947-48 crop years and the world prices for wheat in the 1946-47 and 1947-48 crop years.[12]

Wilson fully expected the Canadian negotiating team would take a long, hard look at the draft clause and that it would be subject to further negotiation, but it was not to be. Gardiner had the agreement in grasp and he wanted it approved immediately by cabinet. The draft had barely arrived when Gardiner intervened to demand its acceptance. He phoned MacKinnon and told him to instruct Wilson to accept it without change. "Wilson can still recall the look of incredulity which swept over Sir Andrew Jones's face as he was told of the acceptance of what was to become the celebrated 'have regard to' clause."[13]

That same morning McIvor was asked to attend cabinet discussions on the negotiations and outlined some of his concerns. Then, in the afternoon, he and A.M. Shaw were called to a meeting with Gardiner who instructed them to negotiate on the terms he had personally reached with Strachey.

Deeply disturbed over the course of events, McIvor wrote a lengthy letter to MacKinnon after he returned to Winnipeg. In a telling protest, McIvor outlined the board's concerns and the points that the negotiating team stressed during the talks. He added that after the June 19 meeting with Gardiner, the Canadian representatives had no alternative but to abandon negotiations on the basis of discussion of the preceding four days. As to the terms laid down by Gardiner, McIvor wrote in conclusion to his letter:

> As far as the Board is concerned, we feel that these instructions do not constitute an adequate basis for a contract with the United Kingdom. As a Board, we do not agree that the quantities should be variable; we think the quantity of wheat included for the crop years 1946-47 and 1947-48 is too high, especially in view of our lack of reserves at the present time, and we feel that the price basis for the third year of the contract is not satisfactory from the producers' standpoint in view of the sacrifices in income which producers will have made by the time the third year of the contract is reached.[14]

Even as the bilateral talks in Ottawa got under way, a new concern arose. Lester Pearson, then Canada's ambassador in Washington, noted in a telegram on June 14, the day the talks opened, that such an agreement would probably prove very unpopular in United States official circles. Norman Robertson, as principal external affairs adviser to Prime Minister King, also warned of the trade implications: "I feel very strongly that the conclusion of such a contract is not in the long-run interests of either Canada or the United Kingdom, and would be in direct conflict with the general policy of freer international trade to which the Government is committed."[15]

King himself had grave reservations as he wrote in his diary of June 19, 1946: "The contract itself while it has advantages with regard to stabilization for the farmers has nevertheless elements which are in the nature of a great gamble, as, for example, the certainty that the British Govt. will pay a higher rate than may be the current rate in a couple of years hence, to make up for their getting wheat at the present time at less than the current rate."[16]

But even as these concerns occupied cabinet on the following day, June 20, Gardiner had telephoned Strachey to inform him that they were agreed on all terms. He then left for the West.

As Pearson had forewarned, the United States had strong objections to the agreement. The implications for Britain were more far reaching than for Canada. The Truman administration had just submitted to Congress for approval a $3.75 billion loan to Britain. Given the critical state of Britain's balance of payments in the wake of the war, approval of that loan was of extreme importance.

On July 1, the U.S. State Department left an aide memoire with the British ambassador in Washington. No reference was made to the pending loan, but the note's implications were obvious. The Americans hoped that the Canada-United Kingdom contract (unless substantially modified) would not be signed. Taking exception to the preferential treatment accorded to Britain and Canada in a long-term arrangement, which appeared to be based on other than commercial considerations, the note said the contract was contrary to accepted proposals for the expansion of world trade and employment.[17]

King was visibly disturbed that Gardiner's phone call to Strachey had compromised cabinet's clear intention to hold conclusion of the contract in abeyance pending formal consultations with the United States. He wired the errant agriculture minister and instructed him not to make any announcement of the agreement. Robertson and Pearson were then instructed to continue talks with American officials to see if the United States could come up with any practical alternative to the Canada-U.K. agreement.

As the informal U.S.-Canada talks continued, the British delayed their reply to the U.S. aide memoire, pending approval in Congress of the loan to Britain. While reports from Pearson and Robertson in Washington indicated that the Americans had little to suggest by way of a practical alternative to the agreement other than to await the outcome of a trade policy conference, King continued to delay action on the contract pending the British reply to the American note.

Finally the U.S. loan to Britain was approved. The British ambassador in Washington left an aide memoire with the U.S. secretary of state on July 19. The British note denied that other than commercial considerations were involved in the contract, and declared that the quantities involved over the four-year period were well within Britain's actual requirements. As to the inference of discrimination, the British government said it was prepared to enter into similar contracts with other suppliers at negotiated terms.[18]

The way was now open for conclusion of the Canada-United Kingdom contract. Following final negotiation on flour quantities, the agreement was signed in Ottawa by MacKinnon and Sir Alexander Clutterbuck, the British high commissioner, on July 24, 1946.

George McIvor was very depressed over the course of the negotiations and declined to turn up at the signing. "The latter stages of the negotiation were most difficult for me. I felt that, between Strachey and Gardiner, that they had taken the negotiations completely out of the hands of both the British committee and ourselves. The British committee felt that way also."[19]

The "have regard to" clause was particularly galling to the chief commissioner. "I'm sure that if that clause had been submitted to us that we would have amended it. We would have fought over it till hell froze over. Have regard to what? It could be interpreted in any number of ways."[20]

Representatives of the Winnipeg Grain Exchange proceeded to Ottawa prior to the signing of the agreement, but, as in September 1943 when the futures market was closed, they failed to get a hearing before the final decision was made. On July 22, George Mathieson, president of the exchange, wrote the prime minister expressing regret over their failure to get an interview. The exchange also circulated a six-page memorandum espousing an expansionary multilateral trade policy and criticizing the contract as a violation of that principle.

W.J. Parker, after his initial criticism, had now come on side with the other pool presidents and welcomed the contract as a bridge toward an eventual international wheat agreement. The pool leaders, however, left it to CFA president Hannam to speak on their behalf. In a press release Hannam commended the agreement as being generally in line with thinking of organized farmers across Canada. At the same time he fired a broadside at the Winnipeg Grain Exchange. Declaring that producers had not been misled by an expensive campaign mounted by the exchange, the CFA release added:

"Wheat farmers know only too well that the men behind such a campaign were those who through the years have prospered in the buying and selling the farmers' wheat under the old speculative system of marketing, and the success of whose campaign would have resulted in the resumption of this system, with prospects of easy profits for themselves."[21]

With the British wheat agreement confirmed, Gardiner moved quickly to institute a second step aimed at guaranteeing stability for the farmer in the postwar transition. It was left to MacKinnon to announce the new policy on July 30, 1946, instituting a five-year pool, but its conception was entirely that of Gardiner. While there was no legal basis for creation of more than a one-year pool under the Canadian Wheat Board Act, Gardiner wanted to relate the terms of British contract to what producers would receive by way of a guaranteed initial payment over the period of that contract. His solution was to raise the $1 guaranteed initial price, previously announced in September of 1945, to $1.35 a bushel over five-years. Participation certificates would entitle producers to share in any surplus that might accumulate with settlement delayed to the end of the five-year period.

Since the Canada-United Kingdom contract covered only a four-year span, the five-year pool was made retroactive to the beginning of the 1945-1946 crop year on August 1, 1945, with termination on July 31, 1950. Inclusion of the 1945 crop in the five-year pool immediately came under fire from the prairie pools. In discussions with farm organization officials on July 24 when the U.K. contract was being signed, Gardiner had suggested an immediate payout of the surplus in the 1945-1946 Wheat Board pool account and creation of a four-year pool commencing August 1, 1946.

However, after the pool officers had left for the West, the government, at the insistence of the finance department, concluded that the terms of the U.K. contract could barely justify the $1.35 guarantee and too great a risk was involved unless the cash surplus in the board's 1945-1946 crop account was added to the pool. Rather than drop the initial payment below $1.35, Gardiner conceded and fell back on the argument that everyone until then had been discussing a five-year plan.[22] The pools did not agree.

Detailing the new policy to the Commons, MacKinnon announced that the initial payment for 1945-1946 of $1.25 would be brought up to $1.35 with an immediate payment of ten cents a bushel on deliveries retroactive to the start of the crop year. "After the ten cent payment has been made—to bring the initial payment up to $1.35—the plan is to place the remaining surplus from that crop in a five-year pool with the succeeding four crops of 1946, 1947, 1948 and 1949. Participation certificates will be issued in the usual way, but the payment on these certificates will not be made until after the conclusion of the five-year pool at July 31, 1950."[23]

The price to domestic mills was left at $1.25 a bushel, with the Canadian Wheat Board still administering drawbacks to the millers on wheat used for domestic purposes for the difference between that amount and 77 3/8 cents. The domestic price was later raised to $1.55 on February 18, 1947, and to $2 per bushel from August 1, 1948 to July 31, 1950.

There was a further complication that the Wheat Board had hoped to avoid. In the confidential memorandum of April 28 commenting on the proposed agreement with Britain, the board had expressed reservations about being forced into a two-price export policy. That eventuality now came into being. MacKinnon announced that "with regard to export prices, the supplies for the United Kingdom will obviously be supplied within the terms of the contract. In sales to non-contract countries, a serious effort will be made to sell at prices roughly corresponding to those of the other principal supplier—now, the United States."[24]

Thus, under the five-year pool, the government imposed a three-price system on the Canadian Wheat Board: the contract price of $1.55 to the United Kingdom; a domestic price of $1.25, with a consumer subsidy from the government adjusting that to 77 3/8 cents; and a non-contract export price which immediately rose to $2.05 in line with U.S. open market prices. Sales to the United Kingdom became Class I wheat and those to other nations were Class II export sales.

But if that was disconcerting for the board, there was a much harder blow for the Winnipeg Grain Exchange in MacKinnon's announcement:

> It will become apparent from what I have just said and from the terms of the United Kingdom-Canada wheat contract that the government considers it wise and advisable to continue the Canadian Wheat Board as the sole purchaser of western Canadian wheat from the producers. The government believes that the great majority of western producers are satisfied, for the present at least, with this method of marketing. The present powers of the Canadian Wheat Board will be extended

under the National Emergency Transitional Powers Act for the duration of this statute. When it expires, the government will direct its attention to the form and authority under which the board's powers may be further continued.[25]

By instituting the five-year pool through an order-in-council under the National Emergency Transitional Powers Act, the government sidestepped the question of the constitutionality of monopoly powers for the board in peacetime. At the same time, it set aside the one-year pooling provision of the Canadian Wheat Board Act by invoking the same Act.

Reaction to the five-year pool was varied. The Winnipeg Grain Exchange said it was gratifying that farmers were assured of a higher price for the past year and for the coming four years, but at the same time took the government to task for selling to the British at a price below the world market and allowing the U.S. exchanges to take the lead in price determination.[26] While the pool leaders welcomed the stability afforded by the enhanced five-year initial payment guarantee, they deplored the retroactive inclusion of the 1945-1946 crop year in the pool.[27]

John Bracken, former premier of Manitoba and now leader of the Progressive Conservative opposition in the Commons, while critical of the agreement and the five-year pool, defused that criticism in his opening remarks following MacKinnon's announcement in the House:

> I rise at this time to criticize the government's wheat policy. But before doing so, let me say this, with respect to the United Kingdom wheat agreement. Any agreement such as this which tends to level out the inequalities, and the wide fluctuation of prices in the past, is a step in the right direction. Even this agreement is better than no agreement at all; because, as the Minister of Agriculture pointed out, those of us who went through the price depression following the last war know the danger of proceeding without some kind of plan to try to avoid wide fluctuations in price.[28]

MacKinnon left it to Gardiner to defend the contract and the five-year pool, which he did with characteristic vigor. For Jimmy Gardiner it was the zenith of his career as the dominant force in government wheat policy. As the wisdom of the United Kingdom agreement was increasingly challenged, his star was in the ascendency. On January 28, 1948, C.D. Howe was sworn in as minister of trade and commerce replacing MacKinnon, who was temporarily transferred to the fisheries portfolio. In his new portfolio, Howe became chairman of the cabinet committee on wheat. While there was mutual respect, there could be no rapport between Gardiner and Howe. In the inevitable clash of two strong wills, it was Howe who emerged the winner.

Howe, a New England born and educated engineer, was already a legendary figure in Canadian politics when he assumed the trade and commerce portfolio. First elected to Parliament in 1935, Howe served in the pre-war years as transport minister. As minister of munitions and supply, Howe mobilized the Canadian manufacturing industry and its expansion during the war years and presided over its transition to peacetime pursuits in the post-war years. While he represented the northwest Ontario riding of Port Arthur, the new trade and commerce minister was no stranger to the western grain trade. Howe graduated from the Massachusetts Institute of Technology in 1908, and emigrated to Canada that same summer to take a post as professor of civil engineering at Dalhousie University. There he became acquainted with Dr. Robert Magill, a philosophy professor who later became chairman of the Board of Grain Commissioners for Canada and still later secretary of the Winnipeg Grain Exchange.

While chairman of the Board of Grain Commissioners, Magill decided on the construction of government inland terminals, and in 1912 persuaded Howe to resign from Dalhousie to advise on the siting and construction of the terminals. This led to the establishment in Port Arthur of Howe's own grain terminal construction company. In that endeavour, Howe was closely associated with leaders in the grain trade, particularly the western co-operative movement. Among the many innovations designed and patented by his company was the Dominion-Howe Unloader. Prior to this invention of the "tilt-car," grain had to be laboriously hand shovelled from box cars.

By the time he made his successful bid for Parliament in 1935, Howe, who was essentially a free enterpriser, had amassed a considerable fortune and a world-wide reputation as an innovative grain terminal builder. He was tough, aggressive, and courageous. When the ship in which he was travelling to Britain in December 1939 was torpedoed by a U-boat in the North Atlantic, Howe manned an oar in a lifeboat until they were miraculously rescued when a Scottish merchant vessel, ignoring strict orders, broke out of convoy to pick up the survivors.

Although he remained a free enterpriser at heart, Howe was

also a pragmatist. He reorganized Canadian National Railways before the war and created the Canadian Broadcasting Commission and Trans Canada Air Lines, later Air Canada. His accession to responsibility for the Canadian Wheat Board was only part of his varied pursuits in the post-war years, which included construction of the St. Lawrence Seaway and formation of Trans Canada Pipe Lines. It was not without reason that this remarkable man became known as "the architect of modern Canada."

Howe believed that crown corporations such as the Wheat Board should be operated as a competitive business, free from political interference as much as possible as long as they were efficiently managed. The Canadian Wheat Board's role was to pursue markets and sell grain in a competitive world market. Setting out his priorities in the Commons, Howe categorically stated: "The intent is maximum marketings, maximum transportation and maximum sales."[29] That philosophy, in large measure, led to the present status and function of the Canadian Wheat Board as it exists today. Ironically, within Howe's insistence that the board be left free to pursue those objectives without distraction lay the seeds that contributed in part to Howe's eventual political defeat. But that is for a later chapter.

If there could be no compromise with Gardiner, the rapport between Howe and George McIvor was immediate. McIvor, who provided continuity on the board throughout the Howe years, had persistently fought for freedom from political intervention in the board's day-to-day business. The chief commissioner now found himself with a minister who understood the grain trade intimately, and with whom he could discuss policy decisions freely. More often than not, when Howe was apprised of a situation or a problem, he would ask McIvor, "How do you think it should be done?" Given a definitive answer, Howe would simply reply, "Well, go ahead and do it." He would then back McIvor to the limit on the decision when questions arose in the House of Commons.[30] The bond of mutual respect and trust was such that McIvor resolved that he would remain with the board as long as Howe was his minister.

Howe's relations with Gardiner were soon resolved. As chairman of the cabinet committee on wheat, he called several meetings of that committee during 1948. But, in the final meetings when domestic issues came to the fore, the previously dominant Gardiner and Howe found themselves confronting each other in the absence of the other two members. Finance Minister Douglas Abbot had other preoccupations, and Glen was absent due to illness. Howe declined to convene further meetings and the committee was formally dissolved by order-in-council on March 17, 1949. The order-in-council revoked that of 1935 which set up the committee and restored sole responsibility for the board to the minister of trade and commerce, as set out in the original Canadian Wheat Board Act.

Thereafter, the Howe-Gardiner rivalry became submerged in the anonymity of cabinet, but emerged publicly in the final settlement of the Canada-United Kingdom wheat contract and the "have regard to" clause. In that traumatic aftermath, Howe once again demonstrated his supremacy in policy decisions.

Immediately following signing of the Canada-United Kingdom agreement, there were discussions across Canada as to the meaning of the "have regard to" clause. Critics said that, in law, it meant nothing. Gardiner replied that whether it meant anything legally or not, "experience had taught us that the United Kingdom always acknowledged her obligations in spirit and I was satisfied she would do so in this case."[31]

When discussion on interpretation of the clause was at its height, Britain's Minister of Food John Strachey accepted an invitation to speak to the Canadian Club in Winnipeg on February 25, 1947. In the course of his address he noted that the Labour government in Britain had come under criticism from the Conservative opposition for irrevocably binding the United Kingdom to an agreement, "which in their view will mean paying a far higher price to the Canadian farmers."[32] After quoting the text of the "have regard to" clause, Strachey added:

> Now these words mean neither more nor less than they say. They mean that the fact that we have bought our wheat from you this year below world prices—and that we may do so again next year—will be one of the factors in negotiating the actual prices to be paid in the third and fourth years. I and my government, and I am quite sure that this applies also to the Canadian government, would resist any attempt to add to or subtract from this clear and definite statement as written into paragraph two subsection (b) of the wheat agreement....[33]

Strachey's words strengthened the expectations of western producers that the prices in the last two years of the contract would compensate in good measure for the concessions they were making at the contract price in the first two years. They also assured Gardiner that his gentlemen's agreement was intact.

Continuation of the bilateral wheat agreement was used later that year as a bargaining ploy by Canada in the negotiation of continuing agreements with Britain on other agricultural products. In November 1947, Britain, in order to conserve hard currency, sought to cancel some of her existing contracts for specific commodities such as eggs and bacon which were available from Denmark for sterling. The Canadian cabinet refused to cancel, holding to its stand that if one contract were cancelled all others would follow, including wheat. It would then be placed on the open market, and food supplies from Canada would all be negotiated afresh based on open market prices.[34]

The British conceded and all of the food contracts remained intact. Tacit public acknowlegement that cancellation of the bilateral wheat contract figured in the negotiations was given by Prime Minister King in announcing renewal of the contracts. "The agreed arrangement provides for the continuance of the wheat agreement with the United Kingdom and for the continuance and renewal of the contracts for livestock products at prices adjusted accordingly."[35]

But whatever the implied intent of the "have regard to" clause, it was left to a new cast of characters to negotiate the final conclusion to the controversial agreement. On November 15, 1948, Mackenzie King resigned from office and Louis St. Laurent was sworn in as prime minister. Just prior to that, Lester B. Pearson was sworn in as secretary of state for foreign affairs. On the British side it was left to Sir Stafford Cripps and Hugh Gaitskill, in the absence of Strachey, to interpret the ambiguous clause.

Its final solution, in a series of dreary consultations over several years, was further complicated by continuing multilateral negotiations on an International Wheat Agreement (IWA) which, in large part, governed the agreed prices in the final two years of the contract. There were a number of mathematical calculations of the presumed loss to western Canadian farmers as a result of the agreement. They ranged from a $700 million estimate of loss by the Winnipeg Grain Exchange to $89 million by governmental sources. The comparison most frequently used by critics of the bilateral agreement calculated a loss of $363,732,000 over the first two years of the agreement, with additional losses in each of the last two years.

The latter figure of $363,732,000 was derived by comparing prices received for Class II wheat—wheat sold to other importing countries—with the $1.55 per bushel, plus 3 1/2 cents carrying charges, obtained under the bilateral contract. In the 1946-1947 crop year the weighted average Class II price was $2.43 and in 1947-1948 it was $2.88. Using that formula, the loss on 169 million bushels delivered to Britain in the first year of the contract would indicate a loss of $142,805,000 and in the second year, on shipments of 170.6 million bushels, would indicate a further $220,927,000 loss.

The carte blanche assumption that the Class II prices could have been obtained on all sales, including those to Britain under the agreement, is difficult to sustain. Canadian exports in that category were minimal fringe sales, reflecting the high prices that importers were willing to pay for small quantities.

Any calculation of losses under the U.K. agreement is further complicated by the diverse price formulas imposed on the Canadian Wheat Board by political fiat. There were no less than five categories of sales, each with variable price formulas, during the term of the five-year pool. Included in that pool, against which the final return to producers was calculated, were the 1949-1950 crop year sales to all importers, including the U.K., at $1.75. During the following four years, sales were divided into four categories: those to the U.K. under the agreement; Class II sales to other importers; exports in the final year to other countries under the International Wheat Agreement; and sales to the domestic market.

An analysis of the distribution of sales under the five-year pool in a table prepared for the 1949-1950 annual report of the Canadian Wheat Board[36] reveals the following: out of total sales of 1.135 billion bushels during the four-year term of the Canada-U.K. agreement, 56 per cent were exports to Britain at an average price of approximately $1.78; roughly 22 per cent went to the domestic market at fixed prices ranging from $1.25 to $2 for an average price of $1.68; slightly over 17 per cent was disposed of through Class II sales at an average price of $2.36; 5 per cent was exported in the final year to countries other than Britain under the IWA at an average price of $1.93.

From this melange of prices the producer received a total return of just under $1.79 at the end of the five-year pool. On the basis of the initial payment of $1.35 at the beginning of the pool, the board accumulated substantial surpluses. As a result interim payments of twenty cents a bushel on participation certificates were made on April 1, 1948, with a further twenty cent interim payment on April 1, 1949. At July 31, 1950, after full allowance for inventory stocks, a surplus of less than four cents a bushel remained for distribution.[37]

Further defying any precise mathematical calculation of presumed losses under the agreement was the fact that in making interim payments totalling forty cents a bushel no differentiation was made as to grades delivered by the producers. In short, a producer delivering the lowest grade of feed wheat received the interim payments, which, added to the initial payment, may have reflected a price above that prevailing on the open market. However, most calculations of loss were based on prices for the top grade.

Critics of the Canada-U.K. agreement have argued that the fringe Class II prices were a clear indicator of what would have been achieved through an open market in the absence of a monopoly board. It could equally be argued, however, that those higher prices were evidence of the efficiency of the Canadian Wheat Board when negotiating sales free of politically inspired bilateral and multilateral agreements and mandatory producer subsidization of the domestic market.

All such simplistic conclusions would, however, ignore the chaotic economic realities in the wake of six years of war. Britain, along with other importing nations and indeed Canada herself, faced acute balance of payments problems. Imports by Britain were made possible by U.S. and Canadian loans and by Marshall Aid. In fact her purchases under the Canada-U.K. agreement were largely with funds from American loans and aid programs. Had Canada not negotiated the firm agreement, albeit at concessionary prices, Britain might well have sought to divert agricultural purchases to sterling areas in order to conserve dollar funds. Also, any increased cost of wheat could well have resulted in more severe bread rationing in Britain, or by inroads on other essential imports. Most certainly Canadian contracts for other agricultural exports, such as bacon and dairy products, would have been terminated or severely cut back.

Had the whole of Canada's wheat exports been disposed of through the open market, the presumption is strong that prices would not have ruled as high as those that were obtained on the fringe. Despite his reservations about the course of negotiations on the Canada-U.K. contract, George McIvor said in retrospect that without the agreement it would be impossible to assess what the situation might have been. "We would have had our ups and downs [in price]. We always had them before and it wasn't going to change. What the net result of the ups and downs would have been I haven't any idea."[38]

Whatever the merits or demerits of entering into the four-year contract might have been, the eventual settlement of the "have regard to" clause led to a bitter confrontation between the two governments involved and precipitated an even more bitter domestic controversy. For McIvor, who had negotiated contracts for hundreds of millions of bushels of wheat over a five-year period during the war without a single complaint on either side, the inter-governmental dispute was a dismaying turn of events.

Negotiation of the price in the third year of the contract pointed out the fallibility of the double entendre contained in the agreement. Since the deadline for determination of the prices in the last two years of the contract fell seven months before the beginning of each of the crop years, it ruled out any possibility of foretelling that any price agreed upon would yield Canada compensation for losses in the first two years. There was simply no way of determining what world prices would prevail that far in advance.

Meanwhile, continuing meetings of the International Wheat Council on a multilateral agreement had shown signs of reaching a successful conclusion. If such an accord were reached, the Canada-U.K. bilateral contract specified that prices under the international agreement would prevail. In the face of that impasse, the two governments agreed upon a price of two dollars for the 1948-1949 crop year, with any differences under the ''have regard to'' clause to be negotiated one year later when determining the price for the 1949-1950 crop year.

In the interval, U.S. President Harry Truman, having been rebuffed by Congress on the signing of a multilateral wheat agreement for 1948-1949, made ratification of an international pact an issue in his uphill battle for re-election. When the principals met to negotiate the price to prevail in the final year of the British contract, Truman's upset victory in the November 1948 election made American participation in an international wheat agreement a near certainty.

It was in this atmosphere that Gardiner proceeded to London in December 1948, to begin negotiations on prices in the final year of the bilateral agreement and to attempt final clarification of the ''have regard to'' issue. Agreement on the contentious Clause 2 (b) continued to be elusive, and when the two governments finally announced agreement on a price of two dollars for the 1949-1950 crop year, it was specified that their representatives would meet not later than July 31, 1950, to settle any obligations under the agreement. When the time came for final resolution of the clause it was Howe, rather than Gardiner, who undertook the assignment. When he proceeded to London in May 1950, Howe took with him a powerful delegation including L.B. Pearson, Dana Wilgress, Norman Robertson, and George McIvor.

In the interim, agreement had been reached in Washington on the 1949 International Wheat Agreement. It was signed by thirty-seven importing countries and five exporting nations—Australia, Canada, France, the United States and Uruguay. Under the agreement, the importing countries undertook to guarantee purchases of 456,283,389 bushels of wheat in each of the four crop years from 1949-1950 to 1952-1953. Britain was the principal importer, undertaking to accept 177,067,938 bushels of that total.

Canada was allocated as the principal supplier with guaranteed sales of 203,069,635 bushels. Basic minimum and maximum prices were set out with a ceiling of $1.80 set for the four years and a floor price of $1.50 in the first year, declining in 10 cent increments to $1.20 in the final year.[39]

On September 9, 1949, the Canadian dollar was devalued by 10 per cent and the ceiling price effectively became $1.98 in relation to the terms of the IWA. Thus, the multilateral agreement overlapped the final year of the bilateral agreement with Britain, and with world prices prevailing at the ceiling in 1949-1950, the $2 price was almost in exact accord.

Howe and his delegation had not journeyed to Britain in May 1950 with the intention of negotiating the "have regard to" clause. Rather, with the four-year bilateral agreement drawing to a close, he sought to consolidate Canada's predominant position in the British market by way of an unpriced quantity guarantee following lapse of that agreement. He had cause for concern in that regard. The critical post-war food emergency had passed with a resurgence in world grain production, and the United States had withdrawn Economic Co-operative Aid funds for British offshore purchases of wheat in Canada. The pendulum was swinging toward recurring surplus.

In the formal discussions on quantity guarantees, Sir Stafford Cripps, heading the British delegation, raised the subject of the contentious "have regard to" clause and took the strong position that Britain had fulfilled all of her obligations in that respect.[40]

While adhering to that stand, the British side had no objection to Howe's public announcement that in 1950-1951 it was reasonable to assume that Canada would sell to the United Kingdom at competitive prices under the IWA, somewhere between 100 million and 120 million bushels of wheat. The British were anxious, however, not to be repesented as having given assurances in regard to wheat purchases in return for a waiver under the "have regard to" clause.[41]

When Howe reported the results of his meeting to cabinet, a lengthy debate ensued. Gardiner continued to maintain doggedly that a moral obligation for further payment existed in the contract. Howe was more inclined to accept the interpretation of the clause put forward by the British. While he agreed with Gardiner that there had been some losses over the term of the contract, Howe preferred to use the analogy of an insurance policy for which too high a premium might have been paid, "because a man who buys an accident policy never claims under it does not mean the policy should not have been taken out, or that the premiums should not have been paid."[42]

A painful series of meetings ensued over the following year. The British firmly maintained their stand that all obligations under the agreement had been expunged. After Howe revealed the British position during questioning in the Commons on June 5, 1950, there was a delayed shock reaction throughout the West. A producer campaign was mounted for further payment, either from the British or from the Canadian government.

In the face of that reaction, Prime Minister St. Laurent undertook a direct intervention on the thorny issue, first to Prime Minister Clement Attlee during a visit to Ottawa, and later in London to Hugh Gaitskill, who had succeeded Stafford Cripps as chancellor of the exchequer. He was singularly unsuccessful in changing the British stand.

Gardiner persisted in his belief that another attempt should be made to reopen the issue. He sought and obtained approval of cabinet to go to London and to take J.H. Wesson, president of Saskatchewan Wheat Pool, with him to present the producers' case. At a meeting with Gaitskill on February 20, 1951, Gardiner failed to move the British. When he suggested that Britain use the unexpended balance of $65 million remaining from Canada's loan to Britain as a final additional payment, Gaitskill replied that he was about to make an announcement that the British government would make no further drawing on the loan. In the light of that, it was not for him to suggest what the Canadian government should do with its own funds.[43]

Shortly after Gardiner reported back to cabinet on his final meeting with the British, St. Laurent announced in the House that the United Kingdom had made it clear that no further payment would be paid under the agreement. The government therefore recommended to Parliament that an amount equal to the balance of the United Kingdom credit, namely $65 million, be added to the sums awaiting distribution under the five-year pool.

The government contribution was equivalent to about 23 cents a bushel on the deliveries made during the last two years of the Canada-U.K. agreement to which the "have regard to" clause had reference. Distributed over all sales under the five-year pool, it was equivalent only to about 4 1/2 cents per bushel. Added to the surplus remaining for distribution by the Wheat Board, it resulted in a final payment of 8.33 cents per bushel, bringing the final return to producers under the five-year pool to $1.833.

The now infamous "have regard to" clause was gone but not forgotten. Both it and the five-year pool remained a controversial issue for years thereafter. Western farm organizations continued to pursue the issue and to seek further payment. They met with no more success than that of the government in its appeals to Britain. "In their rebuff of all further claims, the cabinet could sympathize with the producers to the extent that it, too, had been rebuffed by another government."[44]

Britnell and Fowke stated, "It hardly required the wisdom of hindsight to establish that the Canada-United Kingdom Wheat Agreement had been a thoroughly bad bargain from the beginning."[45] Other historians, such as MacGibbon and Wilson, have evaded such blanket condemnations with a more pragmatic assessment of variables in a complex situation. As for Gardiner, who must bear the brunt of any criticism for lack of legal preciseness in the contract, Wilson has properly noted that in the absence of the hope of creating an international agreement, those who opposed the contract at the outset had no viable alternative forms of market security to offer.

Although he had misgivings over the negotiations leading to the contract and was dismayed by the abrasive bickering in its aftermath, George McIvor said later that Gardiner had only one thought and that was to protect the western farmer. "There is no question about it. It was the highest and most sincere motive that a man can have."[46]

As for the western farmers who had pressed for a multilateral international contract to provide the stability they so ardently sought, there can be little doubt that the bilateral agreement with Britain served as a bridge to that goal in the 1949 International Wheat Agreement. Once it was realized that, for reasons of supply limitations, Canada was unable to enter into similar bilateral agreements with other countries, the importing countries seeking such agreements had a new incentive to support the IWA.

If it had no other salutory effect, it marked the last time that the federal government attempted direct political interference in negotiation of a long-term grain agreement. From henceforth, such negotiations would be left in the hands of the professional grain traders appointed to the Canadian Wheat Board.

GRASPING THE NETTLE

On both pricing and allocation there is a distinct conflict of interest between those who grow oats and barley and those who purchase them for feeding and for other purposes.

— Premier Stuart Garson of Manitoba in a letter to C.D. Howe, March 20, 1948

▪

While preparing to relinquish his long dominance on the political life of Canada in the early months of 1948, William Lyon Mackenzie King was still determined that his Liberal party should continue in power in Ottawa. Thus, at the cabinet meeting held on February 12 of that year, the strategy of legislation to be enacted in advance of the election campaign under a new leader was under active consideration.

Despite his long and constant advocacy of the Liberal philosophy of championing free enterprise against what he considered to be the encroachment of socialism, King could always bend to the wind of political consequences when the occasion demanded. Those political winds were now blowing strongly, from both east and west, toward compulsory marketing of coarse grains by the Canadian Wheat Board.

The cabinet had previously decided on a package of amendments to the Canadian Wheat Board Act, including a pension scheme for the board and its staff, authority to control interprovincial movement of wheat products as well as wheat, and authority to increase the initial payment under the five-year pool. It was now seized with the thorny problem of whether or not to turn oats and barley over to the board.

Within cabinet there was a deep division. The three western ministers, Gardiner, MacKinnon, and Glen, were all strongly of the opinion that unless monopoly powers over coarse grains were given to the board, the party would lose the entire western vote: "The C.C.F. would sweep everything."[1] C.D. Howe, who, as the new minister of trade and commerce, would have the responsibility of piloting the controversial legislation through the House, and Finance Minister D.C. Abbot, were strongly against extending the powers of the board. "They both feel it may further socialistic aims and lead to state marketing of goods, etc."[2]

It was left to King to bend his own Liberal philosophy to the political wind. "I had to give the decision; in doing so, I stated that I thought the Cabinet could not, on a matter affecting Agriculture, go contrary to the strong representatives of three Western Provinces. Howe immediately said: carried, and that ended the discussion on one of the most difficult matters we have had to deal with."[3]

Four days later, on February 16, Howe honoured his commitment. He included the clauses on oats and barley in the amending resolution which he introduced in the Commons. It was hoped that by introducing the amendments as a package the urgency of increasing the initial payment and making a much needed interim payment to producers would help carry the contentious coarse grains clause.

The path had been paved for extension of the Canadian Wheat Board's additional duties the previous year when the government began a systematic replacement, by specific legislation, of powers hitherto exercised under the National Emergency Transitional Powers Act.

In a series of far-reaching amendments to the Canadian Wheat Board Act of 1935 which covered seventeen pages, the government reaffirmed, and to some degree extended, the powers of the Wheat Board which had previously been exercised under the War Measures Act and its successor the National Emergency Transitional Powers Act. Rather than being described as a quasi-independent government body, designed to act as an agent for the grain growers' protection, the 1947 amendments made the specific declaration that "the Board is, for all purposes an agent of his Majesty in the right of Canada, and its powers under this Act may be exercised by it only as an agent of his Majesty in the said right."[4] The 1935 Act had simply specified "the Board shall be a body corporate having capacity to contract and to sue and be sued in the name of the Board."

Under the new statutory authority, the board was given complete control over interprovincial and export movement of wheat, and the Act provided that establishment of wheat delivery quotas were subject to the limitation that the final quota should not be less than fourteen bushels per authorized acre. Another significant feature of the revision was repeal of the clause in the original Act which obliged the board to utilize existing marketing agencies. The amendment empowered the board to "establish, utilize and employ such marketing agencies or facilities" as it deemed necessary for the purpose of its operations. In a concession to the now annual representations of the prairie pools, through the Canadian Federation of Agriculture (with the abstention of United Grain Growers), the right of the government by order-in-council to extend authority of the board to other grains was reinstituted. That provision, contained in the original 1935 Act, had been revoked by order-in-council during the war.

Although the 1947 statutory amendments continued these broad powers only through the period of the Canada-United Kingdom agreement, ending on July 31, 1950, the Canadian Wheat Board was clearly taking on the appearance of permanence. As a result of reaffirmation of its power to acquire, hold, and dispose of real and personal property, the board, on August 31, 1946, purchased the Wheat Pool Building and the Stock Exchange Building at 423 and 407 Main Street in Winnipeg at a cost of $450,000. During the 1947-1948 crop year the properties were renamed the Canadian Wheat Board Building.[5]

The Winnipeg Grain Exchange, whose members had, with cause, looked upon the 1943 suspension of futures trading as a temporary anti-inflationary expedient and had anticipated its reopening at the end of the wartime emergency, were now thoroughly alarmed. A delegation headed by Stanley L. Jones, the exchange president, proceeded to Ottawa to lobby members of the Commons and the Senate to oppose passage of the 1947 amendments. They obtained considerable support from the Conservative Party, which championed the open-market, and from those who had risen to prominence through the grain trade, particularly in the Senate.

After passage of the amendments in the Commons with the weight of the Liberal majority, the most articulate opposition came in the Senate from a group of Liberals led by Senator Tom Crerar. While the Liberal majority in the Upper House prevailed and the measures passed, it presaged an even more rancorous insurrection by Liberal senators the next year when the government sought to institute a constitutional framework for monopoly control of coarse grains.

There was a further contributing factor in the surge of demand for board control of oats and barley in 1947 as the government moved to dismantle price controls instituted during the war. The Wartime Prices and Trade Board had established price ceilings on oats and barley, and the government had also set floor prices which could be implemented, if need be, through the Canadian Wheat Board. As events turned out, the board was required to enter the market to support the floor prices on only two occasions by purchase of oats and barley futures.

With the increased wartime demand from the United States for feed grains in 1943 and with prices on the American market well above the domestic ceiling price in Canada, the Canadian government had been compelled to take measures to retain oats and barley for urgently required domestic usage, particularly in eastern Canada. In order to compensate western farmers for the difference in price they could have received through export, the government empowered the Canadian Wheat Board to collect equalization payments from exporters based on the difference between export and domestic prices. These equalization payments were placed in a fund for distribution to the producers.

Then as the demand for feed grains in both the United States and eastern Canada increased in the face of short crops in both areas, Ottawa extended the equalization payments to western producers on both their commercial deliveries and on authorized farm-to-farm transactions. That action, taken in October 1943, resulted in advance equalization payments of ten cents per bushel on oats and fifteen cents per bushel on barley which were paid at time of delivery.

Under these conditions, advance equalization payments paid to producers exceeded the equalization fees collected on exports. The deficits were absorbed by the federal government. Total advance equalization payments made to prairie producers between the crop years 1942-1943 and 1946-1947 inclusive amounted to $47,755,333 for oats and to $53,726,433 for barley.[6]

The end result of these complicated emergency measures was a strange anomaly. It equated to a two-price system, whereby feed grain prices in the West were higher than the price being paid by eastern livestock producers. On the prairies barley traded at the ceiling price of 64 3/4 cents, plus the advance equalization payment of 15 cents, for a total of 79 3/4 cents a bushel. Similarly with oats, the 10 cent equalization payment was added to the ceiling of 51 1/2 cents for a total price of 61 1/2 cents. In effect it was a subsidy to eastern feeders, who paid only the ceiling price on both grains. At the same time, they were being paid Feed Freight Assistance on their protected supply of western grains. Disenchantment with the situation was shown by a marked decline in livestock production in the West, despite government exhortations to increase production to meet domestic demand and exports under the Canada-United Kingdom contracts. When, on March 17, 1947, the government announced discontinuance of the advance equalization payments and moved to increase the domestic ceiling on oats and barley, concern on the part of eastern livestock and dairy producers mounted.

Dismantling of the price controls was achieved in a unique manner through an order-in-council, P.C. 1292, under authority of the National Emergency Transitional Powers Act. The method employed was to declare the Canadian Wheat Board to be the sole exporter of oats and barley. To give effect to this policy, all stocks of oats and barley in commercial positions were vested in the board. Thus, under the order-in-council, the board acquired title to 29,853,967 bushels of oats at the wartime ceiling price of 51 1/2 cents a bushel, and 20,992,099 bushels of barley at the ceiling price of 64 3/4 cents a bushel.

The order-in-council was given effect on April 3, 1947. The next day the price ceilings were removed, and the maximum price for oats was raised to sixty-five cents a bushel and to ninety-three cents per bushel for barley. Subsequently, the stocks acquired under the former ceiling prices were disposed of by the board at a net profit of $6,596,589 which was credited to the federal treasury.[7] In actual practice, what occurred was that title to the oats and barley, vested in the board by the order-in-council, was sold back to the former owners upon payment of the difference between the old and the new maximum prices. While it was not specifically stated in the preamble to the order-in-council, the government's action was obviously intended to thwart grain traders from acquiring an unwarranted windfall profit from the inevitable relaxation of emergency wartime controls.

Once again the Canadian Wheat Board became the government's chosen instrument to implement an objective.

The net result of discontinuance of the advance equalization payments, and the rise in prices for oats and barley was to restore near parity to feed grain prices vis-à-vis the West and the East. Alarmed over the rise in prices, eastern feeders joined forces with the militant prairie pools in their insistence on granting the Canadian Wheat Board monopoly control of coarse grains.

The concern of the eastern farm organizations was expressed at the annual meeting of the Canadian Federation of Agriculture held in Brockville, Ontario, in January of 1947, where the feed grains issue was discussed at length. With United Grain Growers once again recording dissent, the eastern and western members of CFA passed a resolution seeking board control: "As we have indicated, our dairymen, poultrymen, and livestock feeders are keenly concerned over the rise and fluctuations in the cost of feeds since decontrol, and are urging measures to stabilize these costs."[8]

Thus when the federal cabinet met to decide the issue on February 12, 1948, Mackenzie King realized that his party was facing a political issue of national dimensions. But in deciding to include monopoly control of oats and barley in the 1948 package of amendments to the Canadian Wheat Board Act, the government faced a controversial question of constitutional authority. Inclusion of the authority to delegate control of other grains to the board by order-in-council in the 1947 amendments had gone only part way to facing the constitutional question. If the board handling of coarse grains was on a voluntary basis, then the legislation would be *intra-vires*, or legally permissible under the British North America Act.

However, unlike wheat, the bulk of Canada's feed grains were either fed in the province of origin or moved in interprovincial trade to the East, with very little going to export. Authority for compulsory marketing of oats and barley through the board was therefore questioned. The government solved the constitutional question by making proclamation of the federal legislation conditional upon enactment of complementary legislation by the governments of the three prairie provinces. Legislative action by the provinces would assure beyond a doubt that compulsory marketing of oats and barley through the board, either within provinces or across provincial boundaries, was constitutional. Further, it would assure political acceptance of the policy by the three major producing provinces. The latter consideration may have had more importance than the unresolved legal implications.

Introducing the package of amendments for first reading, Howe said in part:

> It is with this dilemma in mind that we are introducing the present legislation. There is no question of the dominion's constitutional authority to regulate interprovincial trade or export trade in oats and barley, but there is very considerable doubt as to whether that limited power would in itself provide effective control of commodities which are so largely marketed locally. This amendment to the wheat board act will open the door as far as the federal government is concerned. The next step will be to determine whether the three provinces most directly concerned—that is in the prairie provinces—wish to join us in placing compulsory regulation of the trade in oats and barley in the hands of the wheat board.[9]

During debate on first reading, which extended over two sittings, the Conservative opposition moved an amendment to divide the bill into several bills in order that the oats and barley clause could receive separate consideration. For technical reasons the motion was ruled out of order.[10]

The Liberal government came under heavy opposition fire for including in the bill legislation to increase the initial payment to farmers along with that for compulsory marketing in oats and barley. In order to shorten debate, Howe promised to divide the bill in order to permit committee hearings on the controversial issue. When the time came to fulfil that promise during second reading, Howe made the motion to divide the bill, but at the same time, gave a broad hint to the government supporters that it should be voted down.[11]

Only a handful of Liberal members supported Howe's motion, as did the Conservative and Social Credit opposition. The CCF and a majority of the Liberals combined to defeat the motion to split the bill.[12] Inside and outside the House, Howe was accused of engineering defeat of his own motion.[13] The bill, embracing all amendments to the Canadian Wheat Board Act, was then considered in committee of the whole, following which it received third reading on March 19, 1948.

It went before the Senate on March 22, only two days before the Easter recess. If the progress through the Commons had been stormy, it was as a gentle summer breeze in comparison to its ride through the Senate. Senator Crerar who, as a long-time president of United Grain Growers and member of the cabinet committee on wheat, had consistently advocated freedom of choice in marketing for grain farmers, spearheaded a revolt by a group of Liberal members in the Upper House.

Senator Wishart Robertson, as Liberal leader in the Senate, had the task of piloting the legislation through the Upper House. He told Mackenzie King that Howe had lobbied to have the oats and barley clause defeated in the Senate: "Said he had spoken very strongly to Howe who had admitted he had phoned to Lambert or to Crerar to take this course which was a frightful thing for him to have done...."[14]

C.F. Wilson has noted that it was hard to give credence to the charge that Howe was quietly manoeuvring defeat of the bill, since senators Crerar, Lambert, Paterson, Euler and others were in no need of prompting by Howe to defend their lifelong principles: "If, in his confrontation with Howe, Robertson had implicated him in the insurrection, Howe may easily have responded in characteristic fashion to his cabinet colleague by going on the offensive."[15]

Crerar, who, along with Senator Norman Lambert, had acquiesced to the creation of a monopoly Wheat Board in 1943 only under the wartime emergency, joined Senator John T. Haig, leader of the opposition in the Senate, in condemning the bill on second reading. Following that, the bill was referred to the Senate committee on banking and commerce.

Waiting in the hall to testify before the Senate committee, George McIvor suddenly found himself in a quandary. He was about to be put on the spot. The chief commissioner was not entirely in favour that the board should assume compulsory marketing of oats and barley.

> In fact I was rather against it, because I knew of course that this would put the Board in a very difficult position vis'à-vis Eastern Canada. We'd have to act practically wiser than Solomon in fixing our prices. The politicians would be into it both ends. Everything had been pretty clean up to then, and I didn't like the prospect of getting into it.[16]

As he waited outside the committee room, McIvor was approached by Crerar with whom he was very close as a result of their wartime association. Crerar informed him that he was going to ask a question that he thought might embarrass McIvor a good deal. When McIvor asked what the question might be, Crerar said, "I'm going to ask whether you're favorable to the Board handling oats and barley."[17] The chief commissioner informed Howe, who had come along to listen to the proceedings, of the potentially embarrassing development. Howe simply grinned and said, "Well good luck to you."

As McIvor detailed to the committee how the Wheat Board might handle oats and barley, he waited with trepidation for Crerar's questions. But when Crerar's turn came, he failed to ask the dreaded question outright. Instead he launched into a lengthy dissertation on grain handling. Suddenly a senator from Prince Edward Island interrupted to ask a question about a mixed car of grain he had received from which something had been left out. McIvor recalled that, "He certainly got a good answer on that one; it was very extensive." Crerar, having spoken, never got back on his questions before the committee adjourned. McIvor was off the spot to the great delight of Howe.

Despite Crerar's failure to reveal McIvor's apprehensions on the board takeover, he and Lambert gained enough support to have the bill reported back for third reading with a recommendation that the oats and barley clause be deleted from the package. The committee approved the recommendation to delete by a vote of fifteen to eight.[18]

That afternoon it fell to Senator Wishart Robertson, government house leader, to quell the revolt by rallying Liberal support for rejection of the committee report. He succeeded in doing so, but only after watching nine of his fellow Liberals cast their votes with the meagre opposition. The final vote was twenty-five to seventeen for rejection of the report, leaving the oats and barley clause intact.[19] For the most part, the twenty-five Liberal senators who supported the clause were identified with the deficit feeding areas outside of the Canadian Wheat Board designated area. The package of amendments to the Canadian Wheat Board Act received royal assent on the evening of March 24, and the board was in the coarse grains business.

There was to be a delay however. The clauses governing raising of the initial price for wheat, a further interim payment to producers, and establishment of a pension fund for the board and its employees were enacted, but proclamation of the coarse grains clause was held back, pending complementary legislation by the provincial governments.

The political wisdom of the decision taken by Mackenzie King in opting for board control of coarse grains may, to some degree, have been reflected in the returns from the general election held June 27, 1949. The Liberals, under their new leader Louis St. Laurent, scored a resounding victory, winning 190 of the 262 seats in the Commons. On the Prairies, the Liberals staged a resurgence, regaining seats in all three provinces. In Manitoba they swept 12 of the 16 ridings leaving only 1 seat for the Conservatives and 3 to the CCF. In Saskatchewan, where the Liberals had won only 2 seats in 1945, they captured 14 seats, mainly at the expense of the CCF which held 18 seats in 1945. Only one Conservative, John Diefenbaker, was returned to office in Saskatchewan. In Alberta, the Liberals, with five members elected, regained 3 seats from the dominant Social Credit Party.

There was little difficulty obtaining co-operation on passage of complementary legislation from Premier T.C. Douglas of Saskatchewan, where the first CCF government in Canada had recently been elected. Douglas immediately proceeded to enact a Coarse Grain Marketing Control Act, which received royal assent March 25, 1948. The substantive portions of the Saskatchewan Act were very simple: "No producer shall...sell grain...for delivery within the province to any person other than the Canadian Wheat Board."[20] Another section of the Act, however, made an exception for farm-to-farm transactions for feeding purposes.

Manitoba and Alberta delayed action. Manitoba's Premier Stuart Garson was particularly reticent. Although he had initially been in favour of passage of the federal legislation, Garson found himself in a quandary over the need for complementary provincial action. Garson's reticence to enact provincial legislation may have been politically inspired. He was caught in the middle of a bitter controversy between Manitoba Pool Elevators and the Winnipeg Grain Exchange. Also, the powerful Winnipeg *Free Press*, despite its well-known Liberal advocacy, was supporting the exchange and stridently assailing the federal legislation as "a completely totalitarian technique of grain marketing for the country"[21]

Whatever his concerns about the political vulnerability of his own Liberal-Progressive coalition administration, Garson raised some pertinent and prescient questions in several long letters to Howe.

> Is the Wheat Board to be the agent of the producer of oats and barley charged with obtaining the best price possible in all available outlets?

> Or is the Board to be the agency of the Government, buying oats and barley at a price set by the Government for reasons not necessarily related to, and even incompatible with, the securing of the best price?[22]

Garson ended his letter by asking why complementary legislation was not being required from Ontario or Quebec since, without it, eastern farmers could sell their own feed grain at high prices and replace them by price-controlled western grain. It was a concern that was to resurface again in later years in continuing debate over domestic feed grains policies.

Howe's reply gave Garson little comfort by stating: "We would look to the Canadian Federation of Agriculture to recommend prices for oats and barley satisfactory to both producers and feeders."[23] After further correspondence, during which Howe shifted his defence of complementary legislation from legal to political grounds, the Manitoba premier published the exchange and defended his position in a radio address.

In the absence of legislation from Manitoba and Alberta, the federal government continued to withhold proclamation of the oats and barley clause, with the result that a delegation of western members of CFA and the western premiers met with Howe on February 21, 1949, to discuss the coarse grains policy. Howe held his ground on the need for complementary legislation and pointed to an ambiguity in the resolution on coarse grains, passed at the CFA annual meeting in January. The CFA resolution would have required the Wheat Board to sell coarse grains to the best advantage on behalf of producers on the one hand, while, on the other, the federal government would be expected to protect the livestock industry.

Howe told the pools they could accept Wheat Board responsibility for selling to the best advantage without further obligations on the federal government, or they could set up co-operative marketing pools on their own.[24] When Howe reiterated that stand in Parliament on March 14, Alberta and Manitoba shortly thereafter enacted legislation in identical form to that passed in Saskatchewan the previous year. Royal assent was given to the Alberta act March 29, 1949, and Manitoba followed on April 22, 1949. In the interim, Garson had resigned as premier of Manitoba to accept the justice portfolio in the St. Laurent administration. He was succeeded as premier by his former agriculture minister, Douglas L. Campbell. It was Campbell who put through the Manitoba legislation.

On July 20, 1949, the federal and provincial governments jointly proclaimed their legislation. Howe announced that, effective August 1, 1949, oats and barley produced in the three prairie provinces would be marketed through an oats pool and a barley pool operated by the Canadian Wheat Board. Initial payments were set on the basis of the 1949-1950 support prices, announced earlier by the federal government at 61 1/2 cents a bushel for oats and 90 cents for barley basis No. 1 Feed grades in store Fort William or Port Arthur.[25]

For the Winnipeg Grain Exchange it had been a critical and traumatic chain of events. Its continued existence was now in doubt. Deprived of its wheat futures market, and with the prospect that the oats and barley futures market would serve no useful purpose under a board marketing system, there was a division of opinion among members of the exchange as to whether it should continue trading in the residual grains of flax and rye.[26]

It fell to McIvor to relieve the exchange of its dilemma. Upon proclamation of the oats and barley legislation, the Wheat Board was faced with the decision of how the marketing of coarse grains should be carried out. Uppermost in the mind of assistant chief commissioner Bill McNamara, with his background in the Saskatchewan Wheat Pool, was that the Winnipeg Grain Exchange should be closed.

He posed the question to McIvor: "When do we close the exchange?" The reply was immediate: "Never, as far as I'm concerned. Do you expect me to sit between the East and the West on oats and barley?"[27] The chief commissioner was of the opinion that the eastern feeders should pay the market price. He was reinforced in that view by the report of a panel, headed by C.F. Wilson, which reported to the federal interdepartmental committee on external trade policy on problems pertaining to the board marketing of oats and barley. The report, passed on to Howe, said that the board, contrary to the expectations of eastern feeders, had no option under the Canadian Wheat Board Act except to sell western oats and barley in domestic and export markets at the highest available prices.[28]

The Canadian Federation of Agriculture, at its annual meeting of 1948, attempted to present a formula aimed at reconciliation of the conflicting interests between producers and consumers of western feed grains. It proposed "that the Board's domestic operating and selling procedure policy shall carry out the spirit and intent of a general agricultural policy that shall effect a proper relationship between grain and livestock prices, as determined by the Federal Department of

Agriculture after consultation with the Canadian Federation of Agriculture.''[29]

At the same time, the CFA resolution asked that amendments to the Wheat Board Act would ''not disregard the principle that the Wheat Board be an agency operating primarily for the benefit of, and in the interests of grain producers.'' Thus, the CFA formula failed to provide a precise definition of pricing policy and it could not be adopted as a practical policy by the board.

The potential for creation of a serious strain within the CFA itself was inherent in the conflicting aims of the compromise. Under these circumstances, the board fell back upon the recommendation that it follow the intention of the Canadian Wheat Board Act in selling to the producers' best advantage. To do so, the board needed a price indicator and accordingly chose to be guided by the trend in United States markets, particularly the cost of imported feed grains, which were mainly corn.

Thus, on August 4, 1949, the board announced that it intended to ''sell oats and barley freely and to the best advantage.'' In order to do so, the board said it would use the futures market. At the same time it was prepared to make outright sales of oats and barley, in store Fort William, Port Arthur, if buyers wished to purchase on that basis. To give effect to the policy, the board said it would quote prices on principal grades in store at the Lakehead and would establish prices of oats and barley for sale at country points in western Canada and for shipment to British Columbia.[30]

A degree of the acceptance in western Canada of the board takeover of coarse grains was given a year-and-a-half later when a producer plebiscite was held in Manitoba. Faced with a continuing outcry by the private trade, supported by the Winnipeg *Free Press* and the opposition in the legislature, Premier Campbell decided to ''shut them up once and for all.''[31]

As a practicing farmer, Campbell was well aware of the high regard among farmers for the Wheat Board which was then at the zenith of its popularity, notwithstanding the controversy over the Canada-United Kingdom contract. He set about silencing the critics by announcing in the legislature on February 19, 1951, that his government would introduce legislation to provide a producer plebiscite on coarse grain marketing, with the vote to be taken as soon as possible after the results of the 1950-1951 crop year sales by the board became known.

Although taken by surprise, the farm organizations had no

apprehension as to the result. The Manitoba Federation of Agriculture and Co-operation mounted a campaign in support of board marketing. On November 24, qualified farmers were asked to vote yes or no to the question: Do you wish to market your oats and barley as at present? The result was overwhelming. When the results of the referendum were announced, 34,898 farmers out of an eligible 51,803 voters had cast their ballots. Of those, 31,052 voted yes, thereby supporting the board, while a meagre 3,846 voted no.[32]

The Manitoba Co-operator, a weekly newspaper published by Manitoba Pool Elevators was jubilant. It had been carrying on an editorial feud with the Winnipeg *Free Press* and its weekly farm paper the *Prairie Farmer*. Rubbing salt in the wounds after the almost ten to one vote in favour of board handling of coarse grains, the editor declared, "By the tone of its latest editorial dealing with the results of the Coarse Grains Referendum, the Sifton press apparently considers it necessary to whistle like a frightened boy, as they pass the graveyard of interred editorials."[33]

But if the pools and the majority of prairie farm organizations (with the exception of United Grain Growers) found satisfaction in their vindication by the Manitoba vote, eastern farm organizations quickly became disillusioned. Finding that they were not to become parties to domestic coarse grains pricing through participation of the CFA in that process, they soon switched to seeking removal of board jurisdiction over domestic marketing of oats and barley.

Rather than resolving the conflict of interest between coarse grains producers and consumers and bringing peace to the domestic scene, the decision of 1948 opened a Pandora's box of political sprites that were to plague both the government and the Wheat Board long into the future. The forebodings expressed by McIvor within the board and by Garson and others on the political implications inherent in the East-West conflict were to be amply borne out.

It is safe to say that no other agricultural policy question, aside from the bitter debate over the statutory Crowsnest grain hauling rate, has been so divisive on the national scene. This author, as an observer, sat through more than a decade-and-a-half of Canadian Federation of Agriculture annual meetings at which the domestic feed grains policy dominated debate. Accord was never reached, and on one occasion the Quebec delegation rose as a body and left half-way through the meetings, not to return until the next year.

Eastern and British Columbia delegates to CFA, who vigorously opposed any consumer interference in the operation of producer marketing boards operating within their own commodity areas, appeared to have no difficulty in reconciling any inconsistency when they, as consumers of western grains, voted to remove the powers of the Wheat Board on the domestic scene. Even on the prairies, where the majority of farmers unequivocably support the board's role in the export field, the domestic feed grains policy, in its varying forms, has at times split the farm community and served as a wedge for continued debate by minorities seeking a return to the open market.

Given the nettlesome course of political and regional infighting over the marketing of domestic feed grains, which persisted almost without respite into the mid-1980s, it is a fascinating exercise to attempt to analyze the motivations and actions of the principals when control was vested in the board.

As previously noted, the decisive intervention of Mackenzie King in the final cabinet decision was a political expediency, aimed at ensuring the continuity of the Liberal administration under new hands. In bending his own philosophy of Liberal free trade, King convinced C.D. Howe of the need for that same expediency. Both, however, may have taken solace in the apprehension that the method chosen, of demanding "conjoint," or complementary, legislation from the Prairie Provinces, would ultimately negate the need to proclaim the legislation.

King undoubtedly remembered the sequence of events in 1922, when he had bowed once before to prairie producer pressure for reinstatement of the 1919 Canadian Wheat Board. Legislation reluctantly enacted by his government in the face of that pressure foundered, in part, on the failure of one of the provinces, Manitoba, to enact complementary legislation and, in part, on the failure of the other two provinces to recruit competent personnel to head the proposed board. The 1922 legislation lapsed, to the obvious relief of King and other members of his cabinet. Hopefully, that sequence of events would repeat itself with the Liberals benefitting at the polls for enabling legislation that would be thwarted at the provincial level.

In conversations with McIvor, Howe confidently predicted failure to get unanimity on complementary legislation at the provincial level. But the chief commissioner, knowing the mood of the majority of western farmers, disagreed and told his minister it would be overwhelmingly accepted. Howe conceded to the reality after the Manitoba plebiscite and declared, "If that is what the farmers want, then I am with them all the way."[34]

McIvor was apprehensive that the board would be caught between the East and the West on pricing policy. He was relieved when Howe was informed by a panel that the board had no recourse under the Act but to sell to the best advantage of the producer, and the board was allowed to use the facilities of the oats and barley futures market in determining prices vis-à-vis imported American feed grains.

At the producer level in the West, the pools had consistently fought for such a policy since the Canadian Wheat Board Act was first introduced in 1935. As the other major voice in the West, United Grain Growers had just as consistently followed the precepts of its former long-time president Tom Crerar in recommending freedom of choice and opposing extension of the monopoly provisions of the Act.

The powerful voice of the pools was bolstered by the considerable political clout of eastern livestock and dairy interests, who confidently expected that they would have a direct hand in price determination of western oats and barley through the offices of the Canadian Federation of Agriculture. When that failed to transpire, the eastern support was subsequently withdrawn, with abrasive consequences within the federation and on the federal political scene.

The natural opposition of the Winnipeg Grain Exchange requires no analysis, other than to note that their dilemma over continuation of the futures market in the residual grains was relieved by the marketing format chosen by the board. But never before had the exchange come so close to the brink of complete elimination. The irony is that its natural enemy provided the key to survival. In a letter to Howe on March 29, 1949, McIvor had set out alternative methods of handling flax and rye in the event that the government might be forced to intervene to prevent the collapse of those markets should the Winnipeg Grain Exchange cease to function.[35]

There is one other postscript on coarse grains. It is related to the 1947 takeover of all oats and barley in commercial positions by the Wheat Board by order-in-council under the National Emergency Transitional Powers Act. As noted above, the grain held by the private trade was actually vested in the board at the Wartime Prices and Trade Board ceiling price and sold back to the original owners after oats and barley prices rose to a new ceiling the next day. At stake for the private trade was over $6.5 million, and the power of the government to institute the takeover.

An American citizen, Jeremiah J. Nolan of Chicago, had been holding title to forty thousand bushels of Canadian barley since 1943. The barley was stored in various Canadian elevators, and warehouse receipts covering it were in the hands of his agents, Hallet & Carey Ltd., in Winnipeg. Nolan refused to admit the government had power to make compulsory acquisition of his barley and instituted action to obtain possession of the documents of title from Hallet & Carey. Faced with what amounted to a refusal by Nolan to turn over the barley, the board in turn filed a court action against Hallet & Carey for possession of the documents of title and against Manitoba Pool Elevators for the barley itself.[36]

For McIvor, this tangled legal web became a cause célèbre. He alleged that the action taken by Nolan was abetted by a group of the private trade in Winnipeg spearheaded by K.A. Powell. "The trade were not very receptive to this thing [the takeover], but they had no grievance since they had made their margin under the ceiling....I felt that this was a complete effort by the trade to recover money that they were not entitled to."[37]

The case was first heard in Manitoba Court of King's Bench where Chief Justice E.K. Williams ruled in favour of Nolan. It then went to the Manitoba Court of Appeal which unanimously upheld the findings of the lower court. That decision in turn was carried on appeal to the Supreme Court of Canada where Nolan—and the trade—again scored a victory. This time, however, there was a split decision with Chief Justice Kerwin and Mr. Justice Estey dissenting with the majority and ruling for the Wheat Board.[38] As the attorney-general of Canada had been added as a party defendant to the action, a decision now had to be taken in Ottawa as to whether the highly publicized case, having gone down three times, should be taken further.

In line with Canada's continuing determination to sever constitutional ties to Britain, Prime Minister St. Laurent had ruled that no further cases should be taken to the Privy Council in London, except for cases pending. At the meeting of cabinet, held after the Supreme Court decision, nobody was very happy with the Nolan case. "It had gone down three times and they thought that was enough."[39]

McIvor was dismayed over the publicity which was hurting the board due to an action imposed upon it by the government outside of its legislated duties under the Act. He declared that it had become a moral issue and it was the obligation of the government to take the case to the Privy Council. The chief commissioner's determination was reinforced by phone calls from the trade in Winnipeg enquiring when they might receive their cheques. "It was not their money. It belonged to the taxpayers of Canada."[40]

St. Laurent conceded, and the now famous Nolan case became

one of the last Canadian court cases to be taken before the Judicial Committee of the Privy Council. In London, a battery of lawyers including Henry Monk, counsel for the board, presented final arguments. On May 20, 1952, over three years after the action was first commenced, Lord Radcliffe delivered a unanimous judgement in favour of the Canadian Wheat Board. The Nolan case was finally closed.

As the events in the coarse grain sector were unfolding, there were a number of changes in federal legislation and membership on the board. With the Canada-United Kingdom long-term agreement drawing to a close, along with the term of the five-year pool, further amendments were required to the Canadian Wheat Board Act in 1950. The mandate of the board would formally expire on July 31, 1950, under the terms of the 1947 amendments which were passed to accomodate carrying out of those policies.

In the meantime, the International Wheat Agreement (IWA) had come into effect on July 31, 1949, with an expiry date set at July 31, 1953. The government now sought to extend the board's monopoly powers to handle wheat, oats, and barley during the term of the IWA. The necessity for such an accommodation could be argued since the United States, also a participant in the multinational agreement, had no intention of switching to a monopoly marketing system. The Americans preferred, rather, to subsidize wheat exports to the extent necessary to price them at levels eligible for registration under the IWA. The implications of such a policy were, however, much too costly for the Canadian treasury. As we shall see in the next chapter, the American decision was to create a traumatic competitive situation on world markets in which the Canadian Wheat Board was forced to adopt new tactics and seek out new markets.

The amendment extended the mandate of the board to July 31, 1953. It received final reading in the Senate June 15, 1950, but not before it had again come under attack by Senator Crerar. A number of other amendments were also passed along with the extension of the monopoly powers. The statutory initial payment of $1.35 a bushel, along with the five-year pool, had been earlier instituted to provide assurance of an orderly transition from war to peace. The 1950 amendments reverted back to one-year pooling periods, with initial payments set by order-in-council in the light of current market conditions. In addition, the amendments provided for a five-member board, rather than the three specified in the original Act, and the authority to waive surrender to the board of producer participation certificates. The latter amendment marked recognition of the approaching computer age, in which the board could account for total participation payments due each producer without requiring the cumbersome accounting based on surrendered certificates. Provision for five commissioners was in recognition of additional duties imposed by the takeover of coarse grains.

With a return to single-year pooling, there was an extensive re-examination of the pooling mechanism with the result that further amendments to the Canadian Wheat Board Act were passed the following year in 1951. Previously, interim payments that represented upward adjustments in the initial price as indicated by changing market conditions during the crop year had been made in uniform amounts, irrespective of the grade delivered by producers. A wide dispersion of grades, due to difficult harvest conditions during the 1950-1951 crop year, had demonstrated the need to vary such interim payments by grade. An amendment was made to permit this variation under the Act.

Of more critical importance was an amendment to permit timely closing of the pools and distribution of final payments to producers as soon as possible after the end of each crop year. This provision was permissive, rather than mandatory, because of uncertainty over the size of future unsold balances in each pool account. Previously, occasions had arisen where final payments to producers had been delayed for up to three years, since the board was obliged to carry over unsold portions from one crop year to the next and was operating two or more pool accounts at the same time. The 1951 amendment gave the federal cabinet authority to transfer the unsold amount from one pool account to the next after a careful valuation of the inventory to be transferred, "with the principle in mind that the later pool should neither gain nor lose because of the unsold grain transferred to it." Outlining the amendment, Howe conceded that, in actual practice, it might not be possible to eliminate all risks to the pools concerned. "I believe that the House will agree, however, that the proposed method is preferable to holding up the final settlement with producers under each pool until such time as the last grain in that pool has been sold."[41]

Western farmers, who today chafe at the delay in receiving final payments of funds urgently needed for inputs prior to seed the next year's crop, might ponder on the up to three-year wait endured by their predecessors. They will readily identify with the relief of farmers when the amendment permitted prompt closing of the 1950-1951 crop pool, providing a substantial payment in advance of seeding of the 1952 crop.

Having sent the farmers an initial payment of $1.40 on wheat plus an interim payment of 20 cents, a final payment of 25.498 cents, basis the top grade, was authorized on November 19, 1951. Distribution of $104.9 million in final payments on the wheat pool alone proved particularly timely in view of the near disastrous harvest conditions of 1951. Added to this were final payments of $15.1 million on the 1950-1951 barley pool and $9.6 million from the oats pool.[42]

Besides these administrative changes, a rapid change in the personnel of the board took place during the immediate post-war years. C.E. Huntting, who had become assistant chief commissioner in September 1945, to replace D.A. Kane, returned to private business in February 1947. His place as assistant chief commissioner was filled by Bill McNamara, and F.L.M. Arnold was appointed a commissioner. Arnold remained on the board only until May 1948, when he resigned to be replaced by Dr. T.W. Grindley the board's secretary. Because of ill health, Grindley resigned in July 1950, and was replaced by William Riddel, the assistant general manager of Saskatchewan Wheat Pool.

The McIvor, McNamara, Riddel team then remained intact throughout the Howe era, with the addition of a fourth commissioner W.E. Robertson in November 1953. Robertson had been assistant general manager of Federal Grain Limited; his recruitment from the private trade raised criticism from the Parliamentary opposition. McIvor had recommended his appointment to Howe who, in turn, consulted the pools as was his usual custom. The pool executive recognized the need for selection of a man with grain marketing experience and approved. But the newly-founded Farmers Union expressed annoyance that a representative grain producer had not been appointed. Both Howe and McIvor resisted, however, since their overriding concern was to keep board operations out of politics and in the hands of a group with sales expertise who were prepared to operate in low profile.[43]

McIvor was persona non grata with the Farmers Union, a dissident and militant group to the left of the pools and the Canadian Federation of Agriculture, because of his steadfast refusal to consider their demands for a board-administered check-off of Farm Union membership dues on grain deliveries.[44]

THE FATEFUL FIFTIES

The American spirit as yet knows little of moderation, whichever way it turns.

— U.S. Secretary of Agriculture Henry C. Wallace,

America Must Choose, 1934

▪

Of all the world's great natural resources, none matches the Great Central Plain of the North American continent. As a constantly renewable cornucopia of the most vital elements of human survival, it is unique in its variety and in the resourcefulness and vigor of its inhabitants. Out of its rich soil each year has sprung the lifeblood that nurtures and feeds the industrial giant that surrounds it. Its excess output, with a potential far beyond the needs of its fortunate possessors, dominates world trade in wheat, feed grains, oil bearing seeds, and fibres. This unparalleled renewable resource is shared by the United States and Canada but not in equal measure or productive potential.

The evolution of the Canadian Wheat Board, the events which shaped its policies, and its continuing role in the world grain trade and the affairs of the nation cannot be understood without recognition of the disparity of ownership of the Great Central Plain between Canada and the United States. The Canadian Wheat Board designated area comprises only the northern fringe of that huge continental asset.

The Western Plains of Canada are large by world standards, but they are small in comparison to the extent and productive capacity of the share of the Great Central Plain under the stewardship of Canada's southern neighbor. Not only is Canada's share smaller, it is also subject to a more rigorous and uncertain climate. The incidence of frost is earlier in the fall and later in the spring, thereby drastically reducing the number of frost-free days; and the whole of the area falls within the semi-arid portion of the Great Central Plain.

By comparison, the American Great Plain sweeps down from the Canadian border to Texas through a wide climatic spectrum. It is bounded on the east by a large humid and semi-humid environment, which includes the fertile Corn Belt states of Ohio, Indiana, Illinois, Iowa, and Missouri. There, prodigious crops of corn—which alone produce a feed crop six to seven times the total production of all cereal crops in Canada—thrive along with soybeans. The semi-arid to arid area, lying to the west of the Mississippi River, comprises the Northern Plains states of North and South Dakota, Nebraska, and Kansas. The latter state alone produces, on occasion, a wheat crop equalling the total production of wheat in Canada. Added to that are the Southern Plain states of Oklahoma and Texas with equally huge potentials for production of winter wheats.

Bisecting this bounty is a 3,760-mile-long natural waterway, the Mississippi River system. Flowing south from the mid-continental divide in Minnesota to the Gulf States of Mississippi, Arkansas, and Louisiana, it provides access to ports and the markets of the world. In contrast, the land-locked Prairie Provinces of Canada must rely on rail to reach tidewater.

Throughout the early period of the Canadian Wheat Board, to the decade of the fifties, this vast potential to the south had lain sleeping for a variety of reasons. In the period between the two world wars, the United States withdrew into isolationism with a marked tendency to concentrate on its own domestic grain markets. From 1920 to 1929, Canada replaced the United States as the principal wheat exporter, with 31.8 per cent of the world market as compared to 26.4 per cent for the Americans.

Through the period of the Great Depression, from 1930 to 1939, the United States retreated to 10.6 per cent of a reduced world wheat market while Canada remained the principal exporter at 28.3 per cent. As we have seen, during World War II the United States became a net importer of wheat, principally from Canada. However, as the decade of the fifties dawned, the sleeping giant had been revived and stimulated into all-out production. The whole pattern of world grain trade was about to be convulsed in a rapidly changing world as a pent-up sequence of events came together.

Acutely aware of the competitive threat posed by the aroused American potential, George McIvor approached Ezra Taft Benson, secretary of agriculture in the recently elected Eisenhower administration, during one his visits to Washington in 1943. Was the United States going to take its place in the sun, or was it going to revert to its pre-war status in the world grain trade?[1]

Benson, a Mormon and a member of the highest body in the Church of the Latter Day Saints, was a strong moral advocate of non-bureaucratic interference in the farm sector and of letting free enterprise economic forces prevail. His answer was unequivocal. The United States would take its place in the sun.[2]

Further evidence of a looming export confrontation was given when McIvor attended a meeting of the International Wheat Council in London during July 1953. Prior to that date, close co-operation had existed between the Wheat Board and the Roosevelt and Truman Democratic administrations. A decade earlier, the Canadian Wheat Board had established offices in the Pentagon during the war at the invitation of the United States Department of Agriculture. To the end of the war, and during its aftermath, as the United States and Canada worked in close liaison to alleviate food shortages in war-torn countries, the Canadian Wheat Board maintained its office in the USDA premises.

Now, at the London conference, True Morse, head of the U.S. delegation, suggested to McIvor that the point had been reached where it might prove embarrassing to the American government if the Wheat Board continued to maintain its office in USDA premises. McIvor immediately phoned Hume Wrong, the Canadian ambassador in Washington, who offered accommodation for the board representative, Charles C. Boxer, in the Canadian embassy, and the move was made.[3]

One year later, when participants to the International Wheat Agreement met in London to discuss price levels under the agreement in mid-October 1954, signs of American restlessness over growing surpluses emerged. While the delegations agreed to hold the price line, McIvor, reporting back to Mitchell Sharp, deputy minister of trade and commerce in Ottawa, on the tenor of the discussions wrote: "The ghost that seemed to hide behind every door was the fear of the U.S. becoming impatient with sales and disposing of what was often termed their huge surplus by some process of dumping which would seriously affect the whole world's wheat position."[4]

Before describing the emergence of the ghost and the consequences attendant upon its appearance, a short summary of U.S. initiatives and policies dating back to the 1930s is in order.

When Franklin D. Roosevelt assumed the office of president in 1933, replacing the Depression-stricken Hoover administration, the farmers and rural areas were in distress, as were their creditors and farm supply firms throughout the United States. With huge surpluses overhanging a depressed world grain market, the Roosevelt administration sought to provide a mechanism to direct relief to the farmers and, at the same time, institute production controls. The result was the Agricultural Adjustments Act of 1933. The American government was being inexorably drawn by the forces of the Depression into intervention in grain marketing, as was the Canadian government to the north. While the form and pervasiveness of that intervention was to vary between the two nations, Washington's entanglement has persisted to the mid-1980s, despite continuing rhetoric extolling a free enterprise, open-market regime.

Under the Agricultural Adjustments Act, an experiment in "voluntary" acreage controls was undertaken. While voluntary nonparticipating farmers were denied access to income benefits, participating farmers were guaranteed benefit or adjustment payments on that percentage of their wheat used for domestic food, in return for contracting their average wheat acreage. To finance payments to the farmers the U.S. government levied a user tax directly upon the millers which they were obliged to pay upon wheat processed into human food.

Results of that experiment are hard to assess. Drought conditions in the U.S. Dust Bowl, as in Canada, did more to reduce production than the acreage controls. The legislation was struck down by a ruling of the Supreme Court in early 1936, when the user tax was declared invalid. It was replaced by stop-gap legislation, the Soil

Conservation and Domestic Allotment Act, which proved unsuccessful in controlling acreage on a voluntary basis.

Then in 1938 a new Agricultural Adjustments Act was passed in Washington that introduced mandatory wheat acreage controls. This sharply reduced production during the years from 1939 to 1943. Also, in August 1938, Secretary of Agriculture Henry C. Wallace reluctantly introduced export subsidies after a return to normal conditions sharply increased yields following the disastrous drought years. The export subsidies were administered through the Federal Surplus Commodity Corporation. It purchased surplus wheat at the supported U.S. market price and sold it to exporters at the lower world price, thereby enabling them to export abroad. These measures were complemented by a high 42 cent a bushel tariff on imported grain followed by import quotas in 1941.

Despite all these measures, U.S. carryover stocks continued to climb as the outbreak of war in Europe and early German successes denied access to the major export markets. While Agriculture Minister Jimmy Gardiner doggedly contended that what appeared to be overburdensome surpluses of wheat in Canada would be urgently needed at the end of the war (as events proved rightly), planners in the USDA took an opposite view. The Americans would eat their way out of the surplus.

In order to achieve that end, wheat would be processed through livestock. The USDA began a "wheat for feed" program, under which a subsidy was paid on wheat used as animal feed. Under the impetus of that program, wheat used for feeding purposes jumped from 117 million bushels in 1941 to 306 million bushels in 1942, and soared to 518 million bushels in 1943.[5] It will be recalled that, in 1943, there was a turnaround in the Canadian situation. A short crop in the United States, occasioned by adverse weather combined with the acreage reduction program, resulted in the export of over 130 million bushels of Canadian wheat to the U.S. to feed the expanded American hog and cattle herds.

Because U.S. carryover declined from 619 million bushels in 1943 to 317 million bushels in 1944, acreage controls were relaxed; and under the farm price support program, American productive capacity was turned loose. Output of wheat in the U.S. climbed past the billion bushel mark and remained there from 1944 onward. Even with this expansion, the U.S. carryover was further reduced to 279 million bushels at the cessation of hostilities in 1945, and was a scant 100 million bushels entering 1946.

American planners had sadly underestimated the post-war needs in the liberated countries and, with the cupboard virtually bare in the U.S., the Canadian surplus had to be thrown into the breach to relieve the spectre of famine in Europe and the Far East. By July 31, 1946, Canada's wheat carryover was down to a meagre 69.5 million bushels.

As related previously, the United States, Canada, and Australia made a supreme effort to meet the urgent demands uncovered by the final liberation of Europe and the cessation of hostilities in the Pacific area. Competition for export markets was forgotten as Canada and the United States co-operated through the Combined Food Board to co-ordinate all available supplies to meet the urgent need.

During the 1946-1950 period, western Canadian crops narrowly escaped disaster by drought. Canada's export supplies were little more than sufficient to meet the requirements of Britain under the bilateral four-year contract. The United States bore the brunt of the task of supplying the food requirements of her liberated allies and the occupied zones of former enemy countries. To the enduring credit of the United States, that country assumed the lion's share of meeting the world's relief needs through the Marshall Plan and European Relief Aid. In addition to supplying dollars to facilitate purchases by the importers—including British purchases from Canada—the American government spurred production by maintaining high farm support prices and acreage was expanded. In 1947, the United States produced a record crop of 1.359 billion bushels of wheat.

The stage was being set for confrontation in the fateful fifties. After climbing to 504 million bushels in 1948, American exports of wheat began a decline as world production recovered from the ravages of war. One year after that peak was reached, American exports slumped to 299 million bushels in 1949. But the tap of production had been turned on; it was now proving difficult to turn off.

While Canadian wheat crops up to 1950 were considerably below average, falling in the 300 million to 400 million bushel range, crop output in the United States continued in the billion bushel plus range. In both countries, a technological revolution was taking place in agriculture. A pent-up backlog of advancements in the mechanical, biological and chemical fields was being implemented. The damming up of effective demand through a decade of the Depression, followed by wartime scarcities, was loosed by comparative prosperity on the North American agricultural front.

With economic stress and war behind them, and purchasing

power and adequate supplies coinciding, North American farmers eagerly adopted the new technology. In Canada by 1951 there were three times as many tractors per hundred farms as in 1941, five times as many combines, three times as many motor trucks and four times as many electric motors.[6] From 1946 to 1955 Canadian farmers invested $3 billion in new machinery.[7]

With equal alacrity, North American farmers adopted new varieties of grains, fertilizers, and pesticides. As a corollary to those innovations, crop yields and individual farm size increased while farm populations declined. Farms in the Prairie Provinces increased on the average from 405 acres in 1941 to 550 acres in 1956.[8] The average Saskatchewan farm comprised 432 acres in 1941 and 607 acres, or 40 per cent more, in 1956. Persons employed in agriculture in Canada (including self-employed, hired workers, and unpaid family workers) averaged 1,186,000, or 24 1/2 per cent of the total labour force in 1946. By 1956, the number of agricultural workers had fallen to 773,000 or 14 per cent of the total labour force, a decline of 34 per cent in one decade.[9]

Thus, a combination of circumstances and forces were at play and converging in a way that drastically changed the whole face of the world's grain trade. In 1949 the Canadian Wheat Board reported:

> Increased production of wheat in Europe, ample wheat supplies available in exporting countries, the intensity of United States competition, the immediate effects of United States aid to various countries in Western Europe and increasing difficulties in financing international trade, were important factors in the 1948-49 wheat position.
>
> For the first time since the end of World War II, sufficient supplies of wheat were available in exporting countries to meet import requirements. This fact represented an important change in the international wheat position which occurred during the crop year 1948-49.[10]

Despite that pessimistic market outlook, the harvested acreage of wheat in the United States, impelled by price supports and export subsidies, rose to 75.9 million acres during the 1949-1950 marketing year. Having underestimated the requirement for wheat at the end of World War II, the Truman administration now overestimated the impact of the Korean War. Secretary of Agriculture Charles Brannan kept up the production impetus in order to have a cushion of stocks when the Korean conflict ended. Instead of shortages, an avalanche of surpluses developed. Aided by the price supports and export subsidies, U.S. wheat prices averaged 63 cents per bushel higher than the world price during the years July 1, 1949, to July 1, 1953.[11]

On the Canadian prairies, crops rebounded at the beginning of the 1950s. Wheat production, which had averaged 367 million bushels a year from 1946 to 1950, averaged 597 million bushels from 1951 to 1953.[12] In 1952 Canada harvested its largest grain crop to that date with a record 664 million bushels of wheat. It followed upon a 529 million bushel wheat crop in 1951, and was succeeded by a 584 million bushel crop in 1953.

Meanwhile, total world wheat production was rising. World wheat production in 1952-1953 was the highest on record. It was followed by another large world crop in 1953-1954 and the Wheat Board reported:

> Only occasionally it happens that wheat harvests are bountiful the world over and 1953-54 was such a year. All continents harvested excellent wheat crops. Departures from the general trend of generous production were few....The good harvests of 1953-54 followed a year of very large international trade in wheat in 1952-53, and consequently many importing countries were well stocked at the beginning of the crop year with reserves of imported wheat as well as supplies from domestic crops. With some easing of international tensions importing countries generally reduced reserves of breadstuffs which had been carried during the period of the Korean hostilities and in some cases since the end of World War II. These factors combined brought about a readjustment in the world wheat trading position for the crop year 1953-54. The main effect was to lower world import requirements from the levels which had been prevailing in previous years. It so happened that the lessening of import demand coincided with the existence of larger stocks of wheat in exporting countries, and with the offerings of wheat for export by more countries than in any post-war crop year.
>
> As a result of the overall decline in world import requirements, the utilization of stocks of wheat by importing countries, the entrance of some normally importing countries like Turkey and Sweden as exporting countries, and unusually large exports from France, wheat exports in 1953-54 by most of the larger wheat exporting countries were substantially reduced.[13]

The drop in exports brought about by those conditions was drastic. Canadian wheat exports in 1953-1954 slumped to 255 million bushels compared to 386 million bushels in the previous year. American exports fell back to 216 million bushels from 317 million bushels in 1952-1953.[14]

As the carryover of wheat in the United States stair-stepped toward the billion bushel mark in the mid-fifties, there were growing signs that the Americans were undercutting prices. This presented a pricing dilemma for the Canadian Wheat Board. With record Canadian crops, combined with a sharp decline in exports in the 1953-1954 crop year, commercial elevator space was virtually filled with grain at the end of that crop year. The carryover in commercial positions rose from 289.5 million bushels in 1953 to 386.8 million bushels in 1954. This congestion forced a dramatic increase in wheat backed up on the farms. Farm stored wheat leaped from 97.3 million bushels in 1953 to 231.9 million bushels in 1954.

In the midst of this growing crisis, the Liverpool futures market reopened on December 1, 1953. In pre-war years it had been preeminent as a fulcrum for the world's wheat trade. Its revival rekindled hope among the Winnipeg grain traders that the action would lead to a reopening of the Winnipeg Grain Exchange's wheat futures market. However, the Liverpool market folded after several months of trying with no success to obtain volume and liquidity. Its failure was undoubtedly marked in part by a significant shift in world grain trading, whereby single-desk buying and selling agencies, either governmental or quasi-governmental, had begun to dominate.

The tremendous farm carryover and the prospect of small delivery quotas due to reduced world trade were to have political repercussions as the surplus grew. The St. Laurent government had been re-elected in 1953 at some cost to its majority, and Howe was determined to hold the price line.

By the spring of 1954, the Canadian Wheat Board had been dealing at somewhat more than arms-length with the Commodity Credit Corporation (CCC) in Washington, since its representative had moved out of the USDA premises. Liaison had continued on a more formal basis however, and the two agencies were agreed that it would be foolish to embark on a policy of competitive price reductions in the face of the growing surplus. While both the board and the CCC maintained their posted export prices at agreed levels, there was growing evidence that the CCC was extending secret discounts, or greater than published subsidies, in order to promote specific transactions, particularly in the case of flour exports.[15] One of the biggest corporations in the world in terms of its $8 billion capitalization, the

Commodity Credit Corporation paid subsidies to exporters in wheat from government held stocks, rather than in cash.

In 1953, the International Wheat Agreement, signed in 1949, had run its course and had been renegotiated for a further three years. This time, however, the United Kingdom had refrained from participation. The absence of Britain, then the world's major importer, considerably weakened the multilateral agreement.

Throughout the 1952-1953 crop year, the Wheat Board sold wheat for registration under the first IWA at maximum prices provided under the agreement. However, during the latter half of the crop year, Class II prices on wheat sold outside of the agreement began to decline. That decline continued until, on August 10, 1953, the Class II price dropped by 9 3/4 cents breaking through the IWA maximum level. The board then reduced the price on Class I wheat, offered through the IWA, to match the drop in Class II prices.[16]

Prices rose slightly thereafter, but by the spring of 1954 it became obvious to the board that it could not hold the price line. Early in the crop year, the board had responded to the competitive pressures by instituting a number of changes. Selling discounts, or spreads, between No. 2 and No. 3 Northern had been widened to make these grades more competitive. As a further measure to encourage sales of wheat, the board provided, on September 4, 1953, that buyers would have the option of purchasing board wheat at its daily quoted selling price or on a deferred basis. If a buyer chose the latter basis, he had the right to declare the final price up to seven market days after the date of call on shipments from the St. Lawrence or Atlantic ports, and up to fifteen market days from date of loading at Pacific Coast ports.[17]

A similar policy was subsequently applied to Port Churchill where the buyer was given a nine-day leeway. Early in 1954 the board began to quote separate selling prices at the Pacific Coast, the Lakehead, and at Churchill to take into account the internal costs of moving grain to seaboard positions. Despite these measures, the board decided that the price it had been maintaining could no longer be held. McIvor consulted Howe on the dilemma. Fearing a return of the price debacle of the 1930s, Howe opted for a sharp one-step reduction, rather than to embark on a series of reductions which might result in importers holding back purchases as they awaited further declines. McIvor advised that, if this were done, it would have to be as much as ten cents and that it should be done in concert with the Americans. Thus, at the beginning of June, 1954, Deputy Minister of Trade and

Commerce Mitchell Sharp and Bill McNamara went to Washington where they succeeded in reaching agreement with the Americans on separate announcements of a similar ten cents a bushel price reduction.[18]

The move was a wise one. Prices steadied as buyer confidence returned, at least temporarily, in a volatile marketplace. But over the 1953-1954 crop year, Canadian Wheat Board prices had declined from the IWA maximum level of $2.03 to a level of $1.70 1/2 cents on July 31, 1954. Given the widening spreads on lower grades, the selling prices for No. 2 and No. 3 Northern had dropped by 36 1/2 cents a bushel.

However, reaching a compromise with the Americans was only part of the battle. North American prices were coming under heavy pressure from the Southern Hemisphere, where Australia and Argentina were offering stiff competition in the reduced world market. At the Washington meeting, the Canadian and American officials agreed not to reduce prices unilaterally without prior consultation, but it remained for them to come to an understanding with the Australians.

A meeting of the major exporters was held prior to a semi-annual meeting of the International Wheat Council in London later the same month. Australia came to the meetings with the firm conviction that prices should be dropped to the IWA floor price, approximating $1.55 Canadian. The American instructions were fluid. McNamara, who represented Canada, had to exercise all his negotiating skills to persuade the Australians and Americans away from their prepared positions. Convinced that a further reduction in prices would work to the disadvantage of exporters collectively, McNamara held private talks with the other exporters. In a confidential report to Sharp on June 21, 1954, McNamara revealed that he had obtained an informal agreement that the three principal IWA exporters would meet in the United States some time in late August. They had further agreed not to take unilateral price action without prior consultation with each other.[19]

The proposed meeting, held in September 1954 in New York, was satisfactory from the Canadian standpoint. But at the session of the IWC, held in London in mid-October, McIvor had a more difficult time convincing the U.S. and Australia to hold the price line. At a pre-conference meeting of the importers McIvor pointed to a reduction in the quality of the European crop, reduced production in the United States and a crop disaster in western Canada. The 1954 crop on the prairies had suffered from late seeding, due to flooding, retarded development, rust infestation, and frost. This combined to drastically reduce the wheat crop to 282 million bushels, compared with 584 million bushels the previous year.[20] Reporting to Sharp on the New York meeting, McIvor wrote:

> The Americans agreed that the situation had changed in a matter of about six months and in fact mentioned that their own position had deteriorated as far as crops were concerned and that they were now operating under acreage restrictions, the result of which would be a substantial cut in American sowings. They did, however, stress that they were not happy with their sales position and that they would have difficulty in explaining to Congress why they had not reduced prices, if their sales position did not improve substantially.
>
> The Australians also expressed a considerable amount of worry about the loss of sales in traditional markets such as Japan, etc. and complained of the fact that the U.S. was moving in on their traditional markets as a result of give-away programs, sales against currency of the importing country, and other arrangements on which the American government had embarked to dispose of their surplus wheat.[21]

Despite these reservations, the Americans and Australians agreed with Canada that the price line would be held, and it would be made clear at the IWC meeting that there was no thought on the part of the exporters that prices would be reduced. The fears expressed at the meeting by the Australians over inroads by the Americans into their traditional markets were equally shared by Canada. Earlier that year, the U.S. Congress had enacted Public Laws 480 and 665. The Americans were about to turn the whole pattern of world grain trade around and assume a dominant position from which they would not retreat.

Public Law 480 was the most pervasive of the programs instituted by the Americans to dispose of surplus agricultural production. It elevated food surplus distribution to a major role in U.S. farm policy and ultimately in foreign policy as well. Under its various sections, the legislation allowed for disposal of surpluses by barter, payment in non-convertible or ''blocked'' foreign currencies which could not be exchanged for dollars, foreign aid, and other means. Congress authorized a budget of $700 million to finance foreign currency sales over the first three years of the program.

The annual report of the Canadian Wheat Board for 1954-1955

commented, "The effect of the United States disposal program in 1954-55 was to considerably narrow the range of markets for Canadian wheat and to substantially reduce the level of our wheat exports." Over the first three years of the concessionary programs, U.S. exports of wheat doubled, climbing to 548.6 million bushels in 1956-1957. Less than one-third were dollar sales. The remainder, 375 million bushels or 68.4 per cent, were on concessionary terms.[22]

On August 14, 1956, McIvor detailed the extent of the incursion by the Americans into Canadian markets in a letter to Marvin McLain, undersecretary of agriculture in Washington:

> We have recently examined our position in fourteen countries which have been in receipt of wheat under your disposal programs. In these countries our exports so far recorded in our crop year were at the level of 31 per cent of our exports to these same countries in 1953-54, while the United States has increased its exports to 258.4 per cent of the 1953-54 level. This is the sort of thing that continues to disturb us, especially when we can and are maintaining our position in markets where ordinary competitive conditions prevail.[23]

The American concessional sales program arose out of balance-of-payment difficulties in some of the industrialized countries, such as Britain, where foreign exchange controls prohibited convertibility of their currencies. This was even more widespread in the newly-developing and iron curtain countries. The exchange controls discouraged purchases from the hard currency countries, except to the extent of essential transactions to pay for urgent necessities.

As noted above, when the U.S. Congress reconvened in 1954, a number of bills were introduced, each having the common theme of reducing agricultural surplus by selling for payment in local or blocked currencies. These bills eventually took shape in the form of the Agricultural Trade and Assistance Act, commonly referred to as PL 480, the preamble of which declared the policy of Congress to be:

> To expand international trade among the United States and friendly nations, to facilitate the convertibility of currency, to promote the economic stability of American agriculture and the national welfare, to make maximum efficient use of surplus agricultural commodities in furtherance of the foreign policy of the United States, and to stimulate and facilitate the expansion of foreign trade in agricultural commodities produced in the United States by providing a means

> whereby surplus agricultural commodities in excess of the usual marketings of such commodities may be sold through private trade channels, and foreign currencies accepted in payment therefor.[24]

While the administration acknowledged its responsibility under the law to safeguard against "undue disruption" of its own commercial grain trade, and against "undue impairment of the traditional competitive position of friendly foreign countries,"[25] increasingly complicated transactions in implementation of the PL 480 program were to undermine any such safeguards.

Formal Canadian protests against the American surplus disposal programs first took place at the ministerial level during a meeting in Ottawa of the Joint Economic and Trade Committee in September 1955. It was agreed there to set up a Canadian-American consultative committee on grain marketing. The first meeting of that committee was held on October 20, 1955, in Washington.

Public concern in Canada was mounting. In advance of the Washington meeting, there were calls for a firm stand by the Canadian team headed by Mitchell Sharp and including George McIvor and Bill McNamara. In the absence of a firm statement after the Ottawa meeting, the Winnipeg *Free Press* declared that if Canada failed to get a reasonably stated limit to the total rate of the non-commercial disposals the United States would make, "no more than elementary political prudence should dictate that the alternative this time be not a cozy cover-up but a flaming row."[25] Although the Washington meeting was closed, a U.S. State Department official revealed that a flaming row had indeed taken place. He said that while in Ottawa the Canadian ministers had stated their criticism of American marketing methods with lucidity and acidity, the Canadian officials at the Washington meeting had presented their case with vitriol. "He said that in an experience going back over many years he had never heard officials of the Canadian government criticize American policy with such frankness and in such detail."[26]

Despite the vitriol, the U.S. concessional sales persisted in a variety of forms, and at successive meetings of the committee, Sharp and McIvor continued to voice strong protest. At one meeting, held in Washington on January 4, 1957, a PL 480 agreement which McIvor characterized as the "most weird transaction under all surplus disposal arrangements," was outlined. Under the four-way transaction, an agreement would be completed between the U.S. Credit Corporation and the Department of Defence which would enter into a lease agreement with a French builder to build housing for American troops. The French builder, in turn, would sign over his claim to the CCC and a barter contractor would make the foreign currency available to the builder.[27]

At a previous meeting of the committee, held in Winnipeg August 29, 1956, Sharp bluntly warned the Americans that, through sheer desperation Canada might be forced to enter bilateral agreements if the American programs continued. He pointed out that the Canadian government was under considerable pressure to negotiate such agreements and, to the extent that the United States over-stepped the market, Canada would be put into an undesirable position and might be forced to give way to such pressures.[28]

Meetings of the consultative committee dragged on until June 10, 1957. At that final meeting in Washington, Sharp pointed out that Canada's relative carryover position was much more serious than the American in terms of total domestic utilization of wheat. American treasury aid on exports was simply pushing the U.S. surplus problem over to Canada. Sharp said that, up to that point, the Canadian government had been very moderate in its approach to the problem, but they were now being criticized severely on the domestic front for their moderation. In his opinion, the problem was now one of the most serious facing the government. Sharp indicated that there was a feeling in high places that some dramatic action would have to be taken to improve Canada's export position.[29]

The problem was indeed serious in terms of consequences for the Liberal government, at least in western Canada. The political face of the prairies was about to change completely. As American wheat exports expanded under the impetus of PL 480, Canadian exports were reduced and Canadian production was simply backing up on farms. The mood in the West was ugly. The impending election of 1957 was to prove disastrous for the government.

At the end of the 1956-1957 crop year on July 31, 1957, the total carryover of Canadian grains on farms and in commercial storage amounted to 1.108 billion bushels. On farms there were record stocks of 323 million bushels of wheat, 157 million bushels of oats and 81 million bushels of barley, a total far exceeding grains in commercial storage. Producers needed to look no further than their granaries for visible evidence of a surfeit of grain.

As that mountain of grain accumulated on the farms, there were calls for Canada to fight fire with fire by adoption of the American policy of trading wheat for payment in blocked currencies. In

Parliament, the opposition, responding to calls from some farm leaders, recommended that such action be taken. Howe had difficulty in pressing the point that Canadian resources and involvement abroad were minimal by comparison to the United States. Since foreign currencies were not freely convertible, even for the purchase of exchange goods for export to Canada, "selling for local currencies means to us the lending of money to the country without interest, and without a due date." Howe explained that "the United States is selling for foreign currency with this proviso, they leave the foreign currency in the country and use it for certain programs which are usually give-away programs. That is what they mean by selling for local currencies." The currencies could only be used for relief, or for some other purpose previously approved by prior agreement with the recipient country.[30]

While the Canadian treasury could not match the largesse of the United States, the mounting carryover, restricted delivery opportunities, and lower prices resulted in two government measures aimed at easing the resulting restriction of cash flow for hard-pressed western Canadian farmers. They were the Temporary Wheat Reserves Act, 1956 and amendments to the Prairie Grain Producers' Interim Financing Act.

In opting for the latter legislation, Howe sadly underestimated the strength of producer support for cash advances on farm-stored grain. It was the major political error of his long public career. Calls for legislation to provide a system of approved farm storage, under which the Wheat Board would make advances to farmers on farm-stored grain, had surfaced in Parliament as early as 1950. Firmly believing that the board's role was to concentrate on selling grain, and that it should not be diverted from that task by taking on the responsibility of being a banker, Howe resisted the opposition pressure. When a private member's bill calling for such advances was introduced in 1954, the motion was talked out by the Liberals on the grounds that the board's operations should not be complicated by being projected into the credit business. Further, it was argued that any losses arising from the scheme would be at the expense of other producers sharing in Wheat Board participation payments.

That was by no means the end of the issue. By the time the 1955 crop was harvested, it was estimated that 550 million bushels of wheat were stored on farms with only a recently adopted minimal unit delivery quota in force. The lack of cash flow was not only worrying farmers, but merchants, municipalities, and provincial governments as well. That concern prompted a meeting of provincial ministers of agriculture and farm organization representatives in Saskatoon in late September 1955. The meeting decided to send a delegation of twenty of its representatives to Ottawa to meet with the federal cabinet. But when the delegation met with cabinet October 11, 1955, it submitted a brief containing three alternatives; there was no unanimity as to which alternative should be adopted.

The dissent within the delegation marked one of the few occasions on which there was not unanimity among the three prairie pools. W.J. Parker, president of Manitoba Pool Elevators; Ben Plumer, president of Alberta Wheat Pool; and J.E. Brownlee, president of United Grain Growers, favoured government-backed loans through the banks to relieve the producers' plight. J.H. Wesson, president of Saskatchewan Wheat Pool, backed by the CCF government in Saskatchewan, and the Alberta, Manitoba, and Saskatchewan Farmer's Unions, favoured cash advances through the board on farm-stored grain.

Given the division among the farm advisers, Howe consulted with the commissioners of the Wheat Board and his departmental advisers. The board members, faced as they were with a sluggish export market and extreme competition from the United States, had no personal desire whatever to involve themselves in the extension of credit with the risks and expenses involved on advances on farm-stored grain, and they gained the sympathetic ear of Howe.[31]

Henry Monk, the board's legal counsel, also found a number of reasons why the board would be in a weaker position to effect repayment of cash advances than would the chartered banks under the provisions of the Bank Act. Howe opted to make amendments to the Prairie Grain Producers' Interim Financing Act, which had been enacted in 1951 to aid western farmers through a particularly difficult harvest when wet weather that year had caused a large quantity of grain to lay in the fields overwinter. There had been a minimum response to that measure, which involved government-guaranteed loans to farmers through the banks at prevalent interest rates.

At the meeting with the board, where the decision was taken, McNamara noted that unless the government were prepared to absorb interest and administrative charges on the bank loans it would be a major political mistake to have farmers pay interest as they did in 1951. Howe's retort was brusque: "You sell the wheat and leave the politics to me."[32] With the farmer's need urgent, arrangements were made with the banks to make loans up to $1,500 at 5 per cent interest pending passage of the legislation. Having made up his mind to go with the bank loan option, Howe was the most unlikely of men to change his mind.

The 1956 session of Parliament is most remembered for the protracted pipe-line debate; the debate over re-enactment of the 1951 farm bank loan legislation was almost as acrimonious and also degenerated into a prolonged filibuster. All three opposition parties, Progressive Conservative, CCF, and Social Credit, attacked the legislation and called for cash advances. During the prolonged debate, the aggressive Howe intimated that if cash advances were adopted the commissioners of the Wheat Board would resign.

> The chairman of the Board has been in the service of the government for 25 years, his duties associated solely with the marketing of western grain. Associated with him are three very able men who share the work of the Board. I can tell the House that, if the government instructed the Wheat Board to lend money on farm-stored grain and assume responsibility for the lending of that money and its subsequent collection, the four members of the Board would be out of office within a matter of days.[33]

It was a statement made in the heat of Parliamentary battle that was to come back to haunt George McIvor.

Introduced in January, the bill was filibustered on first reading. On second reading in February, the filibuster continued over five days of sittings with 102 speeches. Resistance to the legislation continued even through third reading where John Diefenbaker, shortly to become leader of the Progressive Conservative Party, moved an amendment which would have given the legislation a six-month hoist, effectively killing it. The amendment was defeated, but it was not until February 28 that the bill was given final reading.

The second initiative by Howe to relieve partially the plight of western grain farmers had a far easier passage at the 1956 session. Carrying costs on the carryover of stocks held by the board had risen from ten cents per year in recent years to sixteen cents and threatened to rise to twenty cents. Excessive stocks meant that the board's pool accounts were reduced which, in turn, reduced final payments to the producer. The government now proposed, through the Temporary Wheat Reserves Act, to pay from the federal treasury carrying charges on all stocks held by the board in excess of 178 million bushels a year, representing a normal carryover based on the fifteen-year average prior to 1951. Retroactive to the 1955-1956 crop year, the total treasury contribution for that year was estimated at $32 million. These contributions were to continue into successive crop years until the the carryover dropped to below 178 million bushels.[34] In sharp contrast to the farm loans legislation, debate was brief, and the Temporary Wheat Reserves Act received royal assent on March 7, 1956.

When the 1957 session of Parliament opened, John Diefenbaker had replaced George Drew, who had retired due to ill health, as leader of the Progressive Conservatives. During the throne speech debate, the fiery Diefenbaker attacked the Liberal government for lack of aggressiveness in protesting the PL 480 operations with the resulting loss of Canadian wheat markets and moved a non-confidence vote. The CCF and Social Credit members followed, criticizing the Liberal's wheat policy, the lack of cash advances, and demanding the appointment of a transport controller.

Howe, remembering the filibuster of the previous year, refrained from entering the debate. Indeed, with an election campaign in the offing, he would have preferred not to introduce any further grain legislation during the session. But there were two matters he could not escape. One was the extension of the Canadian Wheat Board Act which was set to expire on July 31, 1957. The other was amendment and extension of the controversial Prairie Grain Producers' Interim Financing Act, which was also due to lapse.

While the bill to extend the Canadian Wheat Board's mandate for a further five years was passed unanimously, debate extended over almost four days largely on matters having little to do with the legislation. Saskatchewan member Ross Thatcher, who had defected from the CCF and was now sitting as a Liberal, intervened in the debate and launched into a tirade against the CCF, whom he described as "professional cry-babies." The acting speaker failed to confine the debate, which turned into an inter-party donnybrook. Howe was finally forced to threaten to cut off debate after one more day: "If it goes through, all right, but if it does not the bill is out." The threat proved effective. A vote was called on second reading and third reading passed that same evening on February 8.[35]

Since all three opposition parties were still calling for cash advances on farm stored grain, debate on amendment of the Prairie Grain Producers' Interim Financing Act threatened to be as prolonged and bitter as that of the previous year. The 1956 version had proved of limited effect. Farmers had taken little advantage of the government-guaranteed loans, with only about

$12 million being disbursed by the banks.

In the interim, the western farm organizations were still unable to agree on a satisfactory system of cash advances. At a meeting in Saskatoon on March 1, 1957, they agreed to a compromise resolution. They did not agree that the interim financing act was "the most satisfactory method for making money available on grain that cannot be delivered," but in view of the late date for having "a more satisfactory plan for cash advances adopted at this session of Parliament," they recommended amendments to the bank loan legislation.[36] Using the lack of unanimity as leverage, Howe wired the heads of the farm organizations for further endorsement of the bill prior to second reading. He then managed to limit debate by reading replies from a majority of the leaders who endorsed the interim loan bill, pending the ability of the farm organizations to produce a satisfactory and agreed recommendation on cash advances.[37] Following a brief discussion in committee of the whole, the bill received third reading and passed.

After a short session, Parliament was prorogued on April 12, 1957, and a general election was called for June 10. Bothwell and Kilbourn, in their biography of C.D. Howe, have summarized the atmosphere that pervaded western Canada during that election campaign:

> World prices were falling away in the face of a vast, subsidized American giveaway program. In 1955, Prairie farmers' net income in Canada was less than half what it had been in 1953, and the granaries of the West were bulging with unsold wheat. Howe's Wheat Board officials were already negotiating for sales in the one potential market that the United States could not touch; but the effects of the first Canadian sales to China were still in the future. Howe and his government in the meantime got blamed for the farmers' plight in the midst of general prosperity. Howe's palliative gesture to the farmers, an increase in government-guaranteed loan limits, was likened by the Saskatchewan provincial Liberal leader to using "a stirrup pump in a brush fire" and denounced as "mere tinkering" by that traditional fashion of Liberalism, the Winnipeg Free Press. When he went west to preach patience for the present and optimism about the future, Howe's message of cheer, coupled with his refusal to consider special subsidies, only roused further hostility.[38]

Although Liberal party organizers, who were more closely in touch with actual farm sentiment, counselled him against appearing before campaign meetings in the rural areas, Howe was not the man to avoid a fight. On May 18, 1957, the determined trade minister went to two campaign meetings in Manitoba. They were both disasters.

At the first meeting in Carman, Howe delivered his prepared address to restrained and polite applause. The first hint of the debacle to follow was given as he left the hall. A farmer thrust a piece of paper into the minister's hand. The note purported to show that it cost seventy-six cents a bushel to grow oats. ''Why'd you cut the price from sixty to fifty-five cents?'' demanded the farmer. When Howe asked him where he got the figures, the farmer replied that it was from ''statistics.'' Howe's response was one that was to live on in Manitoba politics for years to come. ''You look pretty well fed,'' said the trade minister patting the farmer on the stomach with the back of his hand.[39] A Winnipeg *Free Press* reporter present during the incident duly reported it and Howe's remark became a cause-célèbre in the election campaign.

From Carman the Howe party travelled to Morris for the evening meeting held in the crowded auditorium of the high school. The Winnipeg *Free Press* report of the meeting told it all:

> Surplus-suffering Manitoba farmers Saturday night pounced on the man who is responsible for selling Canada's grain crop, turning a carefully planned Liberal rally into a pandemonium of shouts, jeers and raucous booing....Local Liberals said that Mr. Howe had defied their advice to sally forth into the teeth of farm unrest in the grain country. But before he had left the Morris auditorium the teeth had clamped down hard upon him and he had to battle his way off the platform, shouting over choruses of cat-calls and jeers that he was wanted back in Ottawa.[40]

The fallout from the publicity given the proceedings at that meeting was shattering for the Liberals throughout the West. The Liberals, who had dropped from thirty-one seats on the prairies in 1949 to seventeen seats in 1953, now fell even further from favour. In the 1957 election they won only one seat in Alberta, four in Saskatchewan and one in Manitoba for a total of six.

In his own riding of Port Arthur, linked to the prairies by its major grain terminal industry, Howe went down to personal defeat in the election. A giant had fallen, and with him went the Liberal government in Ottawa. The Progressive Conservatives had won 112 seats to 105 for the Liberals. John Diefenbaker's Conservatives formed a minority government in the 265-seat House of Commons.

While there were forces at play other than the prairie discontent over bulging surpluses and low prices for grain, the loss by the Liberals of 11 seats on the Prairies was enough to swing the balance of power in Ottawa.

In the fall of 1957, the Diefenbaker government enacted the Prairie Grain Advance Payments Act, the purpose of which was to provide cash advances on farm-stored grain pending delivery to the Canadian Wheat Board. It was proclaimed on November 25, 1957, and has since remained an integral feature of western Canadian agriculture.

While the Howe era ended in 1957, there were a number of initiatives taken by both the government and the Canadian Wheat Board during the latter stages of that era. In a rapidly changing world, and influenced by the resurgence of the United States in the world's grain trade, the Wheat Board's method of operations and pattern of trade underwent significant change. Those initiatives and changes are the subject of the next chapter.

One postcript must be added to the Howe era. In 1959 the St. Lawrence Seaway was opened. That huge undertaking, financed jointly by the United States and Canada to open up the ports and facilities surrounding the Great Lakes to ocean shipping and to permit enlarged lakers to reach Montreal and the St. Lawrence River ports, was spurred and guided by C.D. Howe. At one period, in the face of U.S. intransigence on proceeding with the project, Howe threatened to go it alone to open up the freshwater seas which lead almost to the centre of the continent.

Prior to construction of the seaway, the larger lake boats had to be unloaded at transfer elevators for reloading into small canal boats in order to transit six small canals along the St. Lawrence River between Lake Ontario and Montreal. The new system of locks and canals allowed deep sea ships 730-feet long with a 75-foot beam and 25-foot draft to travel from the sea to Thunder Bay and large lakers to carry up to one million bushels of grain directly to the St. Lawrence ports. It was a time- and cost-saving boon to western Canadian grain exports and a monument to the determination of C.D. Howe.

NEW HORIZONS

We found that both Canada and Canadian grain are held in very high esteem. Our impression was that we have erred on the side of neglecting these direct contacts, rather than overdoing them. Without exception, we were met on the basis of what could be done to increase our trade in wheat.

— *Grain Trade Mission Report, 1950*

▪

As the agricultural superpower to the south, backed by the muscle of the U.S. treasury, intruded inexorably into the Canadian Wheat Board's traditional markets, the United Kingdom continued as Canada's principal export market throughout the 1950s. But, early in the decade, the Wheat Board turned its eyes toward the Far East, where Japan was emerging from the ashes of war to become the industrial miracle of the century.

George McIvor had pioneered sales of Canadian wheat to the Japanese as early as 1926 when, as Alberta sales manager of the Pool's Central Selling Agency, he had accompanied Henry Wise Wood

A study in contrasts ranging over 100 years. The first export shipment of western Canadian wheat through the Lakehead arrived at the Canadian Pacific Railways terminal at Port Arthur in the autumn of 1883. The grain had to be transferred by wagon from railway cars to a lake vessel because this first terminal elevator at the Lakehead was not yet completed. Capacity of the terminal was 300,000 bushels (8,100 tonnes) and elevation of the grain was accomplished by steam.

on a sales mission to Japan and China. While in Japan, they contracted sales with Mitsui, Mitsubishi, and other trading companies. In those pre-war years, wheaten foods in Japan had been principally noodles and wheat bread was virtually unknown in the Japanese diet. Thus, while significant in terms of the time, only limited sales resulted.

Now, in the aftermath of the war disaster, the Hidden Empire was emerging into world trade and adopting a Western diet. As head of the occupying forces, General Douglas MacArthur began importing

U.S. wheat into Japan in 1946. It was often baked into bread and distributed to school children and civilians. The Japanese found bread convenient and tasty; they ate steadily increasing amounts of it. Before the war, average consumption of flour products in Japan had been thirty pounds per person a year. By 1955, it had tripled to ninety

This picture shows the Prince Rupert Grain Ltd. terminal on Ridley Island at Prince Rupert, B.C. Reputed to be the most highly automated and computerized grain terminal in the world, the $275,000 structure was officially opened on May 16, 1985. It has a capacity of 200,000 tonnes. The vessel shown in the picture is the World Prize, *the first vessel to load at the terminal. It cleared the port on March 18, 1985, bound for China with a test loading of 25,199 tonnes of wheat.*

pounds, and Japan was importing 2.3 million tonnes of wheat a year.

As the United States Department of Agriculture intensified its campaign to encourage changes in the Japanese dietary habits, by sponsoring school lunch programs, training for bakers, and department store exhibits, Canada shared in the upsurge of wheat exports to Japan. McIvor found officials of the USDA to be co-operative in their initiatives to widen the newly expanding market. On one of his frequent trips to Washington, the chief commissioner asked USDA officials if, rather than emphasizing the use of "American wheat," they would simply promote the use of "wheat."[1] The Americans graciously complied with that request. In light of subsequent events they may well have regretted it.

In 1952 and 1953, the Japanese Import Agency made firm purchase commitments with the Canadian Wheat Board for wheat and barley. These commitments were the result of the opening of negotiations between Canada and Japan on a trade treaty, whereby Japan was seeking preferential entry of manufactured goods into the Canadian market.

Recognizing the opportunity for further expansion into the Pacific Rim countries, the Canadian Wheat Board organized a special mission to visit Japan, Hong Kong, the Phillipines, and Southeast Asia. Thus, on January 6, 1954, when the CP Air flight for Tokyo took off from Vancouver airport, Wheat Board Commissioner William Riddell was aboard. Riddell headed the party, accompanied by J.A. Anderson, chief chemist of the Board of Grain Commissioners, and Garson N. Vogel, chief of the grain division of trade and commerce. For the next ten days the team visited leading merchants, millers, and bakers in Japan, stressing the quality, high-protein and bread-making superiority of Canada's hard wheats, since, of all new wheat products circulating in Japan, bread was the most popular. In this area the Americans were at a disadvantage. They had been shipping soft white wheats that flourish close to the U.S. Pacific ports in Washington. Although ideal for Japan's noodles, biscuits, and cakes, the flour of these low-protein wheats was less suitable for bread-making.

Canada was about to take over the bread flour market in Japan. While the Japanese market for wheat had been about equally shared between the U.S. and Canada at the start of the 1950s, Canada would be outselling the U.S. by two bushels to one by 1960, as bread continued to gain in popularity.

Part of that success was attributable to the negotiating skill of C.D. Howe. The Wheat Board trade mission coincided with final negotiations on a trade pact between Canada and Japan. Canada's tariff structure consisted of three tiers of rates: general, most favoured nation, and British preferential. While the Japanese sought a most favoured nation status for her goods entering Canada, she had little to offer in return, since restrictions on imports into Japan were primarily of a regulatory nature involving import prohibitions and import controls.

The Canadian team negotiated a guarantee from the Japanese government for unconditional, non-discriminatory treatment upon entry into Japan of nine key Canadian export commodities, including wheat and barley. These conditions were incorporated into the final agreement on most favoured nation status for Japan signed March 31, 1954, in Ottawa. What was not announced at that signing was that Howe had gone even further to assure Canada's presence in the market for wheat in Japan. On the same day the trade treaty was signed, there was an undisclosed exchange of letters between the Japanese ambassador in Ottawa and C.D. Howe. While the exchange of letters remained separate from the agreement, it was nevertheless a factor in the signing.[2] The letters, which were never placed in the official files, confirmed an agreement on the part of the Japanese to purchase minimum amounts of Canadian wheat and barley over two years at selling prices on a competitive basis. From February 25 to July 1, 1954, Japan agreed to take 200,000 tons of Canadian wheat and 50,000 tons of barley. In the next Canadian crop year, 1954-1955, Japan agreed to take 550,000 tons of wheat and 300,000 tons of barley as a minimum.

The reason for secrecy on the part of both Japan and Canada was obvious. The United States and Canada were competing for the Japanese market. The Americans had just recently made a gift of wheat to Japan as a goodwill gesture, and Japan was a recipient under the PL 480 program. Evidence of the secret agreement has been documented by C.F. Wilson in his unpublished book *C.D. Howe: An Optimist's Response to a Surfeit of Grain.*[3] On March 19, 1954, Dr. C.M. Isbister, director of international trade relations branch of trade and commerce, wrote to A.E. Ritchie in external affairs. "It is our understanding that the letter on wheat will not be made public unless a situation develops in which the government is being criticized for lack of a definite quantitative understanding on sales of wheat to Japan. In particular the letter will not be published or mentioned in the press release when the agreement is signed."[4]

Besides that letter, the department of trade and commerce files contain a draft press release outlining the text of the exchange of notes which is quoted verbatim by Wilson in his unpublished work. The press release was never issued.[5] That surreptitious firm purchase agreement was followed by increased commitments for wheat and barley in the 1955-1956 crop year. When Howe, accompanied by

Mitchell Sharp, visited Tokyo in 1956 he secured an even larger undertaking from the Japanese government. Japan agreed to take a minimum of one million tons of wheat and barley in each of the three years commencing August 1, 1956.

By 1960, the Americans were thoroughly alarmed and prepared a counterassault. The U.S. Commodity Credit Corporation moved stocks of midwest bread wheats to the West Coast under lowered freight rates and offered it for sale to private exporters at prices competitive with those in Vancouver. At the same time, they adopted tactics, pioneered by the Canadian Wheat Board, of bringing Japanese millers and bakers to the United States to demonstrate the qualities of their midwest hard wheats.

Simultaneously, the American state and treasury departments exerted pressure on the Japanese government to rectify its trade surplus situation with the United States. That pressure resulted in the Japanese government's announcement in 1963 that its wheat purchases would be divided equally between the U.S. and Canada. After Lyndon Johnson, whose constituency was a major wheat producing state, Texas, assumed the presidency, the U.S. government made it clear that sufficient export subsidies would be granted to undercut any Canadian price offerings in the Japanese market. These tactics proved effective in the U.S. gaining an increased share of the Japanese market.

The Far East was not the only region in which the negotiation of most favoured nation tariff agreements were used by Howe as a lever to advance sales of Canadian grain. As early as 1952, while the Cold War was at its height, an aggressive Winnipeg-based private company, Northern Sales Co. Ltd., had been probing sales prospects behind the Iron Curtain. As an export agent of the Wheat Board, Northern Sales had some preliminary success with the state monopoly trading countries allied to the Soviet Union.

Then, in 1955, a chink appeared in the Iron Curtain. Secretary of State for External Affairs Lester Pearson was invited to make an official visit to the Soviet Union. Not wanting to have the trip to Moscow appear as a junket, Pearson sought some practical purpose for the visit. An interdepartmental committee was set up to draft an agenda, and a draft trade treaty, reinforced by a firm purchase commitment for wheat, emerged from its discussions.

Thus, when Pearson proceeded to Moscow, he was accompanied by Howe's right hand man, Deputy Minister of Trade and Commerce Mitchell Sharp. Sharp, who began his career with the pioneer grain trading firm of James A. Richardson & Sons in Winnipeg, was a skilled grain agreement negotiator. He had gone on loan from Richardson as an adviser on grain matters to Finance Minister Ilsley during World War II. In his continuing role with government, Sharp attended meetings on the International Wheat Agreements and, as we have seen, was present in the continued negotiations with the U.S. over PL 480.

Sharp used all his skills in the Moscow negotiations when a battle of wits developed between he and I.G. Kabanov, the Soviet minister of foreign trade. The self-sufficiency notion was deeply imbedded in Soviet policy. Premier Nikita Khruschev had embarked upon the vast project of opening up the "Virgin Lands" to the plow in 1953. It was hoped that the millions of new acres in southern Khazakhstan would enable the Soviet Union to become once again an exporter of wheat.

Sharp was aware that Canada had made small sales of wheat to the Soviet Union for shipment from West Coast ports to the northern Pacific port of Vladivostok, which was apparently more economical for the Russians than supplying the eastern reaches of the Soviet Union via the Trans-Siberia Railway. It was on this basis that the agreement was first suggested. Following preliminary discussions on the basis by which most favoured nation status would be accorded to the Russians, Sharp returned to Ottawa carrying a draft agreement. Pearson then proceeded to the Crimea for talks with President Bulganin and Premier Khruschev.

As a result of the Moscow negotiations, a Soviet mission headed by S.A. Borisov, deputy minister of foreign trade, flew to Ottawa in early 1956 to complete the trade agreement. On February 29, 1956, Borisov, Pearson, and Howe signed the most favoured nation treaty, and Borisov and Pearson exchanged letters covering the purchase of wheat. This time there was no need for secrecy. It was duly announced that the Soviet Union had agreed to purchase 1.2 million to 1.5 million tonnes of wheat within the next three years in annual amounts ranging from four to five hundred thousand tonnes. The Russian purchases were to be made at prices and terms on which the Canadian Wheat Board was making sales to its major customers at such time as the Soviet purchases took place.[6] It was a breakthrough that was to pay dividends when harsh climatic conditions in the new Virgin Lands denied Khruschev's hopes of yields beyond Soviet self-sufficiency.

Also, the format of the three-year purchase commitment, coupled with a trade treaty of three years' duration and renewable by negotiation, set a pattern for negotiation with other state-trading nations, notably those of Eastern Europe where similar agreements followed. While still using private trading firms as export agents wherever necessary, the board was now able to expand its "single-desk" selling

Breakthrough. Secretary of State for External Affairs Lester B. Pearson, left, welcomed a Soviet trade delegation to Ottawa on February 2, 1956. S.A. Borisov, Soviet deputy minister of foreign trade, centre, headed the delegation which included Ivan F. Shpedko on the left. The meeting resulted in the granting of most favoured nation trade status to the Soviet Union and the exchange of notes on the first long-term grain agreement with the Russians February 29, 1956. Under the exchange of notes, the Soviets agreed to purchase 1.2 million tonnes of Canadian wheat over the following three years in annual amounts ranging from 400,000 to 500,000 tonnes. That agreement was to lead to more massive purchases in later years when the Soviet emerged as the world's largest grain importer.

technique as the ideal instrument for negotiation with the state purchasing agencies rapidly emerging as the principal buyers on world grain markets. Even in Britain, the number of buyers for the private milling trade had declined to a point where a few negotiators combined around a small table with the board to consummate quarterly purchase agreements.

Coinciding with these events, another departure from previously normal practices in world grain trade was taking place. Access to credit terms was becoming equally as important as price in the negotiation of bilateral agreements. Throughout the history of the Canadian grain trade, commercial practice had required that full payment be made before the grain was discharged into the hold of the buyer's ship. But in 1952-1953, Ottawa authorized a sale of wheat to Yugoslavia under short-term credit, provided by the Canadian exporters as agents of the Wheat Board. The risk was insured by a federal government agency, the Canadian Export Credits Insurance Corporation.

Signed shortly after Yugoslavia had severed its alliance with the Soviet Union, the sale was for 5,477,884 bushels of wheat on the basis of 20 per cent cash and the balance within twelve months of the date of shipment. A second sale to Yugoslavia on credit terms followed two years later for 3,619,989 bushels of wheat with 10 per cent down and the balance within one year. The sales to Yugoslavia were obviously a Cold War concession to that country's defection from the Soviet orbit and not intended as a precedent or shift in policy. Howe's intention in setting up the Canadian Export Credits Insurance Corporation had been solely to assist the manufacturing sector by insuring credit sales, in order to compete with exporters from other countries who had comparable credit insurance available to them.

When, in October 1954, Poland applied for a similar credit purchase, Howe's reaction was negative and the request was refused. His answer to the Polish request was that "no monies have been voted by Parliament for the extension of such credits." The Yugoslavian sale was indirectly explained away by stating that only under very special circumstances, and only on very few occasions, had the facilities of the export credit corporation been used to facilitate the extension of private credit for wheat purchases.[7] In the meantime C.O. Swartz, president of Northern Sales, had been calling on the East European grain importing monopolies and their trade representatives in Washington. At the same time he was exploring the availability of credit, in both West Germany and Canada, to expedite sales behind the Iron Curtain. This led to a renewed application from Poland and similar overtures from Czechoslovakia and Hungary.

Under the pressure of ever-increasing export competition from the American concessional program, Howe modified his resistance to credit sales. In May 1955, the Canadian Wheat Board made a sale of 250,000 tons of wheat to Poland on the basis of 15 per cent cash with the balance payable within one year. In mid-December of the same year the board made a further sale of 100,000 bushels to Poland on the same terms. Early in 1956 there was a similar sale to Czechoslovakia of 300,000 tons with a credit guarantee through the Export Credits Insurance Corporation. One year later, in February 1957, the Polish government, finding some difficulty in obtaining foreign exchange to meet repayment of its credit, and in need of more imports, sent a delegation to Ottawa to seek an extension of the terms of its agreement.

Howe advised Sharp, who was negotiating with the Poles, not to agree to any relaxation of the credit terms unless the Polish government was prepared to make substantial new purchases. The result was a three-year agreement, marking the first extended credit sale authorized by the federal government. Under its terms Poland agreed to purchase 150,000 tons of wheat in each of the crop years 1956-1957 and 1957-1958 on the basis of 10 per cent cash; 30 per cent within twenty-four months; 30 per cent within thirty months; and the remaining 30 per cent within thirty-six months of shipment.

An interesting sidelight to what became known as "Polish credit terms," was that the Soviet delegation, when negotiating their 1956 purchase, insisted on having precisely the same credit terms as those accorded the Poles written into the agreement. Having received that concession, the Russians then punctiliously paid cash on all shipments under the agreement.

As these developments took place, Canadian Wheat Board commissioners and officials were becoming seasoned travellers in the rapidly expanding air age. They fanned out across the globe visiting every important grain market at least once a year.

An amendment to the Canadian Wheat Board Act in 1953 provided a further avenue for promotion of Canadian grain. Provision was included in the amending bill to extend the board's monopoly marketing powers to July 31, 1957, for utilization of unpaid balances which had been accumulating in the board's accounts. These unpaid balances resulted, in large part, from prolonged delays in making final payments on participation certificates in earlier periods, such as during the five-year pool at the end of the war. Removals, deaths, and farm abandonments sometimes created difficulties in locating the claimants to whom payments were due. Thus, despite all reasonable efforts to locate these claimants, surplus funds had been accumulating over the past ten years.

A number of recommendations on disposition of the funds were suggested. They included payment of all funds outstanding after ten years into the current pools; establishment of scholarship funds for farmers' children; sponsorship of scientific research; and contributions to adult education through farm organizations. Howe finally settled on an amendment to the Wheat Board Act which required all outstanding unpaid balances after a period of six years to be paid into a special board fund. Expenditures could be made from the fund for purposes deemed to be of benefit to the producers upon the recommendation of the board, with approval of cabinet.

Under such broad terms of reference, McIvor opted to use the funds principally for sales promotion. He conceived the notion of paying the expenses of grain missions to Canada, whereby groups within the grain importing nations could be exposed to Canadian methods of handling, transporting, and marketing grain.

The first four missions arrived for three-week visits in the summer of 1954 from Brazil, Japan, Ireland, and Switzerland. Then, during the summer and fall of 1955, arrangements were made for five incoming missions from important grain importing countries. The first of these consisted of eight young millers from the United Kingdom, selected by the British National Association of Millers. Their visit extended from August 15 to September 16, and they were shown first-hand the Canadian methods of handling grain, with particular emphasis on the inspecting, grading, storing, and milling operations. The British millers were followed by missions from four Latin American republics, Colombia, Ecuador, Peru, and Venezuela; a mission comprised of four representatives of the grain inspection services of Japan; a fourth mission from the Japanese barley processing industry; and a fifth group of representatives from West Germany.[8]

Another project which utilized the fund was the preparation in the 1953-1954 crop year of a colour film that illustrated important phases of production, transportation, handling, and marketing of Western wheat. The sound track was recorded in seven languages for distribution in importing countries. In 1954-1955, a grant of ten thousand dollars over two years, was made to the University of Saskatchewan for basic research in connection with the physiology of rust.

Incoming missions proved the most popular use of the funds, however, with a further five delegations arriving in 1956 from the Netherlands, Belgium, Czechoslovakia, Norway, and Germany. Success of the missions was so thoroughly demonstrated that the United States and Australia adopted the innovation and made arrangements for similar tours of their countries.

With the onset of mounting surpluses in the early fifties, it became evident that changes would have to be made in the quota delivery system to meet the changing market conditions. Throughout the 1947-1952 period, the first priority had been to get available supplies moved forward as quickly as possible to meet market demands, and only occasional resort was made to delivery quotas. As crop yields jumped at the start of the decade, and competition for markets intensified, it was inevitable that the delivery quota system would have to be used more extensively. Problems had also been encountered with damp and out-of-condition grain from the harvests of 1950 and 1951. Besides changes to enhance equity of delivery opportunities, the board wanted to adapt the system to special marketing situations, such as the need to process out-of-condition grain that might spoil on the farm.

Following a review in early 1953, the board undertook a major revision of the quota delivery system which was announced prior to the 1953-1954 crop year. Under the previous formula, producer's deliveries of any particular grain were limited to a stated number of bushels per acre specifically seeded to that grain. Producer concerns developed over the rigidities within that system. Concern was also expressed that the seeded acreage tended to entrench existing production patterns, since the only way to enlarge the quota base was to seed additional acres to a particular grain, usually at the expense of summer fallow.

The first important change was to broaden the basis of producers' deliveries by including summer fallow as a relevant acreage. Acreage for delivery purposes was designated as specified acreage, which was the combined total of acres that producers in 1953 had seeded to wheat (except durum), oats, barley, and rye, plus acreages in summer fallow. The second major change was to give producers more flexibility in their deliveries of wheat, oats, barley, or rye. This was accomplished by defining the major delivery quotas as a general quota of a stated number of bushels per specified acre. A producer could then deliver wheat, oats, barley, or rye in any combination, up to the limit of the general established quota. The third major change was inclusion for the first time of a minimum number of bushels to be delivered under the general quotas. This was established as a means of assistance to the producers who operated smaller farms throughout the Prairie Provinces.[9] Thus, the minimum right to deliver was five hundred bushels, or a general quota of three bushels per specified acre, whichever was the greater.

There was an inherent danger in this new format that the producer, being master of his choice, would deliver qualities and types of grains in low demand which could eventually clog the delivery system. It was the experience of the board that, under the general quotas, there was a tendency for producers to deliver higher value grains in preference to oats. In order to bring forward types and grades of grain in market demand, the board was obliged to use specific supplementary quotas during the crop year. The board also permitted special carload consignments of malting barley and milling oats.

In advance of the next crop year, further revisions in the delivery quota system were announced in an attempt to provide more equity in monetary returns to the producer on their initial deliveries, irrespective of what grains they chose to deliver. The specified acres and general delivery quotas of 1953 remained, but a system of unit quotas was superimposed on that system. A unit consisted of three bushels of wheat, or five bushels of barley or rye, or eight bushels of oats. The initial quota was then set at 100 units, against which any one, or any combination, of the four grains could be delivered.[10] Roughly based on the disparate bushel weights of the four grains, and current market prices, the unit quota discriminated against wheat in its initial form. The average value of the initial quota of 100 units would return $369 for wheat, $480 for oats, $440 for barley, and $450 for rye.[11] This combination of unit initial quotas and subsequent general quotas was continued from 1953 to 1969. Under it, the Canadian Wheat Board lost a considerable measure of control over the kinds of grain delivered, since the option was with the producer.

Attempts to equalize delivery opportunities as the mountain of surplus grains backed up on the farms was further complicated by an emerging shortage of boxcars to transport grain at critical periods. By the mid-1950s, there were grumblings throughout the West that there was a connection between boxcar shortages and the statutory Crowsnest grain hauling rate. A Social Credit member, Victor Quelch, outlined the concerns in the Commons in 1956: "I know there is a feeling prevalent in the West that perhaps there is some connection between the shortage of boxcars and the Crowsnest rates. They feel that perhaps the railways are not really doing all they can to make more boxcars available, that they are constantly urging a change in the Crowsnest Pass agreement, and that as a consequence they are not doing their utmost to make all the cars available for moving wheat that could be made available.''[12]

Whatever the merits of the emerging criticism at the time, it was an issue that was to plague and hamper the Canadian Wheat Board into the 1980s in its efforts to maximize export sales. While the ''Holy Crow'' was considered a birthright by prairie farmers, the railways increasingly regarded the low statutory rate as a noose around their financial necks, choking off any hope of modernization or expansion in the grain handling network.

The controversial Crow Rate had its origin in the desire of the Canadian Pacific Railway to build a rail line from Edmonton, Alberta, to Nelson, British Columbia, through the Crowsnest Pass in the Rocky Mountains. To do so they sought a subsidy of $3.4 million from the federal government. In consequence, an agreement was entered into in 1897 between the government and the CPR in which the subsidy was granted. In return the railway agreed to move grain from specific prairie points to the Lakehead at a fixed rate in perpetuity. The agreement was confirmed by federal legislation on September 1, 1899.

For a short period at the beginning of the century, rates dropped below the Crow rates as competition from other railways took effect. Then, during World War I, the government allowed the rate to rise in recognition of wartime inflationary forces. However, in 1925, the government reinstituted the Crowsnest Pass rates by statute and extended them to include all grain shipped from any prairie point, on any rail line, to any export port. Based on distance from export position, the Crow Rate dropped by increments from roughly a mid-point on the prairies between the West Coast and the Lakehead. The rate from Regina, Saskatchewan, to the Lakehead was twenty cents per hundred pounds, or roughly one-half cent per ton-mile.

As transportation difficulties began to emerge, Roy W. Milner was appointed transport controller by the federal government on August 21, 1951. He was seconded, on a part-time basis, from the Board of Grain Commissioners of which he was a member. Milner's task was to co-ordinate the Canadian Wheat Board's export commitments with the railways and lake shippers in the amounts required at seaboard to load vessels arriving to lift the grain. During the five years that Milner filled the post he established an enviable record of meeting all export commitments on both coasts without incurring demurrage, and frequently earning despatch money through the timely loading of ships.[13] Despite that the transport controller was heavily criticized by CCF members in Parliament. There were frequent clashes, particularly with Hazen Argue, the CCF agricultural critic.

Argue, a Saskatchewan farmer, made persistent attempts through private members bills to make the transport controller responsible for the allocation of boxcars to individual country elevators on the basis of the producers' choice of delivery point and for equalization of quotas through such allocations. He argued that the powers of the transport controller had not been used in a way that was fair and equitable to producers and which would allow them to deliver to the elevators of their own choice.[14]

As a result of the constant criticism, Howe issued a directive to the Wheat Board in July 1954. In essence, after allowance for marketing requirements and other relevant considerations, the board, in issuing shipping orders, should take into account the relative volume of business done by the competing companies in more normal circumstances where there was an absence of congestion. In following that directive, the board, as far as possible and consistent with ordering out the various grades of grain in quantities needed to meet sales commitments, divided up its shipping orders to the elevator companies in proportion to the relative volume of business they had done in a representative base period before elevator congestion had developed.

In order to discourage public controversy, the board did not reveal its precise formula and left it to the elevator companies to judge whether they were being fairly treated. In issuing its shipping orders the board made the allocations among companies, then left it to them to make the distribution of such orders among its elevators at individual shipping points.

Milner, in turn, simply instructed the railways to allocate cars among competing elevator companies at individual shipping points on the basis of the relative volume of Wheat Board shipping orders held by each elevator at that point. Thus, it could happen that for competitive reasons the companies might concentrate their orders at some points more than others, and the distribution of shipping orders would still not reflect the competitive volume of business done by elevators at a particular point.

Debate and questioning in the Commons and in the standing

committee on agriculture and colonization on the question of car allocations grew more bitter over the period of Milner's tenure as transport controller. Finally, having been appointed chief commissioner of the Board of Grain Commissioners, Milner submitted his resignation on December 17, 1956.

Questioned in January 1957 as to a possible replacement, Howe indicated that it was unlikely that anyone would accept the position in light of the acrimonious treatment accorded Milner. "Mr. Speaker, the minister of Trade and Commerce is well aware of what happened in the meetings of the committee on agriculture during the last session which in my opinion has made the position of transport controller untenable. Whatever recommendations I may make to my colleagues, I cannot mention the name of any man who would accept that position and go before that committee in the capacity of transport controller."[15]

That was the end of transport control. To fill the void, the Canadian Wheat Board established a traffic department which dealt directly with the elevator companies, the railways, and the lake shippers without the intermediation of a transport controller.[16]

Continued discontent in the West over car allocations led to appointment of the Commission of Inquiry into the Distribution of Railway Box Cars by the Diefenbaker government in 1958. The commissioner, John Bracken, formerly premier of Manitoba and a former leader of the federal Progressive Conservative Party, presented his report in December 1958. Among the Bracken report recommendations were: that the allocation of shipping orders to different elevator companies be on the basis of current business earned by each; that the practice of embargoing shipments from full elevators at points where competing elevators have space, and are free to take in new business, be discontinued; that each elevator at a shipping point be kept in a position to compete fairly with the others by the receipt of sufficient shipping orders from its parent company, and sufficient cars from the railway, to keep it from being "plugged" and thus out of business when others are not.[17]

Thus, in the 1958-1959 crop year, the Canadian Wheat Board began administering what became known as the Bracken formula. In order to give practical effect to instructions from the minister of trade and commerce, the board employed a twelve-month moving average of the most recent primary receipts of each company as a basis of car distribution among the various companies.[18]

One further change took place in the mid-fifties when the advisory committee to the Wheat Board was restructured in the summer of 1955. The old advisory committee included a mix of producer and trade representatives. These two groups frequently found themselves in an adversary position regarding advice to the board, with the result that some recommendations were of little value. As a consequence, periods between meetings sometimes extended up to eighteen months. McIvor recommended to Howe that a committee composed exclusively of producer representatives be appointed. The new committee, appointed by the government, consisted of W.J. Parker, president of Manitoba Pool Elevators; J.H. Wesson, president of Saskatchewan Wheat Pool; Ben Plumer, president of Alberta Wheat Pool; J.E. Brownlee, president of United Grain Growers; C.P. Hansen, president of the Saskatchewan Farmers' Union; and R.C. Marler, president of the Alberta Federation of Agriculture.[19]

And, on page twenty-four of the annual report of the Canadian Wheat Board for the 1957-1958 crop year, there were two concise paragraphs marking the end of another era:

> Effective April 30, 1958, Mr. George McIvor resigned as Chief Commissioner. In June, 1958 Mr. W.C. McNamara, formerly Assistant Chief Commissioner, was appointed Chief Commissioner of the Board, and Mr. W. Riddel, formerly Commissioner, was appointed Assistant Chief Commissioner. Mr. W.E. Roberston continued as Commissioner. In July, 1958 Mr. John T. Dallas was appointed Commissioner and assumed his new duties on September 1, 1958. Mr. Dallas was formerly Executive Vice-President and Director of the Continental Grain Company (Canada) Limited.
>
> The Commissioners, officers and staff of the Board wish to record their appreciation of the distinguished services rendered to the Board by Mr. George McIvor. When the Canadian Wheat Board was established in 1935, Mr. McIvor was appointed General Sales Manager. Late in 1935 he was appointed Assistant Chief Commissioner and in 1937 was appointed Chief Commissioner, a position he held until his retirement in April last.

Behind those sparse paragraphs lies the story of an abrasive confrontation. The events leading to McIvor's departure began in the board room of the Canadian Wheat Board Building in Winnipeg in the summer of 1957. During the 1956-1957 crop year the board's asking price for No. 1 Northern wheat, in store the Lakehead, had declined by 11 3/4 cents a bushel down to $1.61 5/8. Part of that decline, 5 1/4 cents, was due to the rise of the Canadian dollar to a premium above the U.S. dollar; the remaining 6 1/2 cents was due to market factors. In addition, the board widened the spreads on lower grade wheats to meet increasing competition from the United States. In June, the spread between No. 5 wheat and the top grade, which had previously been set at 24 cents in January, was widened to 38 cents. As a result the asking price for No. 5 wheat declined to $1.23 5/8.[20]

In July, the board was faced with the decision of whether to recommend spreads in the initial prices to be paid producers during the coming 1957-1958 crop year. On a motion from McNamara, the board recommended to the government that, in relation to the $1.40 initial payment for the top grade, the payment on delivery of lower grades be reduced substantially in order to reflect the lower asking prices. There was one dissenter. Robertson voted against discounting the lower grades, predicting that Prime Minister John Diefenbaker, whose Progressive Conservative government had been elected to office the previous month with a tenuous hold in a minority House, would not accept it. It proved to be a politically perceptive observation. McIvor, having successfully fought the same battle with Jimmy Gardiner in the past, felt that political considerations should be divorced from the practical sales policy of the board. The recommendation went forward to Gordon Churchill, a Winnipeg lawyer who was now minister of trade and commerce in the Diefenbaker administration.[21]

Shortly afterwards, McIvor received a phone call from an agitated Churchill. Would the chief commissioner come to Ottawa? The resulting meeting in Churchill's office, attended by the board's secretary Clive Davidson, was cordial. The Diefenbaker government had indicated its intention to introduce cash advances on farm-stored grain, and methods of administering such a program through the board were discussed. McIvor had been lukewarm to the cash advance proposal and remained so, but offered co-operation. On the question of widening initial price spreads, Churchill conceded. "If it had to be done, it should be done."[22]

As the meeting drew to a close, Churchill suggested to the chief commissioner that the prime minister would like to see him. He proceeded to the prime minister's office, along with Churchill and his deputy minister Mitchell Sharp. McIvor was unaware that Diefenbaker had been drawn into the price spread issue. "Diefenbaker and I had had a relationship and I thought it was just going to be; 'How are you George,' and that kind of thing.'' That illusion was quickly shattered; McIvor found Diefenbaker in a towering temper. The prime minister immediately launched into a screaming tirade. Shaking his finger at McIvor, he accused the chief commissioner of playing politics and attempting to embarrass and undermine the new administration by lowering initial prices. McIvor was completely taken aback. ''They wouldn't love it in the West, but we had done it before when we had to. I could only reply that I had never played politics in my life, at this time or any other time.''[23]

As the tirade continued, Churchill, despite his earlier concession on the question of spreads, stood quietly by. Sharp attempted to come to McIvor's defence. Probably more suspect than McIvor of allegiance to Howe and the former Liberal administration, Sharp was abruptly told to shut-up.

As the initial assault subsided, McIvor pointed out that the pricing decision had been taken by the board in line with its requirement under the Act. Diefenbaker then asked if there was any way that the decision could be reversed and the initial payments on the lower grades raised. McIvor replied that Churchill, as the minister responsible for the board, could write a letter instructing the board to restore initial prices to their former level. If there was a loss on the lower grades, due to the advance payment being higher than achievable market prices, then the government should assure the board that the losses would be made up from the federal treasury, rather than diluting final payments on the higher grades in the pool. Churchill was instructed to write the letter.

The crisis, insofar as the farmer was concerned, was over. For McIvor it was not. Accustomed to support from C.D. Howe on board decisions, he was disappointed in the silent acquiesence of Churchill to the humiliating confrontation. Outside the office, Churchill apologized for the prime minister's outburst, pointing out that Diefenbaker was under great strain and that he was also worried about Mrs. Diefenbaker, who had suffered a fall during a recent overseas trip. McIvor simply replied, ''I'm not taking that from anybody.'' As he walked away the decision had been made. He would resign.[24]

Back in Winnipeg, McIvor called a meeting of the board and informed them of his intention. However, despite his antipathy to the board's administering cash advances on farm-stored grain, it was a critical time for the farmers and he wanted to finalize the regulations under which the new program would be implemented. He and Clive Davidson worked out final details of the program. Then, on

Saturday morning, November 16, 1957, McIvor went to the office and dictated his letter of resignation.

On November 25, the Prairie Grain Advance Payments Act went into effect. Under it the Canadian Wheat Board administered interest-free advances on farm-stored grain up to a maximum of $3,000 to each permit holder. The advances were repaid by the farmer on delivery of grain as quotas opened up. In the first year advances totalled $35,203,467, of which only $2,660 remained outstanding at the end of the crop year.[25] Once again, the Wheat Board was the chosen instrument of government to administer a program outside of its direct sales role. Over the years the cash advance system proved invaluable to farmers, particularly in years when elevator congestion developed. In the 1968-1969 crop year the advances totalled $151,852,319 and in the next year they totalled a record $272,777,516. Over the first nineteen years of operation, cash advances totalling $1,144,297,368 were made with a very low percentage of defaults.[26] Availability of cash advances on farm-stored grain afforded the board greater latitude in establishing delivery quotas to meet its market needs, without the same degree of concern for the cash requirements of producers.

As the once controversial cash advance legislation was going into effect, McIvor returned to Ottawa. His official letter of resignation had precipitated another agitated phone call from Churchill. The concerned trade minister asked McIvor to reconsider, but the decision remained firm. After his meeting with Churchill, McIvor went to lunch at the Chateau Laurier Hotel with Mitchell Sharp.

After lunch, McIvor was about to leave for the airport when a bellboy informed him he was wanted on the phone. Sharp guessed correctly; it was the prime minister's office. Would the chief commissioner cancel his flight and meet with Mr. Diefenbaker? McIvor reluctantly agreed, and proceeded to the prime minister's office. He found Churchill, "waiting like an office boy," in the hall. In the prime minister's office, Diefenbaker sought the reason for McIvor's resignation and asked him to stay on. Not wishing to resurrect the previous acrimonious meeting, McIvor explained that his pension was small, the plan having only been instituted a short time previously, and he wished to make provisions for his family through other endeavours. Finding McIvor firm in his decision, Diefenbaker revealed the canker of suspicion that lay behind his earlier explosive outburst: "Howe put you up to this. He said in the House that you would resign if cash advances were implemented." McIvor replied that, while he was lukewarm to the board's administration of cash advances and remained so, he had not threatened to resign. He added, "On the subject of Mr. Howe, everybody who ever worked for him not only had a deep regard for him but had a deep affection, and I'm one of them."[27]

Finally, at the request of the prime minister, McIvor agreed to stay on until the next April. In the interim, Lester Pearson issued an ill-timed challenge to Diefenbaker to call an election. It was gleefully accepted, and on March 31, 1958, the Progressive Conservatives swept to an unprecedented victory winning 208 seats in the 265-seat Commons. The solid Tory wave swept the Prairies clean of opposition members except for one CCF member in Saskatchewan. Jimmy Gardiner was one the casualties and retired from politics.

George McIvor, honoured with the Cross of St. Michael and St. George at the end of World War II, for distinguished service during that crisis in world affairs, departed without fanfare to begin a new career at the age of sixty-four. His honorarium, received from the board shortly thereafter, was five thousand dollars. On the day McIvor left the Canadian Wheat Board, he became chairman of the board of Robin Hood Flour Mills Limited in Montreal, a position he occupied for the next twelve years. He also became a director of the Canadian Imperial Bank of Commerce and a director of Crown Trust, before retiring to Calgary in his later years.

The warm friendship that had developed between he and C.D. Howe continued until New Year's Eve 1960. Shortly before the bells heralded 1961, Howe died in Montreal while watching the Saturday night hockey game on television. One of the other major players in the affairs of the Canadian Wheat Board during the decade, Mitchell Sharp, seeing the handwriting on the wall, had resigned as deputy minister of trade and commerce. Howe obtained a position for him with Brazilian Traction. However, Sharp was to return to the scene later.

Thus, as the Canadian Wheat Board went through the late fifties and into a dramatically changing world market in the sixties, there was a change in the cast of leading players. On the board, there was a marked difference in personality and philosophic outlook between George McIvor and his successor William C. McNamara. McIvor, with his courtly manners and quiet diplomacy, guided the board through its difficult, and sometimes uncertain, early years when the government tried to disentangle itself from involvement in grain marketing. In the midst of the crisis of wartime conditions and in its aftermath when available supplies had to be rationed among the nations in need, he earned a reputation of fairness and won many friends for Canada around the world. It was said that George McIvor could reject a request and have the petitioner leave the office thinking he had been granted a favour.

While he and McNamara differed on many occasions, McIvor obviously respected McNamara's negotiating and marketing skills. Those skills were to be needed in the next decade, when the gregarious McNamara, an ever-present cigar clenched in his teeth, negotiated new and expanding export markets for Canadian grain. The scene was set for change. Despite their differences, both men may have been the right men for their times.

POSTSCRIPT

This volume has traced the history of the Canadian Wheat Board to a point approximately midway in its first half-century. We have covered an era dominated to a large extent by one remarkable man, George McIvor. In the first half of this endeavor to bring an understanding of the board's role and place in Canada's broader agricultural policy objectives, the author has had the benefit of a rich source of previously published material to guide him — particularly that of Charles Wilson and other observors of the early years. While research and writing on the second half of the first fifty years has been completed, those chapters largely break new ground. In short, while many undertakings and initiatives that have impinged on the Wheat Board's operations have been reported, speculated, and commented upon in the popular press, there has not been a definitive recording of the background to those events. In being granted free and unimpeded access to the files of the Canadian Wheat Board, I found myself alone in unexplored territory.

In consequence of that privilege granted by the commissioners of the Canadian Wheat Board, my research led me into heretofore unpublished personal correspondence, office memoranda, minutes of the board and of the advisory committee to the board, minutes of grain agreement negotiations, and other previously classified material that might prove sensitive in the short term. Many of the principal personalities involved in that unfolding sequence of events remain on the national and international scene. It may be that, had some of them foreseen that their personal reactions were to be published, they would not have ventured them into the record, or upon consideration altered what was said or written. The dilemma that presents itself here is that the record would be incomplete without those personal reactions, which enliven and enrich any history.

Recognizing a similar sensitivity in publication of his history of Canadian agriculture up to 1951, Wilson wrote:

> Little would have happened had it not been for the conflicts of view and abrasions of personalities. In the heat of action some derogatory remarks have been written or said, and descendants of the principal characters can possibly still take umbrage at repetition of what is already historical record. This need not be, however, for there comes a time when an adversary's confrontation is transformed into an enduring compliment. In instances set out here, that metamorphosis should already have taken place.[1]

Unfortunately, many of the fractious issues which have marked the western Canadian agricultural policy scene in relatively recent years have not yet been fully resolved at the time of this publication, and that metamorphosis may not yet have taken place. On the other hand, any history of the Canadian Wheat Board would not be complete, nor would it be accepted with credulity, if it were written in isolation from such issues as the Crowsnest Pass grain-hauling rate debate, Feed Freight Assistance, the domestic feed grains policy, rail line abandonment, hopper car acquisitions, rationalization of the country elevator system, and even the relatively distant Operation Lift controversy. Many cannot view these issues dispassionately, particularly farmers and their diverse organizations and political policy makers, both past and present, at the provincial and federal levels. While resolution, or implementation, of those issues lies in the political sphere outside of the legislated jurisdiction of the Canadian Wheat Board, each has a direct bearing upon its continuing day-to-day operations. Yet, on each the board maintains an apolitical stance.

Therefore, in recognition of any personal sensitivities that may remain, it has been decided that the later years leading up to the fiftieth anniversary will be outlined only in a brief review. It may be that, in the future when personal and government material is considered less sensitive, a more complete and definitive publication of those latter years will be possible.

Until that time, a brief review is in order since, in many respects, the end of the McIvor era marked a turning point in the history of the board.

With world production and trade in wheat and coarse grains rapidly expanding, Canada and the United States were still co-operating on holding the price line through informal meetings and through the International Wheat Agreement, which had been renegotiated in 1959 with thirty-seven countries participating. However, American exports, financed largely through concessional sales under P.L. 480 and other programs, were taking an increasing share of that expanding market entering the decade of the 1960s. While Britain remained Canada's principal market, there were ominous signs of change in traditional European trade which had so long dominated the importing side of the market. In the European Economic Community the first steps toward what became the Common Agricultural Policy were underway in a surge toward increased self-sufficiency. For the Canadian Wheat Board, new strategies were needed in a rapidly changing world.

William C. McNamara, chief commissioner Canadian Wheat Board, June 1958 to February 1971.

As chief commissioner, William McNamara began an aggressive reorganization of the departments and administrative structure of the board and took steps to bring the widely dispersed staff under one roof. Despite the fact that the mandate of the board was still being extended for five-year periods, property was acquired adjacent to the Main Street building for expansion, and plans were made for acquistion of a large mainframe computer to handle the board's complex records and payments to producers.

Then in September 1960, McNamara instigated a search for a new market in China. The result, achieved after thirty-one days of negotiations in Hong Kong and Peking, was the first long-term agreement with the People's Republic of China. Signed in Peking on April 22, 1961, the pact provided for shipment of up to five million long tons of wheat and one million long tons of barley between June 1, 1961, and December 31, 1963. Announcement of the sale was made six days later in Hong Kong by Agriculture Minister Alvin Hamilton. That breakthrough was to result in a steady and continuing relationship into the 1980s. It marked an historic precedent in that it was the first time the board extended credit through commercial sources: the board was authorized to borrow from the banks to finance the sales; the loans were backed by a guarantee from the federal government.

It was followed by another major breakthrough in September 1963 with the largest single sale by the board up to that period. In Ottawa's Chateau Laurier Hotel, McNamara and Leonid Matveev, chairman of the Soviet Union's Exporkhleb state grain-trading agency, signed a contract for delivery of 5.3 million long tons of wheat and 500,000 tons of flour to the Soviet Union over the following 10 1/2 months. The board had made earlier sales to Russia, dating back to the 1957-1958 crop year, but they had been minimal amounts from Canada's West Coast to the Soviet Union's Pacific port of Vladivostok. From 1963 onward, sales to the Russians, while somtimes intermittent, were massive.

As Canada expanded sales into these new markets, strains became evident in the pricing co-operation between Canada and the U.S., which was enforcing the pricing provisions of the IWA that had been renegotiated in 1962. The world's grain trade was now clearly divided into what was classified as the "Three Cs": commercial, communist, and concessional. In the United States, there was openly expressed discontent, since, when reserve stocks were sold outside of the IWA, the American exports were on concessional terms while Canada's sales were primarily into commercial markets, particularly to the communist countries where the Americans were locked out by law. Early in 1965, the U.S. abandoned the route of co-operation and began to use its economic power competitively by the use of increased export subsidies. In the ensuing price war, the pricing formula of the IWA disintegrated.

As the decade progressed, attempts were made to revive the ailing International Wheat Agreement, which was extended by protocol for one-year periods up to July 31, 1967, when the price and quantitative obligations under the pact ceased. Following the Kennedy round of negotiations of the General Agreement on Tariffs and Trade, another attempt was made at international co-operation in the world grain trade, and on July 31, 1968, the International Grains Agreement (IGA) came into effect. In the interim, before the IGA was implemented, Canada attempted to stem the price decline by holding within the agreed limits of the proposed arrangement. It was at a heavy cost: Canada's share of the world wheat trade in the 1967-1968 crop year dropped to a new low of 17.9 per cent, as compared to 26.3 per cent in the previous crop year. In the face of intensified price competition and export subsidization, particularly by the EEC and the U.S., Canada continued to attempt to make the IGA a viable instrument. Finally, in March 1969, the Canadian Wheat Board informed the Prices Review Committee of the IGA that it could no longer strictly observe the agreement's minimum price provisions.

The IGA was a dead instrument. In the dog-eat-dog environment of world markets, Canada entered the new decade of the 1970s in an atmosphere of bleak frustration. International wheat supplies hit record levels, after three consecutive years of record world wheat crops. As prices slid downward, Canada's carryover of grain was at record levels. On the Prairies, farm bins were bursting with over half a billion bushels of wheat and another half-billion plugged commercial storage facilities.

During this period the Canadian Wheat Board was finally recognized as a permanent institution. On August 1, 1967, the sections of the Canadian Wheat Board Act requiring the legislated powers of the board to be reviewed at five-year intervals were repealed and no new sections to replace them were enacted.

A further complication for the board during the disruptive decade of the 1960s was a growing inadequacy in the transportation pipeline to export positions. Surge demands, arising from the huge sales to the Soviet Union in 1963 and 1965, had put a severe test on the shipping and handling system. In response to that emergency, the government appointed a Grain Transportation Committee chaired by the chief commissioner of the Canadian Wheat Board. It included the chief commissioner of the Board of Grain Commissioners, the vice-presidents of the railways, and the presidents of three representative grain companies.

As a result of a two-year study by a Grain Transportation Technical Group, appointed by the committee, a proposal emerged for a "block shipping system" to make the most efficient use of country and terminal elevator storage and handling facilities. The study also recommended that the Wheat Board, the major claimant on grain transportation, take the initiative in the continuous planning of grain movement and in keeping up-to-date inventory of the kinds and grades of grain in all positions. At the same time the board would maintain regular consultations with the railways and elevator companies on planning of the board's shipping programs in order to assist them in planning their own operations.

After the establishment of two test blocks in early 1969, the whole of the Wheat Board designated area was integrated into forty-eight shipping blocks covering 1,431 shipping points. Assisted by the board's upgraded computer capability, the block-shipping system led to a substantial reduction in the in-transit time for cars between loading and unloading. This resulted in a faster turnaround, enhancement of marketing opportunities, and more efficient operation of country elevators.

The arrival of the seventies coincided with the entry on the agricultural policy scene of a thirty-six-year-old former dean of law and former Rhodes scholar, Otto Lang. Elected in the Saskatchewan riding of Saskatoon-Humboldt in the federal election of June 25, 1968, Lang was given responsibility for reporting to Parliament for the Canadian Wheat Board in late 1969. He was to retain that responsibility for ten years while holding a number of diverse portfolios in the federal cabinet over the following years. The fledgling minister inherited a grim and apparently deteriorating situation. For the first time ever, the 1968-1969 report of the Canadian Wheat Board showed deficits in all of the pools, including wheat, oats, and barley. Prices were deteriorating and payments from the treasury under the Temporary Wheat Reserves Act were at record highs. Disillusioned with the inflation-eroded Crowsnest statutory grain hauling rate, which they regarded as a tightening noose on their economic viability, the railways were retiring aging boxcars without replacement at an alarming rate, and the branchline system in western Canada was rapidly deteriorating. From 1963 to 1973 the number of six-foot door, general purpose boxcars in the fleet declined from 88,200 to only 48,200.

One of the first actions by the new minister was formation of the Grains Group in Ottawa, which consisted of personnel seconded from the departments of agriculture, industry, trade and commerce, transport and foreign affairs. That new planning body was immediately assigned a number of priority study projects, including a feasibility study on modernization of the elevator and transportation system, and the most effective systems for marketing oil seeds and oats and barley. Foremost among the immediate problems assigned to the Grains Group was an urgent review of production patterns in western Canada. That review was to lead to the controversial Operation Lift (lower inventory for tomorrow), instituted at the start of the 1970-1971 crop year. The Lift program was aimed at a drastic reduction in prairie wheat acreage. To achieve that end, farmers were offered acreage payments for land diverted to summer fallow and perennial forage. At the same time, farmers not participating in the program found their quota delivery opportunities for wheat severely limited. As a result, the area sown to wheat in western Canada fell from 24.4 million acres in 1969 to 12 million acres in 1970.

Despite the critical domestic and international situation, 1970 was a year of intensive activity at the board. A three-member committee, headed by E.A. Boden, vice-president of Saskatchewan Wheat Pool, was set up in January to review the quota delivery system. An information department was established in January, and a new market analysis and development department was set up in March to keep abreast of research and developments and to recommend long-term market development programs. In line with the restructuring of the organization, the board doubled its computer capacity to keep up with the work load. Commissioners and employees of the board fanned out to sixty-three countries on sales missions during the year in a drive to widen Canada's market base.

In September, the board appointed a Canadian Grain Marketing Review Committee to evaluate Canada's system of selling grain under existing marketing conditions. In October, responsibility for the administration of all new sales of grain under medium-term credit of up to three years was transferred to the board. And, in that same month, Bill McNamara retired from the board after twenty-five years of service — nine of them as chief commissioner. He was appointed to the Canadian Senate two days later on October 7. (McNamara was succeeded as chief commissioner by G.N. Vogel in early March 1971.)

The report of the Boden committee on delivery quotas, delivered to Lang in early 1970, resulted in a broad revision of the quota system. The recommendations virtually revolutionized the delivery quota system. They were instituted in two stages at the start of the

1970-1971 and 1971-1972 crop years. The committee's primary objective was to bring into country elevators at the right time the kinds, qualities, and quantities of all grain required to compete effectively for market demand, and in the long-term interest of the agricultural industry, it must reflect market demand back to producers. The allocation of delivery opportunities for grain in demand among producers as equitably as possible, was declared to be a desirable secondary objective, if consistent with the need to bring forward the right grains at the right time.

Garson N. Vogel, chief commissioner Canadian Wheat Board, March 4, 1971 to September 30, 1977.

The report of the board-appointed Grain Marketing Review Committee, submitted to the board on January 12, 1971, endorsed the report of the Boden quota review committee, saying that only to the degree consistent with efficiency of marketing should quotas be used for the equitable allocation of the available market among producers. The Grain Marketing Review Committee also called for a grains income stabilization policy to be operated outside of the jurisdiction of the Wheat Board, and for revised quality standards, including protein grading, and for a continuing presence in the export barley market.

Armed with the review committee reports, Lang instituted an aggressive series of legislative programs in Parliament in 1971. While his program for a Western Grains Stabilization Fund, with contributions from both farmers and the government, foundered on a Parliamentary impasse, changes in grading and the delivery quota system were instituted by order-in-council and went into effect at the start of the 1971-1972 crop year. With these changes the board was now able to offer wheat on a specific protein guarantee basis, and to call forward more efficiently the types, qualities, and quantities of grain in market demand.

Lang's ill-fated stabilization bill was reintroduced in late 1974. It was finally passed into law on April 1, 1976, with its provisions retroactive to January 1, 1976. At its inception, all Canadian Wheat Board permit holders were enrolled in the Western Grains Stabilization Program, but those not wishing to participate were given the option of withdrawal up to December 31, 1978. Participating farmers contributed to the fund through a levy of two per cent on their sales of the six major grains, which was deducted at the time of delivery. The federal government matched those payments on a two-for-one basis, contributing two dollars for each dollar paid in by the producer. Payments from the fund were triggered when the net cash flow to western farmers fell below the average of the previous five years. With amendments over the years, the fund, administered by the Western Grain Stabilization Administration, provided assistance to the participating farmers in those years when income from grain farming dropped. At the same time, the Canadian Wheat Board was relieved of the necessity of attempting to support producer income, as had sometimes happened in the past, and was freed to concentrate on selling aggressively in the competitive world market.

By late 1971, the gloomy outlook that had pervaded on entering the 1970s was gone. After the Lift-reduced 1970 crop of 336 million bushels of wheat and record sales in the 1970-1971 crop year, the previous massive carryover was declining, and inroads had been made by the board into the world barley market. In May 1971, the Soviet Union, despite the assurance of a large crop of its own, had entered into a large purchase from Canada. Only logistical problems in the handling and transportation system limited the board's ability to make sales. One thing marred the outlook: the United States was not sharing equally in the expanding world market and was holding down the world price by means of export subsidies. Then, the 1971 fall-sown Soviet winter wheat crop suffered a serious setback. In February 1972, the board consummated a further large contract with Exporkhleb. However, due to strikes, work stoppages, and a severe winter with snow slides and derailments, the Wheat Board had to defer delivery into 1973 of 1.5 million long tons of wheat.

Canada's delivery system was now totally committed, and Argentina and Australia were virtually withdrawn from the market due to forward commitments and short crops. Representations were made by the board to the United States, which now had a virtual run at the market, to eliminate their export subsidies. Then the harsh winter on the Russian steppes was followed by a searing summer drought, and the Soviets, now in dire need, turned to the United States as the sole source for their requirements. Even as ministerial-level talks between the Russians and the Americans were underway in Washington on a grain trade agreement in early July, Exporkhleb officials had begun a frenetic round of purchases from the multinational grain traders. What was to become known as The Great Grain Robbery was underway. Secretary of Agriculture Earl Butz later testified before a committee of the House of Representatives that neither his department or the private traders knew how much the Russians were booking, ''nor were the Russians talking.'' Within a period of just over one month, Exporkhleb entered into contracts with the multinationals for 17.5 million tonnes of U.S. grain and 1 million tonnes of soybeans. Each of the traders, in turn, contacted the USDA to make sure the export subsidies would be maintained before entering into the contracts.

The enormity of the Soviet purchases did not fully emerge until late August, at which time prices on the U.S. exchanges went wild. Meanwhile, the U.S. was selling huge amounts of wheat at a subsidized $1.63 a bushel. Finally, on August 25, 1972, the USDA gave the international traders a one-week period of grace to register their past sales, during which time the wheat export subsidy would be raised to 47 cents a bushel. After that, the export subsidies would be discontinued. For the Canadian Wheat Board, with exports reaching to the capacity of the handling system, the depressing factor of the U.S. export subsidy on world grain prices had been removed. The board's monthly asking price for top grade wheat, in store Thunder Bay, rose from $1.79 1/2 a bushel at the start of the 1972-1973 crop year to $3.56 1/4 at the close.

In spite of the rapid run-up in world prices, the following two years became a crisis of lost opportunity for western Canadian farmers. Nagging transportation problems, which had persisted from before the opening of the 1973-1974 crop year, came to a head early in that crop year. At the outset of the 1973-1974 crop year it appeared that the quantities of grain available would be the main limiting factor for board sales. On August 1, 1973, the outward carryover of wheat was at its lowest level in twenty-one years. Stocks of wheat, on which carrying charges were payable by the board, had dropped below 178 million bushels, the point at which a ''sunset'' clause in the Temporary Wheat Reserves Act was triggered. The Act, passed in 1954, was dead, and no carrying charges were payable by the federal treasury for any subsequent crop year. As it turned out, the limiting factor was the quantity of grain that could be moved to export positions. As world prices climbed to new records, labor-management disputes flared into strikes and stoppages in almost every sector of the grain handling and transportation industry. In March 1974, the board estimated that 50 million bushels in sales had been lost to Prairie farmers because the board had been unable to take advantage of potential sales due to the uncertainty of delivery to export positions because of stoppages.

Worse was yet to come. The litany of strikes and work stoppages in the 1974-1975 crop year appeared to be endless. There were strikes and stoppages on the railways, at the port terminals, on the Great Lakes ships, and by government grain inspectors. When the appalling toll had been totted up at the end of the crop year, labor-management disputes in various parts of the system had affected grain shipments on 143 out of 220 working days, representing 65 per cent of the working time based on a five-day work week and excluding holidays. In a world market of unlimited opportunity and high prices, Canada's wheat exports slid back to 394,559,463 bushels, for an all-time low of 17.1 per cent of the world trade. While the work stoppages were the major culprit, the damage was exacerbated by the lack of transportation facilities to make up the shortfalls following those stoppages. Meanwhile, the long-awaited window of opportunity was closing. Having hit a high of $6.07 1/8 a bushel in November and December 1974, the board's asking price for No. 1 CWRS wheat slid progressively down to $4.70 1/4 at the close of the 1974-1975 crop year. The damage went beyond the immediate financial losses. Canada's reputation as a reliable source of supply, built up so painstakingly in the past, suffered a severe blow.

Even though transportation problems had crippled Canada's potential on the booming world market, the inventory was running low. In 1974, the prairie grain crop suffered from adverse weather conditions in virtually every stage of development from seeding to harvest. As a result, the western crop fell 18 per cent below the 1973 level. Of equal concern to the reduced yields was the poor quality of the crop, a large portion of which was harvested in tough and damp condition. It was followed by a more satisfactory but still below average crop in 1975. The board found itself living from hand-to-mouth, and was withdrawn from the market for long periods, due to the supply and quality limitations. The supply turnaround came in 1976 when a record crop was harvested in western Canada, but the world price had gone into a decline. However, the Wheat Board, anticipating a price drop, scored a coup by selling over 4 million tonnes of wheat to the private trade for forward shipment at slight discounts to the card price prior to the price break in the fall of 1976.

For the board, the entire decade of the 1970s was a tumultuous one, dominated by a fluctuating yet rapidly expanding world grain market, and by studies and ad hoc initiatives aimed at rehabilitating the ailing transportation and handling system that was thwarting Canada's ability to exploit the potential of the growing world grain trade. On the international scene, trade in wheat rose by 70 per cent between 1969 and 1979; trade in coarse grains by 156 per cent, oilseeds by 81 per cent, and rice by 65 per cent. Taken together, world trade in all grains in 1979, amounting to 245 million tonnes, was more than double that of the previous ten years.

In the face of the railways' reluctance to replace the declining grain car fleet, the federal government, in late 1972, purchased 2,000 modern 100-ton steel hopper cars, to be held in trust for the Crown by the Canadian Wheat Board. As pressure grew in Parliament over the failure of the railways to meet the requirements for the movement of grain to export positions, Otto Lang announced an agreement for the rehabilitation of 2,400 boxcars with federal funds in March 1974. Two months later, Lang announced a government purchase of a further 4,000 hoppers, 1,600 of which were seventy-ton aluminum hoppers to cope with load limitations on secondary branch lines. It was to be a continuing process. By 1985, the board-administered hopper fleet was to swell to over 19,000 cars, with the purchase or lease of 15,192 by the federal government. A further 2,000 were bought by the Wheat Board, and the provinces of Saskatchewan and Alberta each purchased 1,000 hoppers.

The nagging transportation crisis of the mid-seventies also sparked a series of commissions and enquiries into the state of the aging prairie rail network. Appointed in mid-April 1975, a five-member commission headed by Mr. Justice Emmett Hall conducted hearings across the West and two years later presented an extensive report on rationalization of the system. Meanwhile, a Washington, D.C., consultant, Carl M. Snavely, was conducting a study to determine the costs and revenues of grain traffic and their relationship to the general operations of the railways.

Although recommendations with respect to the emotionally charged issue of the Crowsnest statutory grain-hauling rate were specifically excluded from its terms of reference, the Hall commission came down firmly for its retention. The commissioners also found little merit in the concept of a system of large inland terminals serviced by unit trains, and recommended that the Wheat Board be given a more prominent role in total co-ordination of grain transportation. Few of the Hall report recommendations were acted upon. Lang had intimated as early as 1972 that the "Holy Crow" might be reviewed. In January 1974, the minister sparked a debate that was to flare across the Prairies over the next decade, by declaring that, legislation setting artificially low rates for grain movement had to be reconsidered. Although he had a precise blueprint for reform of the Crow rate, Lang had retired from the political scene before that objective was achieved. He was defeated in the general election of May 22, 1979, and became an executive in a private Winnipeg grain company in August of that year.

Lang left behind another controversial legacy in his reform of the domestic feed grain policy in 1974. Monopoly control by the Wheat Board of feed grains sold into the domestic market had been a subject of bitter debate at national farm meetings for over two decades. When the Canadian Federation of Agriculture was unable to formulate a compromise between the various regions, Lang intervened. Following an interim policy in the 1973-1974 crop year, an open market policy for domestic feed grains was introduced on August 1, 1974. While the board remained as the sole purchaser and seller of export feed grains, western farmers were given the option to deliver feed grains to the board or to the open market for domestic consumption.

Introduction of the optional domestic marketing policy exacerbated debate over the allocation of rail cars between the board and the private trade, particularly in periods of restricted availability of cars. In August 1978, the advisory committee to the Wheat Board appointed a committee to review the delivery quota system. As a result the board was empowered to administer delivery quotas on domestic off-board feed grains, which went into effect on August 1, 1979. There was an immediate outcry from the Winnipeg Commodity Exchange, and, in October 1979, the federal government announced the formation of the Grain Transportation Authority (GTA). The GTA became operational in mid-March 1980, and assumed responsibility for procurement and allocation of grain cars between the board and the private trade. Following that initial allocation, the block shipping staff of the Wheat Board worked out the detailed shipping plans to move the grain from specific prairie areas to its destination.

Other initiatives of the Lang era included introduction of a two-price policy for wheat and a change to an elected advisory committee to the Wheat Board, rather than a government appointed one as in the past. The two-price wheat policy was first introduced in 1971. Under it domestic millers paid $1.95 1/2 a bushel for wheat, which was above the prevailing world market price. When world prices rose the next year, the millers continued to pay $1.95 1/2, but farmers were reimbursed to a base price of $3 a bushel by payment of $1.04 1/2 from the federal treasury. As world prices climbed above the $3 level later the same year, Lang introduced a seven-year program in September. Under it domestic millers paid $3.25 a bushel for wheat, and a consumer subsidy was paid by the government to the board on the difference between $3.25 and the world price up to a maximum of $1.75 a bushel. In effect, if the export price of milling wheat rose above $5 a bushel during the seven-year period, the producer would be sharing with the government in subsidizing domestic consumer prices. In return he was guaranteed a domestic floor price of $3.25 for the seven-year period. With variations over the years, the two-price system remains in effect.

Adoption of an elected advisory committee to the board resulted when Lang accepted representations from the farm organizations. The Wheat Board designated area was divided into eleven electoral districts in 1975, and board permit holders were sent a list of candidates and a mail-in ballot. Successful candidates were then appointed to a four-year term on the committee.

At the Wheat Board, the transportation-plagued seventies were a period of change and planning for the future when improvements in the system would allow unrestricted access to expanding world markets. In September 1977, Gerry Vogel retired to accept a post as executive director of the World Food Program in Rome. He was succeeded as chief commissioner by W. Esmond Jarvis, co-ordinator of the Ottawa Grains Group and associate deputy minister of agriculture. The board was pressing for expanded facilities at the West Coast to service the growing markets on the Pacific Rim, and a number of internal studies were underway to assess Canada's grain market potential to 1990. As a result, export targets of 30 million tonnes of grain and oil seed exports were forecast by 1985, growing to 36 million tonnes by 1990. There was skepticism that prairie production could be expanded to meet that challenge. But, as the decade drew to a close, there were clear signs that the goals might be reached.

By 1979, active planning had begun for construction of a large new export terminal at Prince Rupert, to be undertaken by a consortium of grain companies. Work was underway on upgrading the permanent prairie rail network, and the fleet of modern grain hopper cars was expanding rapidly. And, across the Prairies, rationalization and consolidation of the country elevator system had reached new impetus. Between 1971 and 1978, the number of primary elevators in western Canada declined by 30 per cent — from 3,423 to 2,423 — and future projections were for a further reduction to 1,750. At many of the consolidated delivery points, new and modernized high-throughput elevators were constructed or old installations upgraded to handle higher volumes. A board incentive program resulted in the addition of 10.4 million bushels of storage capacity to the Vancouver terminals.

The Wheat Board's promotional program to bring missions from around the world to study and learn about Canada's grain industry was supplanted by a permanent Canadian International Grains Institute. Located in a new Canadian Grain Commission Building, the educational facility opened in 1972, following a proposal by the Wheat Board and the Canadian Grain Commission. Within the board itself, a new weather and crop surveillance section had been set up to assimilate and analyze meteorological data and crop conditions around the world. The market analysis and development department was reorganized, and testing was undertaken on new varieties of grains which were contracted with producers and then tested in overseas markets to assess their acceptability. Computerized handling of the multiplicity of paperwork, so essential to the grain trade, was being upgraded and expanded.

Moving toward the 1980s, a wave of marketing euphoria swept the North American Great Central Plain. The sluggish world prices which began in 1976 ended in the closing months of 1979. Throughout the seventies, global trade had expanded dramatically, particularly for coarse grains. World wheat trade grew from 54,851,000 tonnes in 1970-1971 to 93,154,000 tonnes in 1980-1981. In the same period, world coarse grain trade leaped from 43,900,000 tonnes to a peak of 108,800,000 tonnes in 1980-1981. At the U.S. Outlook Conference in late 1979, there were optimistic predictions that the upcoming decade would tax the capacity of American farmers to meet unlimited opportunities in the growing world market. A sale of 25 million tonnes of U.S. grain to the Soviet Union in the fourth year of a bilateral agreement seemed secure. With strengthening prices and sales opportunities, the huge American production capacity was turned loose.

In late December Soviet troops invaded Afghanistan. On January

4, 1980, President Jimmy Carter invoked an embargo on all outstanding wheat, corn, and soybean contracts with the Soviet Union. Grain prices dropped in the ensuing fallout. The other exporting countries, with the exception of Argentina, pledged co-operation in the embargo by undertaking to supply no more than "normal and traditional" quantities to the Russians. However, the embargo had minimal effect, since the Soviet Union still managed to import 30.9 million tonnes of grain in the 1979-1980 crop year. By the time the embargo was lifted by President Ronald Reagan, the United States had been relegated to a residual supplier to the Soviet market.

Meanwhile, world wheat trade, having peaked at 100,881,000 tonnes in 1980-1981, levelled off over the next three years. The world coarse grains market went into a decline, dropping from the 1980-1981 peak of 108.8 million tonnes to 90.7 million tonnes by 1983-1984. World grain prices once again went into an abrupt slide. In the background, a simmering dispute between the United States and the EEC was flaring into open warfare. Spurred by subsidized price guarantees, wheat production in the EEC climbed dramatically, and, by the early 1980s, the Europeans became the third largest wheat exporter in the world, capturing 14.5 per cent of the trade by the use of export subsidies. With the U.S. share of the market declining, the Americans struck back with a subsidized "blended credit" program in 1982.

In this increasingly competitive world grain trade environment, the Canadian Wheat Board was moving toward the 1985 target of 30 million tonnes of Canadian grain exports, with the constrictions on the transportation bottleneck gradually loosening. Despite stagnating world markets, the record was in sight by the end of the 1982-1983 crop year with exports of 29.4 million tonnes. The next year the target was exceeded, with 30.7 million tonnes of exports. Achievement of the export target one year ahead of schedule was blunted, however, by steadily declining world prices in the face of an increasing trade war between the EEC and the Americans.

Canada's steadily increasing exports were aided by three successive years of bumper crops, and by a slowdown in other parts of the economy which freed railway rolling stock for grain transport. Canadian production hit 42 million tonnes in 1981, followed by an all-time record crop of 45.5 million tonnes in 1982. Although production slid 5 million tonnes to 40.5 million tonnes in 1983, it was still 5 million tonnes over the previous ten year average. Then, in 1984, drought struck the western Canadian crop, and prairie grain production slumped back to 35.6 million tonnes. With a record low carryover on hand, only 20.5 million tonnes was available for export after taking domestic requirements into account. In the Canadian Wheat Board's fiftieth anniversary year, total exports of western grains had fallen back to 23.3 million tonnes, and the carryover was further reduced to record low levels. However, in the face of growing carryovers of grain in the United States and in Western Europe, reduced crops in other exporting countries no longer exerted any influence on world prices. A burning drought in Australia in 1982 had cut that country's wheat production back to 8.9 million tonnes, the lowest level in ten years, but prices continued their slide.

At the start of the 1985-1986 crop year, the U.S. carryover of wheat and coarse grains stood at 88 million tonnes — almost 66 per cent of the world carryover. In the EEC the carryover of 24.3 million tonnes, approximated a further 18 per cent of world stocks. The EEC was capturing a growing percentage of the world wheat trade by means of export subsidies at times as high as $60 to $70 per tonne, while the U.S. share of the markets was dropping, President Reagan signed a new farm bill into law in late 1985. Expected to cost the U.S. treasury $57 billion over the following three years (some sources unofficially set the cost nearer the $70 billion mark), the bill drastically lowered the loan rate, which effectively set a floor price on which American grain traded on world markets. At the same time, American producers who participated in an acreage reduction program were promised support payments well in excess of world prices. The subsidy trade war between the U.S. and EEC had reached new heights. Meanwhile, wide areas of the western Canadian crop had been hit for the second year by drought and an outbreak of grasshoppers. Prairie farmers found themselves in the worst possible scenario — reduced yields and slumping prices.

Thus, when the Canadian Wheat Board celebrated its fiftieth anniversary on July 7, 1985, it faced new challenges in a sluggish world market armed with the lowest carryover in thirty years. It could look back, however, at sales totalling 727,608,168 tonnes of wheat, oats and barley over the previous forty-nine crop years. From those sales, over $72 billion ($72,216,961,494) had poured back into western Canada.

Sales of wheat, the major export grain, had brought a return of over $60.5 billion ($60,590,409,368). For that massive return to Canada's economic well-being, the federal treasury had been called upon only once to make up a deficit in the wheat pool after the board assumed monopoly control in 1943. It amounted to $39,787,979 in the 1968-1969 crop year, when Canada held the price line in a vain attempt to shore up the faltering International Grains Arrangement. By comparison to the multi-billion dollar support programs in other major export countries, that contribution by the government to the operations of the Canadian Wheat Board must be considered infinitesimal. It amounted to only six-tenths of one per cent of the $668,625,682 in sales in the year in which it was incurred, and less than seven one-thousandths of one per cent (.000657) of total wheat sales since 1935.

Deficits in the barley pool, consciously inspired by a decision at the political level in an effort to diversify western production and break into the expanding world feed grain market, were larger on a percentage basis. However, at $30,115,034, it amounted to only three one-hundredths of one per cent of sales totalling over $10 billion ($10,213,828,350). Taken together with several small deficits in the oats pool, Canadians had benefitted to that immense $72 billion plus contribution to the nation's balance of payments at a cost from the treasury of only approximately one-hundredth of one per cent of total sales towards operation of the Canadian Wheat Board. The remainder of the costs for the board's operations—99.99 per cent—were borne by the farmers of western Canada through deductions on their sales.

The board's report to producers for the 1984-1985 crop year noted that the modest celebration of its first half-century had not coincided with a good year for western Canadian producers:

> This report covers the marketing of your 1984 crop grain. As you receive it, the Board is in the midst of facing even greater challenges in marketing your 1985 crop. With the recent passage of a new U.S. farm bill, which lowers world prices but maintains U.S. farm income, we cannot offer hope for an immediate improvement in prospects for our producers.
>
> While this is the unfortunate reality for the near term, we are not as pessimistic as some in the longer term. There is a "herd instinct" in the world grain market and, at the moment, the instinct is to be pessimistic, even though the facts sometimes indicate otherwise. With a continuing growth in world population, and continued improvements in living standards, world grain consumption has nowhere to go but up. The increases may be more moderate than in the past, and it will continue to be marked by year-to-year fluctuations, but the trend will still be there.[2]

Facing that future, the Canadian Wheat Board appeared to be well-equipped to meet the challenge when it should come. After the bitterly fought demise of the Crowsnest Rate by passage of the Western Grain Transportation Act on November 14, 1983, the railways, now guaranteed compensatory rates for hauling grain, had begun a spate of upgrading and rail building. While debate over the method of payment of a ''Crow benefit'' by the federal government was continuing, double tracking and tunnel building relieved the bottleneck on the treacherous route through the Rockies to the West Coast. At Prince Rupert, a $275 million state-of-the-art grain terminal was officially opened on May 16, 1985. The highly-computerized structure was expected to increase West Coast export capability by 20 per cent, and was seven hundred kilometres closer to Pacific Rim countries. The block shipping system had been fine-tuned to a train-run system for greater efficiency. Combined with computerization, this resulted in drastically reduced turnaround times for grain cars. Modernization and upgrading of the primary elevator system also added to increased efficiencies.

While the immediate outlook on the glutted and price-depressed world market was grim, the most highly integrated computer co-ordinated sales and grain gathering system of any exporting nation was rapidly coming into place in western Canada to meet future eventualities.

APPENDICES

APPENDIX A

Commissioners of the Canadian Wheat Board 1935 — 1985

Chief Commissioners

John I. McFarland; August 14, 1935-December 3, 1935

James R. Murray; December 3, 1935-July 1937

George H. McIvor, July 1937-April 30, 1958; assistant chief commissioner, December 3, 1935-July 1937

W.C. McNamara; June 1, 1958-October 5, 1970; appointed commissioner September 1945 and as assistant chief commissioner February 1947

G.N. Vogel; March 4, 1971-September 30, 1977; appointed commissioner

September 1, 1964, and assistant chief commissioner July 1, 1969
W. Esmond Jarvis; October 3, 1977

Commissioners

D.L. Smith; assistant chief commissioner, August 14, 1935-December 3, 1935
H.C. Grant; August 14, 1935-December 3, 1935
A.M. Shaw; December 3, 1935-August 31, 1938
R.C. Findlay; assistant chief commissioner, July 1938-October 26, 1939
W. Charles Folliott; August 1938-March 13, 1943
C. Gordon Smith; assistant chief commissioner, October 26, 1939-December 1944
D.A. Kane; June 1, 1943-September 1945; assistant chief commissioner December 1944-September 1945
C. E. Huntting; December 1944-February 1947; assistant chief commissioner, September 1945-February 1947
F.L.M. Arnold; February 1947-May 1948
T.W. Grindley; July 1948-July 1950
William Riddel; August 1, 1950-September 30, 1965; assistant chief commissioner, June 1958-September 1965
W. Earle Robertson; November 1952-December 31, 1964
John T. Dallas; September 1, 1958-January 1, 1961
J.B. Lawrie; December 22, 1961-June 30, 1969; assistant chief commissioner, October 1, 1965-December 22, 1961
R.L. Kristjanson; October 1, 1965-; assistant chief commissioner, January 1, 1976
C.W. Gibbings; July 1, 1969-December 31, 1982
J.L. Leibfried; January 1, 1976-December 31, 1985
F.M. Hetland; January 1, 1976-
W.H. Smith; April 7, 1984-

APPENDIX B

Canadian Wheat Board Advisory Committee 1935-1985

First advisory board appointed August 14, 1935, but disbanded on December 3, 1935: Paul F. Bredt, L.C. Brouillette, Brooks Catton, Lew Hutchinson, Robert McKee, C.H.G. Short, Sidney T. Smith
Advisory board reconstituted August 27, 1940, appointed by the Governor-In-Council

D.A. Campbell, Toronto, Ont.; August 1940-July 1947
Fred H. Clendenning, Vancouver, B.C.; August 1940-July 1955
Paul Farnalls, Halkirk, Alta.; August 1940-July 1955
Lew Hutchinson, Duhamel, Alta.; August 1940-February 1955
J.A. McCowan, Summerberry, Sask.; August 1940-July 1955
D.G. McKenzie, Winnipeg, Man.; August 1940-July 1941
Rosario Messier, Contrecoeur, Que.; August 1940-September 1943
Fred Pettypiece, Auld, Ont.; August 1940-July 1955
R.C. Reece, Winnipeg, Man.; August 1940-February 1946
A.C. Reid, Winnipeg, Man.; August 1940-January 1948
J.H. Wesson, Regina, Sask.; August 1940-July 1960
R.C. Brown, Pilot Mound, Man.; August 1941-July 1955
Theo Roy, Montreal, Que.; September 1943-July 1955
C. Gordon Smith, Winnipeg, Man.; March 1946-February 1949
C.E. Hayles, Winnipeg, Man.; January 1948-1952
D.I. Walker, Toronto, Ont.; August 1948-August 1955
J.C.A. Nijdam, Winnipeg, Man.; February 1949-September 1952
R.R. Emerson, Winnipeg, Man.; September 1952-July 1955
K.A. Powell, Winnipeg, Man.; September 1952-July 1955
J.H. Brownlee, Winnipeg, Man.; July 1955-1961
C.P. Hansen, Saskatoon, Sask.; July 1955-July 1957
R.C. Marler, Edmonton, Alta.; July 1955-July 1957
W.J. Parker, Winnipeg, Man.; July 1955-November 1970
Ben Plumer, Calgary, Alta.; July 1955-July 1957
A.P. Gleave, Biggar, Sask.; August 1957-July 1965
G.L. Harrold, Lamont, Alta.; August 1957-May 1975. (see also Elected Advisory Committee).
A.W. Platt, Edmonton, Alta.; August 1957-July 1960
A.M. Runciman, Winnipeg, Man.; July 1960-May 1975
C.W. Gibbings, Regina, Sask., November 1960-July 1969
J.I. Stevens, Morinville, Alta.; August 1960-May 1972
R.R. Atkinson, Landis, Sask.; December 1965-May 1975. (see also Elected Advisory Committee).
E.K. Turner, Regina, Sask.; July 1969-May 1975. (see also Elected Advisory Committee).
H.B. Sneath, Winnipeg, Man.; November 1970-May 1975
Mrs. E.C. Hartle, Leroy, Sask.; May 1972-May 1975
W.D. Lea, Jarvie, Alta.; May 1972-May 1975. (see also Elected Advisory Committee).
Ivan McMillan, Craik, Sask.; May 1972-May 1975
S.G. Mitchell, Dawson Creek, B.C.; May 1972-May 1975
L.E. Parker, Ste. Agathe, Man.; May 1972-May 1975. (see also Elected Advisory Committee).

Elected Advisory Committee

During the 1974-75 crop year the appointments of members of the previous Advisory Committee were terminated and a new committee was elected by producers in eleven electoral districts. Successful candidates were appointed for a four-year term by the Governor-In-Council in accordance with Section 10 of the Canadian Wheat Board Act.

L.E. Parker, Ste. Agathe, Man., District 1; May 1975-
Donn Mitchell, Douglas, Man., District 2; May 1975-January 1983
Everett Murphy, Estevan, Sask., District 3; May 1975-January 1979
Vic. Althouse, Kelvington, Sask., District 4; May 1975-January 1979
E.K. Turner, Regina, Sask., District 5; May 1975-January 1983
R.R. Atkinson, Landis, Sask., District 6; May 1975-
Avery Sahl, Mossbank, Sask., District 7; May 1975-
Ted Strain, North Battleford, Sask., District 8; May 1975-
Orville Reber, Burdett, Alta., District 9; May 1975-January 1983
G.L. Harrold, Lamont, Alta., District 10; May 1975-December 1977
W.D. Lea, Jarvie, Alta., District 11; May 1975-January 1979
Allan Smith, Red Deer, Alta.; District 10; appointed to complete term of G.L. Harrold from March 1978 to January 1979
C.A. Hookenson, Kisbey, Sask. District 3; January 1979-
M.G.W. Halyk, Melville, Sask., District 4; January 1979-
K.D. Galloway, Fort Saskatchewan, Alta., District 10; January 1979-
H.A. Dechant, Fairview, Alta., District 11; January 1979-
Brad McDonald, Strathclair, Man., District 2; January 1983-
Harold Yelland, Porcupine Plain, Sask., District 5; January 1983-
C.F. Thurston, Bow Island, Alta., District 9; January 1983-

APPENDIX C

Ministers Responsible to Parliament for the Canadian Wheat Board 1935-1985

W.D. Euler, minister of trade and commerce, (Lib.); October 31, 1935-May 10, 1940

James A. MacKinnon, minister of trade and commerce, (Lib.); May 10, 1940-January 18, 1948

C.D. Howe, minister of trade and commerce, (Lib.); January 18, 1948-June 21, 1957

Gordon Churchill, minister of trade and commerce, (PC); June 21, 1957-October 11, 1960

Alvin Hamilton, agriculture minister, (PC); October 11, 1960-April 22, 1963
Mitchell Sharp, minister of trade and commerce, (Lib.); April 22, 1963-November 3, 1966
Robert H. Winters, minister of trade and commerce, (Lib.); November 3, 1966-April 22, 1968
Charles M. Drury, minister of industry, trade and commerce, (Lib.); April 22, 1968-July 5, 1968
Jean-Luc Pepin, minister of industry, trade and commerce, (Lib.); July 5, 1968-October 15, 1969
Otto E. Lang, minister without portfolio, July 1968 to September 1970; minister of manpower and immigration, September 1970 to January 1972; minister of justice, January 1972 to June 1979; minister of transport, September 1975 to June 1979, (Lib.); October 15, 1969-June 4, 1979
Donald F. Mazankowski, minister of transport, (PC); June 4, 1979-March 3, 1980
Senator Hazen Argue, minister of state, (Lib.); March 3, 1980-June 30, 1984
Lloyd Axworthy, minister of transport (Lib.); June 30, 1984-September 17, 1984
Charles Mayer, minister of state, (PC); September 17, 1984-

APPENDIX D

Weights and Measures

Throughout this volume various, and sometimes apparently arbitrary, references appear in relation to tonnages and volumes of grain in the area of sales, production and inventories; i.e., tons, long tons, metric tons (tonnes). This is occasioned in large part by the use of imperial weights and measures on the domestic scene in the recent past, and before the introduction and use of metric calculations in Canada. Since there is some uncertainty as to the preciseness of the terminology in the documents examined, we have used the exact words encountered in the archival material. It has been quoted precisely as written at the period in question. For the guidance of readers, the more commonly used weights and measures for agricultural commodities in domestic and world markets are set out here along with conversion factors.

1 short ton = 2,000 pounds
1 long ton = 2,240 pounds
1 tonne (metric ton) = 2,204.622 pounds

Bushel weights: wheat, soybeans = 60 pounds; corn, sorghum, rye, flaxseed = 56 pounds; barley, buckwheat = 48 pounds; oats = 38 pounds.

Factors for converting domestic and metric weights

wheat, soybeans; 1 tonne = 36.7437 bushels
corn, rye, sorghum, flaxseed; 1 tonne = 39.368 bushels
barley, buckwheat; 1 tonne = 45.9296 bushels
oats; 1 tonne = 58.016 bushels
Example: wheat at $160 a tonne - $160 divided by 36.7437 = $4.3544 per bushel.

NOTES

INTRODUCTION

1. Louis Aubrey Wood, *A History of Farmers' Movements in Canada*, p. xvii.
2. Vernon C. Fowke, *The National Policy and The Wheat Economy*, p. 26.
3. *Ibid.*, p. 2.
4. Hopkins Moorehouse, *Deep Furrows*, p. 72.
5. C.F. Wilson, *A Century of Canadian Grain*, pp. 45, 46.
6. *The Diary of Alexander James McPhail*, pp. 113, 114.
7. Tim Josling, *Intervention and Regulation in Canadian Agriculture*.
8. Compiled from International Wheat Council statistics.
9. J.D. Forbes, R.D. Hughes, T.K. Warley, *Economic Intervention and Regulation in Canadian Agriculture*, p. 85.

CHAPTER ONE

1. Charles F. Wilson, *Grain Marketing in Canada*, p. 73.

2. W.E. Jarvis, Address to the Western Canadian Wheat Growers Association, Calgary, January 8, 1986.
3. *Ibid.*

CHAPTER TWO

1. Taped interview George McIvor.
2. Britnell and Fowke, *Canadian Agriculture in War and Peace*, p. 71.
3. J.H. Ellis, *The Ministry of Agriculture in Manitoba*, p. 305.
4. *Ibid.*
5. Britnell and Fowke, *Canadian Agriculture in War and Peace*, p. 73.
6. D.A. MacGibbon, *The Canadian Grain Trade 1931-51*, p. 21.
7. *Ibid.*, p. 9.
8. Taped interview George McIvor.
9. Leonard D. Nesbitt, *Tides in the West*, p. 48.
10. R.B. Bennett papers.
11. *Ibid.*
12. *The Diary of Alexander James MacPhail*, entry for November 14, 1930, pp. 227, 228.
13. *Ibid.*, November 22, 1930, p. 230.
14. Winnipeg *Free Press*, December 4, 1930.
15. Swanson and Armstrong, *Wheat*, pp. 134, 135.
16. Winnipeg *Free Press*, December 30, 1930.
17. Harald S. Patton, *The Canadian Wheat Pool in Prosperity and Depression*, pp. 12, 13.
18. R.B. Bennett papers.
19. *Ibid.*
20. *Ibid.*
21. C.F. Wilson, *A Century of Canadian Grain*, pp. 416-418.
22. *Ibid.*, p. 421.
23. *Ibid.*, p. 434.
24. R.B. Bennett papers.
25. Taped interview George McIvor.
26. Leonard D. Nesbitt, *Tides in the West*, p. 264.
27. Taped interview George McIvor.
28. *Ibid.*
29. R.B. Bennett papers.
30. *Free Press Evening Bulletin*, October 28, 1933.
31. *Ibid.*
32. R.B. Bennett papers.
33. *Ibid.*
34. *Ibid.*
35. Garry Fairbairn, *From Prairie Roots*, p. 136.
36. R.B. Bennett papers.
37. *Ibid.*
38. *Ibid.*
39. *Ibid.*

40. Minutes of the Council of the Winnipeg Grain Exchange, November 1934.
41. *The Manitoba Co-operator,* June 1935, p. 3.

CHAPTER THREE

1. *The Manitoba Co-operator,* June 1935, p. 3.
2. *Ibid.*, p. 14.
3. Taped interview George McIvor.
4. George McIvor, Address to the Calgary Ranchmen's Club, May 7, 1976.
5. Taped interview George McIvor.
6. C.F. Wilson, *A Century of Canadian Grain,* p. 472.
7. Taped interview George McIvor.
8. R.D. Colquette, *The First Fifty Years,* p. 188.
9. Winnipeg Grain Exchange, *Wheat Marketing Fallacies,* p. 11.
10. *Ibid.*, p. 14.
11. Canada Royal Commission to Enquire Into Charges Against Manitoba Pool Elevators, *Report,* 1931, p. 32.
12. C.F. Wilson, *A Century of Canadian Grain,* p. 467.
13. House of Commons *Hansard,* June 10, 1935, p. 3458.
14. Clive B. Davidson, *Wheat, Politicians and the Great Depression,* p. 35.
15. R.K. Finlayson, *That Man R.B. Bennett,* quoted by C.F. Wilson, *A Century of Canadian Grain,* p. 472.
16. Clive B. Davidson, *Wheat, Politicians and the Great Depression,* pp. 30, 31.
17. T.W. Grindley, *Canada Year Book 1939,* Dominion Bureau of Statistics.
18. R.B. Bennett papers.
19. Winnipeg *Free Press,* March 1, 1935, p. 1.
20. *Ibid.*, p. 5.
21. *Ibid.*, March 2, 1935, p. 23.
22. House of Commons *Hansard,* June 12, 1935, p. 3561.
23. R.B. Bennett papers.
24. *Ibid.*
25. Clive B. Davidson, *Wheat, Politicians and the Great Depression,* p. 31.
26. Winnipeg *Free Press,* June 10, 1935, p. 1.
27. *Ibid.*
28. Taped interview George McIvor.
29. House of Commons *Hansard,* June 13, 1935, p. 3585.
30. *Ibid.*, p. 3592.
31. Winnipeg *Free Press,* June 13, 1935, p. 1.
32. House of Commons *Hansard,* June 12, 1935, p. 3577.
33. Clive B. Davidson, *Wheat, Politicians and the Great Depression,* pp. 33, 34.

34. House of Commons *Hansard*, June 13, 1935, p. 3597.
35. *Ibid.*
36. *Ibid.*, June 12, 1935, p. 3581.
37. *Ibid.*, June 13, 1935, p. 3598.
38. Winnipeg *Free Press*, June 13, 1935, p. 1.
39. *Ibid.*, June 15, 1935, p. 1.
40. *Ibid.*, June 14, 1935, p. 6.
41. *Ibid.*, June 28, 1935, p. 1.
42. *Ibid.*
43. Special Committee on Bill 98, *Canadian Grain Board Act, Minutes and Proceedings of Evidence*, June 28, 1935, p. 362.
44. F.W. Hamilton, *Service At Cost*, p. 164.
45. Special Committee on Bill 98, *Canadian Grain Board Act, Minutes and Proceedings of Evidence,* June 20, 1935, p. 84.
46. *Ibid.*
47. R.K. Finlayson, *That Man R.B. Bennett*, p. 203.
48. Taped interview George McIvor.
49. *Ibid.*
50. Winnipeg *Free Press*, July 2, 1935, p. 1.
51. *Ibid.*
52. Senate *Hansard*, 1935, p. 473.
53. *The Manitoba Co-operator*, July 1935, p. 13.
54. C.F. Wilson, *A Century of Canadian Grain*, p. 473.
55. Cabinet Document 44-51, October 11, 1950, Privy Council office files.
56. D.A. MacGibbon, *The Canadian Grain Trade 1931-1951*, pp. 36, 37.
57. C.F. Wilson, *A Century of Canadian Grain*, p. 475.
58. *The Manitoba Co-operator*, July 1935, pp. 7, 13.

CHAPTER FOUR

1. R.B. Bennett papers.
2. Douglas Campbell, interview by the author in July 1984.
3. R.B. Bennett papers.
4. *Ibid.*
5. *Ibid.*
6. Canadian Press Despatch, Regina, September 17, 1935.
7. An Act to provide for the Constitution and Powers of the Canadian Wheat Board.
8. T.W. Grindley, *The Canada Year Book 1939.*
9. R.B. Bennett papers.
10. *Ibid.*
11. C.F. Wilson, *A Century of Canadian Grain*, p. 481.
12. D.A. MacGibbon, *The Canadian Grain Trade*, pp. 72, 73.
13. R.B. Bennett papers.

14. C.F. Wilson, *A Century of Canadian Grain*, p. 483.
15. *Ibid.*, p. 483.
16. D.A. MacGibbon, *The Canadian Grain Trade*, p. 73.
17. Winnipeg *Free Press*, October 10, 1935.
18. *Ibid.*, October 11, 1935.
19. *Ibid.*, October 14, 1935.
20. C.F. Wilson, *A Century of Canadian Grain*, p. 485.
21. *Statutes of Canada*, 1 Edward VIII, Chapter 12.
22. C.F. Wilson, *C.D. Howe*, p. 11.
23. Winnipeg *Free Press*, November 1, 1935.
24. Report of the Royal Grain Inquiry Commission, 1938, p. 103.
25. C.F. Wilson, *A Century of Canadian Grain*, p. 507.
26. *Ibid.*, p. 507.
27. Leonard D. Nesbitt, *Tides in the West*, pp. 227, 228.
28. R.B. Bennett papers as quoted by C.F. Wilson, *A Century of Canadian Grain*, p. 507.
29. *Ibid.*
30. Taped interview George McIvor.
31. C.F. Wilson, *A Century of Canadian Grain*, p. 509.
32. *Ibid.*, p. 508.
33. *Report of the Canadian Wheat Board, Crop Year 1937-38*, p. 2.
34. *The Manitoba Co-operator*, March 1936, p. 5.
35. *The Story of Stabilization*, published by the Committee in Charge of McFarland Luncheon, Calgary, Alberta, 1936, Frontispiece.
36. *Ibid.*, p. 13.
37. *Ibid.*, p. 22.
38. C.F. Wilson, *A Century of Canadian Grain*, p. 546.

CHAPTER FIVE

1. D.A. MacGibbon, *The Canadian Grain Trade*, p. 75.
2. Taped interview George McIvor.
3. C.F. Wilson, *A Century of Canadian Grain*, p. 516.
4. Report of the Royal Grain Inquiry Commission, 1938, p. 196.
5. Winnipeg *Free Press*, December 4, 1935, p. 1.
6. Special Committee on the Marketing of Wheat and Other Grains, *Proceedings and Evidence*, May 1, 1936, p. 268.
7. *Ibid.*, pp. 260, 261.
8. *Ibid.*
9. Minutes of Canadian Wheat Board Meeting, December 11, 1935.
10. *Report of the Canadian Wheat Board, Crop Year 1935-36*, pp. 4 & 10.
11. Winnipeg *Free Press*, December 20, 1935.
12. House of Commons *Hansard*, February 10, 1936, p. 53.
13. *Report of the Canadian Wheat Board, Crop Year 1935-36*, p. 7.
14. W.L.M. King papers, Public Archives of Canada.

15. C.F. Wilson, *A Century of Canadian Grain*, p. 528.
16. Winnipeg *Free Press*, August 29, 1936.
17. W.L.M. King papers.
18. House of Commons *Hansard*, March 17, 1937, p. 1866.
19. *Ibid.*, March 18, 1937.
20. C.F. Wilson, *A Century of Canadian Grain*, p. 535.
21. *Report of the Canadian Wheat Board, Crop Year 1935-36*, p. 2.
22. Taped interview George McIvor.
23. *Report of the Canadian Wheat Board, Crop Year 1936-37*, p. 2, 3.
24. W.L.M. King papers.
25. Taped interview George McIvor.
26. *Report of the Canadian Wheat Board, Crop Year 1937-38*, p. 3.
27. C.F. Wilson, *A Century of Canadian Grain*, Appendix 7.
28. Report of the Royal Grain Inquiry Commission, 1938, p. 183.
29. *Ibid.*
30. *Ibid.*, p. 194.
31. *Ibid.*, p. 206.
32. C.F. Wilson, *A Century of Canadian Grain*, pp. 629, 630.
33. W.L.M. King papers.
34. C.F. Wilson, *A Century of Canadian Grain*, p. 560.
35. W.L.M. King diary, July 26, 1938.
36. *Ibid.*
37. Winnipeg *Free Press*, August 5, 1938.
38. *Ibid.*, August 8, 1938.
39. Cabinet Document 44-51, October 11, 1950, Privy Council office files.
40. C.F. Wilson, *A Century of Canadian Grain*, p. 583.
41. House of Commons *Hansard*, January 12, 1939, p. 4.
42. *Ibid.*, February 16, 1939, p. 1037.
43. *Ibid.*
44. Submission by Committee on Markets and Agricultural Readjustments, March 1939, CWB Library.
45. W.L.M. King diary, March 1, 1939.
46. *Ibid.*, March 3, 1939.

CHAPTER SIX

1. George McIvor, Address to the Calgary Ranchmen's Club, May 7, 1976.
2. W.L.M. King papers.
3. Taped interview George McIvor.
4. *Ibid.*
5. W.L.M. King papers.
6. Taped interview George McIvor.
7. W.L.M. King papers.
8. *Ibid.*

9. Taped interview George McIvor.
10. *Ibid.*
11. *Ibid.*
12. George McIvor, Address to the Calgary Ranchmen's Club.
13. *Report of the Canadian Wheat Board, Crop Year 1940-41*, p. 25.
14. Taped interview George McIvor.
15. *Report of the Canadian Wheat Board, Crop Year 1940-41*, p. 5.
16. Taped interview George McIvor.
17. *Ibid.*
18. *Ibid.*
19. Britnell and Fowke, *Canadian Agriculture*, p. 204.
20. *Report of the Canadian Wheat Board, Crop Year 1940-41*, p. 4.
21. House of Commons *Hansard*, March 12, 1941, p. 1464.
22. Britnell and Fowke, *Canadian Agriculture*, p. 206.
23. *Ibid.*
24. "Less Wheat in 1941 Will Help Win the War," Pamphlet, Ottawa: King's Printer, 1941.
25. Britnell and Fowke, *Canadian Agriculture*, pp. 2, 3.
26. *Report of the Canadian Wheat Board, Crop Year 1941-42*, pp. 2, 3.
27. House of Commons *Hansard*, March 9, 1942, p. 1123.
28. *Report of the Canadian Wheat Board, Crop Year 1942-43*, p. 1.
29. C.F. Wilson, *A Century of Canadian Grain*, p. 773.
30. Taped interview George McIvor.

CHAPTER SEVEN

1. Taped interview George McIvor.
2. C.F. Wilson, *A Century of Canadian Grain*, p. 776, and taped interview with George McIvor.
3. Taped interview George McIvor.
4. *Ibid.*
5. Canadian Wheat Board Trade and Commerce File 20-141-11.
6. Taped interview George McIvor.
7. Britnell and Fowke, *Canadian Agriculture*, Table V.
8. Minutes of the Council of the Winnipeg Grain Exchange, November 3, 1943.
9. *Ibid.*
10. C.F. Wilson, *A Century of Canadian Grain*, p. 787.
11. Britnell and Fowke, *Canadian Agriculture*, p. 216.
12. C.F. Wilson, *A Century of Canadian Grain*, p. 1053.
13. *Report of the Canadian Wheat Board, Crop Year 1944-45*, p. 2.
14. C.F. Wilson, *A Century of Canadian Grain*, p. 750.
15. Taped interview George McIvor.
16. *Ibid.*
17. Britnell and Fowke, *Canadian Agriculture*, p. 219.
18. D.A. MacGibbon, *The Canadian Grain Trade*, p. 118.

19. *Western Weekly Reports*, Vol. 3, 1944, p. 338.
20. Interview with Henry B. Monk, July 1984.
21. *Dominion Law Reports, 1945*, 2 D.L.R., Toronto: Canada Law Books Ltd., p. 155.
22. *Report of the Canadian Wheat Board, Crop Year 1944-45*, p. 13.
23. C.F. Wilson, *A Century of Canadian Grain*, p. 814.
24. Winnipeg *Free Press*, March 3, 1945.
25. C.F. Wilson, *A Century of Canadian Grain*, p. 1047.
26. *Ibid.*, p. 843.
27. *Report of the Canadian Wheat Board, Crop Year 1945-46*, p. 1.
28. *Ibid.*
29. *Ibid.*, p. 2.
30. *Ibid.*, p. 12.
31. House of Commons *Hansard*, September 19, 1945, pp. 289, 290.
32. *Ibid.*, p. 290.

CHAPTER EIGHT

1. C.F. Wilson, *A Century of Canadian Grain*, p. 855.
2. *Ibid.*, p. 852.
3. *Ibid.*, pp. 855, 856.
4. *Ibid.*, p. 856.
5. Minutes of the Wheat Committee of Cabinet, May 2, 1946.
6. Canadian Wheat Board. *Observations on Proposed United Kingdom Wheat Contract, April 26, 1946*. Trade and Commerce File 20-141-11.
7. Canadian Federation of Agriculture, *Farmers Meet the Cabinet*, March 28, 1946.
8. Winnipeg *Free Press*, May 23, 1946.
9. Minutes of the Advisory Committee to the Canadian Wheat Board, January 9, 1947.
10. House of Commons *Hansard*, August 15, 1946, p. 4834.
11. C.F. Wilson, *A Century of Canadian Grain*, p. 859.
12. House of Commons *Hansard*, August 15, 1946, p. 4848.
13. *Ibid.*
14. W.L.M. King papers.
15. *Ibid.*
16. *Ibid.*
17. *Ibid.*
18. *Ibid.*
19. Taped interview George McIvor.
20. *Ibid.*
21. W.L.M. King papers
22. C.F. Wilson, *A Century of Canadian Grain*, p. 883.
23. House of Commons *Hansard*, July 30, 1946, p. 4036.

24. *Ibid.*
25. *Ibid.*, p. 4037.
26. Winnipeg *Free Press*, July 31, 1946.
27. Canadian Co-operative Wheat Producers Limited, *Director's Report 1945-46.*
28. House of Commons *Hansard*, August 14, 1946, p. 4811.
29. C.F. Wilson, *C.D. Howe*, p. 613.
30. Taped interview George McIvor.
31. Cabinet Document 44-51, October 11, 1950, Privy Council office files and in C.F. Wilson, *A Century of Canadian Grain*, p. 1099..
32. House of Commons *Hansard*, March 8, 1951, p. 1062.
33. *Ibid.*, p. 1063.
34. C.F. Wilson, *A Century of Canadian Grain*, p. 928.
35. House of Commons *Hansard*, December 18, 1947, p. 423.
36. *Report of the Canadian Wheat Board, Crop Year 1949-50*, pp. 8,9.
37. Britnell and Fowke, *Canadian Agriculture*, pp. 224, 225.
38. Taped interview George McIvor.
39. International Wheat Agreement, 1949, Canada Treaty Series No. 10, 1949.
40. House of Commons *Hansard*, June 5, 1950, p. 3221.
41. *Ibid.*, March 15, 1951, pp. 1306, 1307.
42. *Ibid.*, March 12, 1951, p. 1169.
43. C.F. Wilson, *A Century of Canadian Grain*, p. 1030.
44. *Ibid.*, p. 1043.
45. Britnell and Fowke, *Canadian Agriculture*, p. 225.
46. Taped interview George McIvor.

CHAPTER NINE

1. W.L.M. King diary, February 12, 1948.
2. *Ibid.*
3. *Ibid.*
4. *Statutes of Canada*, 11 George VI, Chapter 15, p. 61.
5. *Report of the Canadian Wheat Board, Crop Year 1947-48*, p. 16.
6. D.A. MacGibbon, *The Canadian Grain Trade 1931-1951*, pp. 110, 111.
7. *Ibid.*, p. 111.
8. Canadian Federation of Agriculture, *Farmers Meet the Cabinet*, February 1948, p. 3.
9. House of Commons *Hansard*, February 27, 1948, p. 1678.
10. *Ibid.*, pp. 2112, 2113.
11. D.A. MacGibbon, *The Canadian Grain Trade*, p. 187.
12. House of Commons *Hansard*, March 19, 1948, pp. 2411, 2412.
13. Winnipeg *Free Press*, March 23, 1948.
14. W.L.M. King diary, March 24, 1948.
15. C.F. Wilson, *A Century of Canadian Grain*, p. 972.

16. Taped interview George McIvor.
17. *Ibid.*
18. Senate *Hansard*, March 24, 1948, p. 309.
19. *Ibid.*, p. 316.
20. *Statutes of Saskatchewan*, 12 George VI, Chapter 66, March 25, 1948.
21. Winnipeg *Free Press*, March 22, 1947.
22. Province of Manitoba, *Manitoba's Position on Oats and Barley Marketing*, 1948.
23. *Ibid.*
24. C.F. Wilson, *A Century of Canadian Grain*, p. 973.
25. *Report of the Canadian Wheat Board, Crop Year 1949-1950*, pp. 10, 11.
26. C.F. Wilson, *C.D. Howe*, pp. 132, 133.
27. Taped interview George McIvor.
28. C.F. Wilson, *C.D. Howe*, p. 133.
29. Canadian Federation of Agriculture, *Farmers Meet the Cabinet*, February 1948.
30. *Report of the Canadian Wheat Board, Crop Year 1949-50*, p. 12.
31. Interview with Douglas L. Campbell, November 1984.
32. *The Manitoba Co-operator*, November 29, 1951, p. 4.
33. *Ibid.*
34. Taped interview George McIvor.
35. C.F. Wilson, *C.D. Howe*, pp. 133, 134.
36. *Western Weekly Reports*, 6 WWR (NS), p. 30.
37. Taped interview George McIvor.
38. *Western Weekly Reports*, 6 WWR (NS), p. 25.
39. Taped interview George McIvor.
40. *Ibid.*
41. House of Commons *Hansard*, March 8, 1951, p. 1052.
42. *Report of the Canadian Wheat Board, Crop Year 1951-52.*
43. C.F. Wilson, *C.D. Howe*, p.22.
44. Taped interview George McIvor.

CHAPTER TEN

1. Taped interview George McIvor.
2. *Ibid.*
3. *Ibid.*
4. Canadian Wheat Board files.
5. USDA Statistics.
6. DBS, *Handbook of Agricultural Statistics*, August 1955, Part III, Trends in Canadian Agriculture, p. 12.
7. W.M. Drummond and W. Mackenzie, *Progress and Prospects in Canadian Agriculture*, 1957, p. 22.
8. Census of Canada figures.

9. Britnell and Fowke, *Canadian Agriculture*, p. 409.
10. *Report of the Canadian Wheat Board, Crop Year 1948-49*, p. 1.
11. Don F. Hadwiger, *Federal Wheat Commodity Programs*, p. 187.
12. *Report of the Canadian Wheat Board, Crop Year 1953-54*, p. 2.
13. *Ibid.*, p. 1.
14. *Ibid.*, pp. 1, 2.
15. C.F. Wilson, *C.D. Howe*, p. 321.
16. *Report of the Canadian Wheat Board, Crop Year 1953-54*, p. 8.
17. *Ibid.*
18. C.F. Wilson, *C.D. Howe*, pp. 321, 322.
19. Canadian Wheat Board Trade and Commerce File 20-25, Telegram 700, June 21, 1954.
20. *Report of the Canadian Wheat Board, Crop Year 1953-54*, p. 2.
21. Canadian Wheat Board files.
22. Commonwealth Secretariat.
23. Canadian Wheat Board files.
24. Activities under Public Law 480, 84th Congress 1st Session, House of Representatives Document No. 62, p. 2.
25. C.F. Wilson, *C.D. Howe*, p. 366.
26. Winnipeg *Free Press*, October 19, 1955.
27. *Ibid.*, October 21, 1955.
28. Canadian Wheat Board Trade and Commerce File 10:66:1, Volume 1, Notes on a meeting between United States and Canadian officials in Washington, January 4, 1957.
29. *Ibid.*, Winnipeg, August 29, 1956.
30. *Ibid.*, June 10, 1957.
31. House of Commons *Hansard*, May 17, 1955, pp. 3843-46.
32. C.F. Wilson, *C.D. Howe*, p. 487.
33. *Ibid.*
34. House of Commons *Hansard*, January 16, 1956, p. 127.
35. *Ibid.*, February 3, 1956, pp. 845-847.
36. *Ibid.*, February 8, 1957, p. 1124.
37. *Ibid.*, March 13, 1957, p. 2161.
38. C.F. Wilson, *C.D. Howe*, p. 524., p. 2161.
39. Winnipeg *Free Press*, May 19, 1957, p. 11.
40. *Ibid.*

CHAPTER ELEVEN

1. Taped interview George McIvor.
2. C.F. Wilson, *C.D. Howe*, p. 432.
3. *Ibid.*, pp. 431-434.
4. *Ibid.*
5. Canadian Wheat Board Trade and Commerce File 4-J2-8, Volume 1.
6. House of Commons *Hansard*, February 29, 1956, pp. 1661, 1662.
7. Canadian Wheat Board Trade and Commerce File 4-P6-3A, Volume 4.
8. *Report of the Canadian Wheat Board, Crop Year 1954-55*, p. 14.

9. *Ibid., Crop Year 1953-54*, p. 3.
10. *Ibid., Crop Year 1954-55*, p. 3.
11. C.F. Wilson, *Grain Marketing in Canada*, p. 236.
12. House of Commons *Hansard*, May 2, 1956, p. 3500.
13. C.F. Wilson, *C.D. Howe*, p. 571.
14. House of Commons *Hansard*, May 14, 1954, p. 4611.
15. *Ibid.*, January 30, 1957, p. 800.
16. C.F. Wilson, *C.D. Howe*, p. 594.
17. *Inquiry into the Distribution of Railway Box Cars*, p. 61.
18. *Report of the Canadian Wheat Board, Crop Year 1958-59*, p. 3.
19. *Ibid., Crop Year 1954-55*, p. 27.
20. *Ibid., Crop Year 1956-57*, p. 9.
21. Taped interview George McIvor.
22. *Ibid.*
23. *Ibid.*
24. *Ibid.*
25. *Report of the Canadian Wheat Board, Crop Year 1947-48*, pp. 2, 3.
26. *Ibid.*
27. Taped interview George McIvor.

POSTSCRIPT

1. C.F. Wilson, *A Century of Canadian Grain*, preface (unnumbered xxii).
2. *The Canadian Wheat Board Report to Producers on the 1984-85 Crop Year*, p. 3.

SELECTED BIBLIOGRAPHY

General Works

Britnell, George E., and Fowke, Vernon C. *Canadian Agriculture in War and Peace*. Stanford, Calif.: Stanford University Press, 1962.

Colquette, R.D. *The First Fifty Years: A History of United Grain Growers Ltd*. Winnipeg: Modern Press, 1957.

Davidson, Clive B. *Wheat, Politicians and the Great Depression: Two Memoirs*. Winnipeg: Natural Resources Institute, University of Manitoba, 1976.

The Diary of Alexander James McPhail. Harold A. Innis (ed.) Toronto: University of Toronto Press, 1940.

Ellis, J.H. *The Ministry of Agriculture in Manitoba, 1870-1890*. Winnipeg, Manitoba: Department of Agriculture (Economics and Publications Branch), 1970.

Fairbairn, Garry Lawrence. *From Prairie Roots: The Remarkable Story of Saskatchewan Wheat Pool*. Saskatoon: Western Producer Prairie Books, 1984.

Finlayson, R.K. *That Man R.B. Bennett* n.p., n.d.

Fowke, Vernon C. *Canadian Agricultural Policy, The Historical Pattern.* Toronto: University of Toronto Press, 1946.

______ *The National Policy and the Wheat Economy.* Toronto: University of Toronto Press, 1957.

Grains & Oilseeds: Handling, Marketing, Processing. Third Edition, Revised. Winnipeg: Canadian International Grains Institute, 1982.

Hadwiger, Don. Frank. *Federal Wheat Commodity Programs.* Ames, Iowa: Iowa State University Press, 1970.

Hamilton, Fred W. *Service At Cost: A History of Manitoba Pool Elevators, 1925-1975.* Saskatoon: Modern Press, 1978.

Josling, Tim. *Intervention and Regulation in Canadian Agriculture: A comparison of costs and benefits among sectors.* Ottawa: Economic Council of Canada, Technical Report No. E/14, March 1981.

MacGibbon, Duncan Alexander. *The Canadian Grain Trade.* Toronto: The Macmillan Company of Canada Ltd., 1932.

______ *The Canadian Grain Trade 1931-1951.* Toronto: University of Toronto Press, 1952.

Moorhouse, Hopkins. *Deep Furrows.* Toronto and Winnipeg: George J. McLeod Ltd., 1918.

Morgan, Dan. *Merchants of Grain.* New York: Penguin Books, 1980.

Nesbitt, Leonard D. *The Story of Wheat.* Calgary: Alberta Wheat Pool, 1953.

______ *Tides in the West.* Saskatoon: Modern Press, n.d. [1962?]

Patton, Harald S. "The Canadian Wheat Board in Prosperity and Depression." Central Selling Agency booklet reprinting article from N.E. Himes (ed.) *Economics, Sociology and the Modern World: Essays in Honor of T.N. Carver.* Cambridge: Harvard University Press, 1935.

______ *Grain Growers' Co-operation in Western Canada.* Cambridge: Harvard University Press, 1928.

Swanson, W.W. and Armstrong, P.C. *Wheat.* Toronto: Macmillan, 1930.

Wilson, Barry. *Beyond the Harvest.* Saskatoon: Western Producer Prairie Books, 1981.

Wilson, Charles F. *A Century of Canadian Grain: Government Policy to 1951.* Saskatoon: Western Producer Prairie Books, 1978.

______ *C.D. Howe: An Optimist's Response to a Surfeit of Grain.* Ottawa: Grains Group, 1980.

______ *Grain Marketing in Canada.* Winnipeg: Canadian International Grains Institute, 1979.

Wood, Louis Aubrey. *A History of Farmers' Movements in Canada.* Toronto: Ryerson Press, 1924.

Government Documents, Publications and Reports

Canada. House of Commons. *An Act to Provide for the Constitution and Powers of the Canadian Wheat Board*, George V, July 5, 1935.

Canada. House of Commons. *Hansard*. Selected years 1930 to 1984.

Canada. House of Commons. Special Committee on Bill 98, Canadian Grain Board Act. *Proceedings and Evidence*. Ottawa: King's Printer, June 28, 1935

Canada. House of Commons. Wheat Committee of Cabinet Minutes, 1946.

Canada. Privy Council. Office files.

Canada. Report of the Inquiry Into the Distribution of Railway Boxcars, Ottawa, 1958.

Canada. Report of the Royal Commission to Enquire Into Charges Against Manitoba Pool Elevators, Ottawa, 1931.

Canada. Report of the Royal Grain Inquiry Commission, Ottawa, 1938.

Canada. Senate. *Hansard*. Selected years 1930 to 1984.

Canada. Transport Canada. *Western Grain Transportation: Report on Consultations and Recommendations,* (J.C. Gilson Report).

Canada. Transport Canada. Committee of Inquiry on Crow Benefit Payment. *Report*, March 1985 (Mr. Justice Gordon C. Hall).

Canada. Transport Canada. Grain Handling and Transportation Committee. Grain and Rail in Western Canada, 1977 (Mr. Justice Emmett Hall).

Canada. Wheat Board. Minutes of the Advisory Committee to the Canadian Wheat Board. Crop years 1940-41 to 1983-84.

Canada. Wheat Board. Minutes of the Canadian Wheat Board. Crop years 1935-36 to 1984-85.

Canada. Wheat Board. Reports of the Canadian Wheat Board. Crop years 1935-36 to 1984-85.

Canada. Wheat Board, Trade and Commerce files.

Drummond, W.M. and Mackenzie, W. *Progress and Prospects of Canadian Agriculture*. Ottawa: Queen's Printer and Controller of Stationary, 1957.

Forbes, J.D.; Hughes, R.D.; Warley, T.K. *Economic Intervention and Regulation of Canadian Agriculture. A Study Prepared for the Economic Council of Canada and its Institutes for Research and Public Policy.* Ottawa: Canadian Government Publishing Centre, 1982.

R.B. Bennett papers. Public Archives of Canada.

U.S., Congress, House, Subcommittee on Livestock and Grains of the Committee on Agriculture, Sale of Wheat to Russia, 92nd Cong. 2nd Ses., 1972.

U.S., Congress, Senate, Committee on Government Operations, Permanent Subcommittee on Investigations, *Russian Grain Transactions,* 93rd Cong. 2nd Ses., 1974.

W.L.M. [Mackenzie] King papers. Public Archives of Canada.

Winnipeg Grain Exchange. Minutes of the Council, 1934.

Winnipeg Grain Exchange. *Wheat Marketing Fallacies*. n.p., n.d.

Newspapers

Free Press Evening Bulletin, 1933
The Manitoba Co-operator, 1935 to 1985
The Western Producer
Western Weekly Reports
The Winnipeg Free Press, 1930 to 1984 (Manitoba Archives)

Interviews

Taped Interviews: George McIvor, Honourable Otto Lang, R.L. Kristjanson, Frank T. Rowan, C. Gordon Earl.

Verbal Interviews: Douglas L. Campbell, Henry Monk.